BARRIO LIBRE

Gilberto Rosas

Barrio Libre

*Criminalizing States and Delinquent Refusals
of the New Frontier*

Duke University Press Durham and London 2012

© 2012 Duke University Press
All rights reserved
Printed in the United States of America on acid-
free paper ∞
Designed by C. H. Westmoreland
Typeset in Arno Pro with Lato display
by Tseng Information Systems, Inc.

Library of Congress Cataloging-in-Publication Data

Rosas, Gilberto
Barrio Libre : criminalizing states and delinquent
refusals of the new frontier / Gilberto Rosas.
p. cm.
Includes bibliographical references and index.
ISBN 978-0-8223-5225-9 (cloth : alk. paper)
ISBN 978-0-8223-5237-2 (pbk. : alk. paper)
1. Crime—Mexican-American Border Region.
2. Gangs—Mexican-American Border Region.
3. Youth—Mexican-American Border Region
—Social conditions.   4. Illegal aliens—Mexican-
American Border Region—Social conditions.
I. Title.
HV5831.M46R66 2012
364.10972′1—dc23   2012011568

To my mom and dad, Niki, Kora, and Teo

Crime is a coup d'état from below.

—MICHEL FOUCAULT, "On Attica: An Interview"

The tradition of all dead generations weighs
like a nightmare on the brains of the living.

—KARL MARX, "The Eighteenth Brumaire of Louis Bonaparte"

We're the fucked ones. But we're free . . . free, motherfucker.
I'm in the Free 'Hood and I'm free now and I will be free forever!

—CHAVO

CONTENTS

Acknowledgments ix

INTRODUCTION
The Criminalizing Depths of States and Other Shit 3

CHAPTER 1
Other Nightmares and the Rise of the New Frontier 29

CHAPTER 2
Against Mexico: Thickening Delinquency of
the New Frontier 55

CHAPTER 3
Low-Intensity Reinforcements: Cholos, Chúntaros, and
the "Criminal" Abandonments of the New Frontier 73

INTERLUDE
Post–September 11 at the New Frontier 89

CHAPTER 4
Against the United States: The Violent Inaugurations and
Delinquent Exceptions of the New Frontier 95

CHAPTER 5
Oozing Barrio Libre and the Pathological Ends of Life 115

INTERLUDE
Nervous Cocks at the New Frontier 133

CONCLUSION
The New Frontier Thickens 137

Notes 147

Bibliography 163

Index 183

ACKNOWLEDGMENTS

I have always imagined writing my acknowledgments as an exorcism, a banishing of the burdens and abstraction of "the book," which haunts junior scholars in the social sciences and the humanities, as it becomes "my book." But this enterprise is far more than a release or a sigh of relief. The book generally and the acknowledgments specifically are a recognition of the collective nature of intellectual labor: the pounds of intellectual, political, and emotional flesh, of critical feedback and shared knowledges. In other words, it is the humbling realization that I stand on the shoulders of giants, and it is to them I give thanks.

My greatest debt goes to the youths I have called Román, Margarita, Shorty, Bolillo, La Negra, Skinny, Victor, Tocayo, Jesús, Victoria, Loco, Willi, La Morena, and many, many more who lived—and some of whom died—in Barrio Libre. How you pained me. How you fascinated me. How you challenged me. How you taught me. How you haunt me. I will always feel that I never did enough. I still look for you.

I am deeply grateful to my family—or "kin," in the parlance of anthropology. My parents, Gilbert and Cecilia Mora Rosas, and my sister, Monica Rosas, have been vital to my seeing this project come to completion. Korinta Maldonado's astute insights and her patience with my multiple rewrites likewise have helped me see this project to its end.

I am indebted to the activist intellectuals in community organizations in the Tucson and Nogales region, particularly Raquel Rubio Goldsmith and Guadalupe Castillo, of Coalición de Derechos Humanos, and Jennifer Allen, of the Border Action Network. Their critical assessments and grounded knowledges suffuse this manuscript and reminded me of the "other side" of the border. It can bring people together to fight injustice.

Working on the sharp borders of anthropology and Latino studies proves tenuous without the friendships, knowledges, and support of my mentors, colleagues, friends, and critics. At the University of Texas, Austin, José Limón taught me what ethnography could be. The guidance and challenges of Ricardo Ainsle, Richard Flores, Shannon Speed, and Kamala Visweswaran proved invaluable as my ideas congealed into what was a dissertation. Also invaluable were the always critical interrogations of Ted Gordon, Charles Hale, and Martha Menchaca. Mary Weismantel and Michaela di Leonardo challenged me and professionalized me as I reformulated the project, when I was a Mellon Postdoctoral Fellow in Latino Studies at Northwestern University. So did my colleagues in the Department of Anthropology at the University of Illinois at Urbana-Champaign (uiuc). They include: Nancy Abelmann, Alma Gottlieb, Janet Keller, Steven Leigh, Martin Manalansan, Ellen Moodie, Andy Orta, Marc Perry, Charles Roseman, and Arlene Torres, and I offer a special acknowledgment to a fellow anthropologist of the border, Alejandro Lugo. I am similarly indebted to my colleagues in uiuc's Department of Latino Studies, particularly Julie Dowling, Edna Viruell-Fuentes, Jonathan Inda, Mireya Loza, Isabel Molina, Richard Rodriguez, and Rolando Romero. I must thank other colleagues at uiuc as well, such as William Castro and Erik S. McDuffie. At the University of Chicago, the Center for the Study of Race, Politics, and Culture, under the skilled leadership of Ramón Gutiérrez, provided an intellectual home away from home, and Ramón patiently gave me invaluable feedback.

I am indebted to the members of the University of Texas diaspora for their interrogations and queries, but mostly for the lasting friendships of fellow travelers such as Mohan Ambikaipaker, Ben Chappell, Pete Haney, B. C. Harrison, Olga Herrera, Mireya Loza, Mariana Mora, Jennifer Najera, Vivian Newdick, Laura Padilla, Marc Perry, Junaid Rana, Virginia Raymond, Sandy Soto, Michael Trujillo, and Anthony Webster. Similarly, the Advanced Seminar in Chicano Research at the University of Texas has been instrumental and inspirational in this project. The seminar's members included Estevan Azcona, Manolo Callahan, Emmet Campos, Rebecca Gamez, Alan Gomez, Pablo Gonzalez, Marco Iñiguez, Veronica Martinez, Dana Maya, Isa Quintana, Russell Rodriguez, Lilia Rosas, Cristina Salinas, Geoff Valdes, Cristobal Valencia, and Teresa Velasquez.

I must also acknowledge Leigh Binford, Nicholas De Genova, Timothy Dunn, Jonathan Hill, Ruben Martinez, Josie Saldana, Carlos Velez-Ibanez, and particularly Ralph Cintron, who read, critiqued, and helped me navigate the process. I also wish to thank Ken Wissoker at Duke University Press for his guidance and keen insights, as well as his choice of poignant, incisive, and helpful anonymous reviewers.

Conversations in my seminars "The U.S.-Mexico Border" and "States and Governance" at Northwestern University, the University of Chicago, and the University of Illinois likewise prove prescient. Finally, I have had the pleasure of working with high-caliber graduate students, including Claudia Holguin, Amaziah Suri, and again Cristobal Valencia. They are well on their ways to being great colleagues, if they are not already there.

An earlier version of chapter 2 appeared as "Policing Life and Thickening Delinquency at the New Frontier" in the *Journal of Latin American and Caribbean Anthropology* 16, no. 1 (2011): 24–40. Similarly, portions of chapter 3 originally appeared in "Cholos, Chúntaros, and the 'Criminal' Abandonments of the New Frontier" in *Identities: Global Studies in Culture and Power* 17, no. 6 (2010): 695–713.

BARRIO LIBRE

1. Looking out from Barrio Libre, Nogales, Sonora. Photo by author.

The Criminalizing Depths of States and Other Shit

The photo (fig. 1) captures a necessary fissure in the US-Mexico border and a glaring gap of its enforcement. It is a sewer, a site of human waste rendered an opening into and out of the "dark" world of Barrio Libre, and it is where this ethnography begins. Long imagined as the site for "dark," Machiavellian operations of state power,[1] these scatological interconnections underneath Nogales, Sonora (in Mexico), and Nogales, Arizona (in the United States), stage the criminalizing effects of global asymmetrical neoliberal processes—processes that drive bodies across increasingly militarized international boundaries such as those between Mexico and the United States, and processes that push me to plumb the depths of state power in an age of globalization, new or actually renewed security warfare, and corporeal excess.

This sewer tunnel begins a couple of kilometers south of the international boundary at a ditch in a decaying, impoverished neighborhood of Nogales, Sonora, not far from an abandoned bullfighting ring. As the southbound traffic zooms past and border inspections clog the northbound traffic, I follow my guides into the darkness of what they imagine as Barrio Libre. Sergio, a fourteen-year-old, reaches under his clothing, pulls out a flashlight, and urges me to stay close as we join the northward flow of bodies rendered brown seeping under the international boundary. Sergio blasts N.W.A.'s "Fuck da Police" on his Walkman, which he has recently purchased with money he earned through violent means. He mugged an unfortunate migrant, who was attempting to undermine the border through this very passage.

We pass names of several of the youth of Barrio Libre scrawled in iridescent spray paint on the cement walls of the sewer: Juanita, Juanatos, Monica, Salvador, El Trabeiso, Igor, Román, El Chamuco, San-

tos, Willi, Santana, Garocho, La Morena, La Negra, and many more. Another text in large gold letters reads: "Barrio Libre." More graffiti captures my attention: "Cristo te Odia por eso te dio la vida" (Christ hates you that is why he gave you life). And what I will term later in this book as the pathological ends of Barrio Libre make an appearance in the graffiti: "Vivir para ser libre o morir para no ser esclavos" (Live to be free or die so as not to be slaves). The latter was originally written by Práxedis G. Guerrero, a Mexican miner, intellectual, and anarchist, during the Mexican Revolution (1910–20).

The uneven floor of the sewer tunnel is covered with sand, rocks, and pools of foul water. My clothes quickly grow damp with perspiration, partly from the humidity of the sewer system and partly from the exertion of jumping over the puddles. Next to us, more water — called aguas negras *(black waters) — rushes through the sewer. Another subterranean scripture stands out: "Barrio Libre," and below it "Bajadores total" (The Free 'Hood,[2] all Muggers).*

Above us, the border wall that a special US military unit reinforced and extended with sections of mobile runways from the first Persian Gulf War severs Mexico from the United States. Above us, Mexico's Grupo Beta — a special police force marking the country's modern foray into policing of its northern border as it was transformed into a frontier in the aftermath of the North American Free Trade Agreement (NAFTA) — and the increasingly militarized US Border Patrol, customs officers, and other police forces regulate the passage of bodies through the international boundary. Yet such police campaigns or local exercises of sovereignty in the global age are only part of this history.[3] In spite of such vast regimes of policing, neoliberal flows of illicit bodies circumvent this new frontier, configuring a shifting politics of difference that is turning increasingly violent.

In the sewer, I find myself fearing for my life, wondering about violence, worrying about shit. My guides tense as we approach a door that marks the international boundary. Yes, even here, the border, or what I take as the new frontier, runs deep. Grotesquely twisted iron bars, which had been designed to hinder — if not stop — such underground flows, have been ripped away from the ground and signal that the authorities were aware of this passageway. I crouch down and follow my guides. We penetrate the darkness of this antiborder space. We flow through the opening, seeping into the United States unofficially, illegally, sans documentation. A bearded figure demands to know what we are doing in this subterranean, borderless world. My guides converse

with the angry old man for a few minutes. After their brief conversa-
tion, the youths decide that the journey is too dangerous. We turn back
toward Mexico and ooze again under the international boundary.

We come to a manhole and push ourselves upward and into the civil
society of Nogales, Sonora. Local traffic police called transito *immedi-*
ately confront us. Rumors about police violence permeate Barrio Libre.
Stories of beatings and extortion press on the youth, incite them, pro-
voke them, and define them in perverse relationship to that oppression
and related ones.

An officer yanks the hair of one of the youths and throws him up
against a wall. We are questioned. We are searched; hands run up and
down our bodies and into their crevices. But here my US citizenship
marks my privilege. I manage to pull out and flash my passport. They
let us go and warn me not to be found in the tunnels again: "Son muy
peligrosos" (They're very dangerous). Days later, Román tells me that
had I not had my passport, "they would have hit you so hard you would
have wished you were dead," a collapsing of death and punishment
that is part of the modus operandi of the new wars of late neoliberal
sovereignty making.[4]

Such exercises of policing and related practices of violence speak
to the multiple productions of the contemporary Mexico-US border,
what I call the new frontier. It includes myriad official and unofficial
exercises of state power, such as the reports that Grupo Beta scrawled
"Beta Rifa" (Beta Rules) and "Cuidado Delincuentes" (Careful Delinquents), deep in the underground terrain of Barrio Libre, and the
youths' frequent encounters with the United States Border Patrol.

No Rio Bravo — or Rio Grande, if one hails from north of the border — separates Nogales, Sonora, from Nogales, Arizona. Rather, the
rolling hills of the desert valley, so susceptible to droughts and floods,
cradle the two communities together. Historical memory and landscape point to their long-standing continuities, residual affiliations,
relationships, and vibrant kin networks, all of which disrupt the border. The aligned downtown boulevards of the two cities; the architecture of the Nogales, Sonora, church that complements the museum in
Nogales, Arizona; the streets that end on one side of the international
boundary and pick up again on the other side — all illustrate the sovereign dismemberment of territory from territory and of people severed
in two, as do the frustrated murmurings of "ambos Nogales" (both
Nogaleses) among elder residents of the two communities. Indeed, a

US consul wrote in 1924: "the two towns are practically one, one street separates them."[5]

When my ethnographic fieldwork began at the end of the twentieth century, Nogales, Sonora, like other border communities had a significant tourist industry. In Nogales, Sonora, sunburned tourists would buy tequila, carved Oaxacan animal figurines, blankets, hats, and T-shirts proclaiming "Viva Mexico" and the benefits of tequila drinking. Elderly hawkers, wearing cowboy hats, would haggle with tourists in bright pastel tops and shorts. The latter would comb the curio shops, the artisan and taco stands, and restaurants. Younger hawkers would don mirrored sunglasses and black baseball caps emblazoned with the figure of Michael Jordan, a marijuana leaf, or text such as "Sonora," "Red's Trucks," or "Chicano." They would bark in border English: "Come en. . . . Come en. . . . Look around" or offer "pharmaceuticals . . . cheap." Bars that at one time used to spill over with Mexican revolutionaries would sell buckets of beer and, increasingly often, the flesh of young women. At night, as in Juarez and Tijuana, the bars and discothèques of Nogales, Sonora, would thump contemporary top-forty music in seeming orchestration with the bodies of "the undocumented" yearning to cross this new frontier.[6] Yet the ruins of neoliberal globalization and vast new nightmares of insecurity in both Mexico and the United States have gradually diminished this once-thriving scene.

Barrio Libre coalesced in the tourist zone in the late 1990s, seeping between legitimate and violent ways of reproducing themselves. They would panhandle, sell trinkets and candy, or wash the windshields of cars in the slow northward-bound traffic. They were denigrated, called variously *las ratas* (the rats), *los delincuentes* (the delinquents), *los cholos* (gangsters), and the less noxious but nonetheless popular misnomer "tunnel kids," as well as far more vulgar names. Their underground practices—oozing under the border through a sewer system, mugging migrants, and other "pathological" practices—alarmed law enforcement and health authorities of Nogales, Arizona, and Nogales, Sonora, while fascinating the media and certain travel writers.[7] The youths ranged in age from nine to sixteen when I first began working with them. Those who have survived are young adults now.

The ruins of the North American Free Trade Agreement (NAFTA) include a *maquiladora* force that has nearly quadrupled in Nogales, Sonora, Mexico, since 1990. These artifacts of Mexico's submission to a global economy import components and raw goods from the United

States and other wealthy nations. Products are finished at the maquiladoras and exported back across the border for sale. As of 2000, border factories employed 105,000 people, up from 43,000 in 1993 in a capitulation to a new order of things. More than 300,000 people now call the new frontier town of Nogales, Sonora, home. For the vast majority of them, the only affordable housing is the *colonias*, typically makeshift neighborhoods that erupt overnight from the desert floor of the post-NAFTA landscape. They sit precariously on the steep hillsides. They have poor drainage, abet erosion, aggravate monsoon-like flooding, and are blamed as sources of surface and groundwater pollution. The people in such communities drink water from trucks and store it in barrels salvaged from the dump or nearby factories, as the city's fifty-year-old water distribution system crumbles under global pressures. And the old, leaky, and often broken sewer infrastructures seep waste from the makeshift latrines into the soil and runoff into the washes, from where it flows downhill into Nogales, Arizona. Contaminants such as ammonia, heavy metals, and other toxins have been found in the water supply. A number of diseases are related to the quality and quantity of available water. Some are waterborne diseases that are transmitted by pathogens ingested in drinking water.[8]

Many of the youth in Barrio Libre were the sons and daughters of local maquiladora workers. Others came from other communities in Sonora, Sinaloa, Chiapas, or other states in Mexico, and a few hailed from Central America. They had come to this new frontier either on their own or with their families, following the mammoth disruptions that the liberalization of national economies had wrought in much of Latin America, particularly in the countryside. They supplemented their incomes from legitimate work violently; they would mug and terrorize migrants trying to circumvent the new wars of border sovereignty in the fetid darkness of the sewer system.

That is, Barrio Libre flowed under the low-intensity warfare that border policing has become, a kind of warfare that dramatizes the necessarily incomplete nature of sovereignty in the age of late neoliberal globalization. It is a kind of warfare that collapses the distinctions between the police and the military, between regulating life and killing it. This kind of low-intensity warfare has become instrumental in the making of sovereignty in the neoliberal or putatively post-neoliberal age, and it births intense historically and politically charged nightmares of insecurity among the citizens of the United States and, increasingly, Mexico.[9] Such nightmares about others in the United

States and about certain others in Mexico as related dominant knowledges that animate both countries, fueled the youths' dense sensations of fury, defiance, deep marginality, and dangerous, unbridled, unfettered freedoms. Barrio Libre and its complex coproduction in relation to the nation-states of Mexico and the United States attest to how, in an age of globalization, certain people are made subjects to nation-states and their accompanying power relations through direct and indirect political violence.

The youths of Barrio Libre, having oozed under the border, embodied such nightmares. Having flowed in the darkness under the border through such moist, wet sewers, they would then stow away on trains to travel to a "real" Barrio Libre in Tucson, Arizona. Some sixty miles to the north, it is home to Mexican Americans, Native Americans, and Mexican migrant populations. Its porous boundaries have expanded and contracted in accordance with the needs of the larger Tucson community for Mexican migrant labor.[10] From the point of view of the denizens of Barrio Libre, such movements constituted what it meant to be in the Free 'Hood. To dwell in it was to be "from here and from there," as Margarita, one of the young women, once explained.

To dwell in the Free 'Hood was also to be terrorized and to terrorize. It was to suffer the humiliations and denigrations; to be beaten by Mexican police forces and to be incarcerated; to be called a rat and other vulgarities; to be refused employment and health care in Mexico based on their unkempt appearance and cholo stylings; it was to be abandoned at the margins of two nation-states during low-grade regimes of warfare and dispossession. To dwell in Barrio Libre was also to mug Others who sought to circumvent the militarized campaigns of sovereignty in the world above, the new migrants of post-NAFTA Mexico, commonly denigrated as *chúntaros* or *cheros*,[11] as the established boundary entered a free trade–induced crisis in the 1990s and later thickened amid neoliberal Americans' post–September 11 nightmares of terrorism, undocumented migration, and *other* kinds of criminals.

Timothy Dunn's influential *The Militarization of the U.S.-Mexico Border* speaks to these campaigns of sovereignty. It documents the massive investment in manpower and technology at the border as an example of the repatriation of low-intensity conflict theory and practice to the United States. Originally developed as a response to guerrilla insurgency in the Third World by the Kennedy administration, low-intensity conflict (LIC) reached its full form during the Reagan administration as a counterinsurgency doctrine in Central America in the early 1980s. Dunn outlines LIC by citing a 1986 US Army Training Report: low-intensity conflict is a limited political-military struggle to achieve political, social, economic, or psychological objectives. It is generally confined to a geographic area and is often characterized by constraints on the weaponry, tactics, and level of violence.[12] He argues that many key aspects of LIC have coincided with numerous facets of the militarization on the US-Mexico border.[13] Moreover, US officials have described unauthorized migration and illegal drug trafficking from Mexico to the United States as a "national security" issue.[14] Such anxieties exemplify how nightmares of contaminations engulf increasingly depleted nations-states and their reliance upon an incomplete, pseudo-domestic or pseudo-foreign warfare against transgressing and contaminating others.[15] Increasingly, elements of the Mexican government seem to be adopting similar strategies of warfare.

That is, state legitimated campaigns of sovereignty and security, as well as the accompanying pervasive multiple representations and anxieties and cultural imaginaries about them, signal the tenuous, incomplete, and fragile control of territory and population in the global age. Sovereignty in the neoliberal age does not constitute the classic monopoly over the relations of violence of modern social theory. Rather, violence and other death-producing technologies become key techniques of rule and governance. Militarized policing and other irregular forms of warfare have become central both to the daily production of sovereignty and in their very incompleteness to the daily governance of Others.

Such tactics speak to the unspeakable, the now taken for granted violence of the new frontier. It ranges from the "killing deserts," where more than five thousand corpses and countless partial human remains attest to the violence of trying to enter the United States "illegally"; to quasi-licensed hunting of migrants by the Minutemen and other vigilante groups;[16] to the widespread acknowledgment of human trafficking, including some through dark, underground crossings and "darker" criminal networks; to the violence exercised against the young women disappeared from the streets of Ciudad Juarez, Chihuahua, their bodies later found mutilated and abandoned in the desert.

Fears of the undocumented migrant turned terrorist or parochial peasants turned vengeful, violent, armed narcogangsters attest to the radical transformation of livelihoods amid neoliberal globalization and its new security concerns. Indeed, such sentiments of unease and insecurity amid the flows of "contaminating" bodies at the new frontier may explain the reaction of border guards to my attempt to enter Nogales, Arizona, from Nogales, Sonora, through the official port of entry.

When they ask me my business in Mexico, I explain that I am a scholar, conducting research on the street youth of the border. Their scrutiny of me intensifies. One of the officers responds, "Oh, you're a scholar? Do you mean the tunnel rats? Do you have identification?" They escort me to what is called secondary inspection.

Another young man is also trying to cross into the United States. I hear him ask the officer if he recognizes him from yesterday, but the officer ignores him. The young man is bent over the metal table next to me. The officers demand that I pull the end of my shirt out of my pants and remove my shoes. A tall, blond agent stands close behind me. He quickly runs his hands along my body and inner thigh to my groin, frisking the crevices of my body.

"Sir, are you carrying over $10,000?" another officer asks.

I shake my head no.

"Sir, who do you work for?" This routine line of questioning attempts to establish whether I am a threat to national security or some other criminal menace, such as a smuggler of contraband, particularly drugs. I repeat the script, so well rehearsed now. I again explain to the officers, "I research the street kids of Nogales, Sonora."

"That requires money," he says. A second officer rifles through my backpack. And the new taken-for-grantedness of institutionalized violence of the state as sovereignty made against others exacerbates such exercises of power.

I explain further that I also consult for a nonprofit organization that attempts to intervene in the lives of those of Barrio Libre.

"You're . . . a consultant?" the first officer asks.

As I had learned growing up in and in between El Paso, Texas, and Ciudad Juárez, and spending many years in and in between southern Arizona and northern Sonora, such officials seek simple responses to complex questions.

Such "border inspections," a concept theorized by Alejandro Lugo, reify power relations of the order of nation-states.[17] They bring a semblance of official order to sovereign powers beleaguered by the flow of commodities, bodies, flora, and fauna both licit and illicit in nature, while reaffirming preexisting overlapping asymmetries, such as white over brown, men over women, and certain classed power relations.[18] They exemplify how certain "technologies of control" render states legible in the age of globalization.[19] For the officers and for many people of the US-Mexico border region, the category of "Mexican" equates to a life of poverty, one that is often mistaken as being from "over there," south of the border.[20] Although many in my family experienced such conditions, I did not, thanks to my parents' success and good fortune.

But this technology of control proves even more complex. My official groping hails an unspoken complicity, a public, officially mediated performance of our respective straight masculinities and part of *my* criminalized state. At the necessarily jagged fringes of this new frontier, gendered, racial, and sexualized orders are reconstituted.[21]

Barrio Libre: Criminalizing States and Delinquent Refusals of the New Frontier interrogates the rise—or the descent—of these new delinquent subjects. They coalesced on the borders of the streets of a community of the new frontier and the dark moist passageway and other dark fissures of always incomplete militarized policing practices in an age of neoliberal government. The descent of the youth into Barrio Libre thus reveals the criminal depths of state power in the age of neoliberal globalization. In oozing under the processes whereby neoliberal states stabilize themselves in legitimate displays of violence, institutionalized in the law and instantiated in the figure of the police, migrants generally and the youths specifically foreground the necessary incompleteness of neoliberal borders-cum-frontiers. It licenses a range of sovereign exercises against racialized, pathologized, and gendered Others, capturing the mobilization of a certain category of people deemed to be excluded from national membership and caught in the practices of policing and low-intensity warfare as sovereignty making, a sovereignty that is necessarily incomplete. Neoliberal sovereignty is forged on people deemed to be on the margins of the state,[22] in the practices of policing as sovereignty making. The emergence of Barrio Libre shows the centrality of actual borders and frontiers in instigating and replenishing nightmares about Others.

That is to say, the constellation of discourses, practices, and images that constituted the youths' delinquent or criminal territorialization of Barrio Libre is not an object of positivist study that I comprehended ethnographically. Rather, it was produced in the sense of Marx, "birthed" in the sense of Foucault. Barrio Libre reveals the dense relationship among neophyte criminalities and warfare as sovereignty

making and governance. Amid such low-intensity militarized policing occurring at the border, the high-intensity "dark," Barrio Libre
took root. The youths' painful descent into the Free 'Hood reveals
how players opt to participate in "black markets" and exercise "dark"
means in order to exploit these neoliberal reconfigurations of state
power and refuse the new order—in this case, the stripping away of
sovereign protections from the displaced or more specifically migrants
in an age of neoliberal flows.

All too often such flows are thought of as moving from south to
north. But this and related perspectives negate the flows of weapons
from the United States southward: there are some 6,600 gun shops in
the four US states that border Mexico. Of the 11,000 guns turned over
to the Bureau of Alcohol, Tobacco, Firearms and Explosives (ATF)
by Mexican forces in 2009, almost 90 percent were traced to US gun
shops.[23] And there are the criminal bodies, the youths who are incarcerated, imprisoned, or deported and exported from the US penal
system across the Americas. This is to say that a perverse proximity—a social relation—emerges between the articulations of pressurized chaos of Barrio Libre and Mexican and US militarized policing
regimes and related exercises of sovereignty, a process that has only
intensified or thickened following September 11, 2001.

The New Frontiers of Race

The youths' practice of preying on bodies in the process of becoming
"alien" contaminates the normative scholarship about the border
and certain traditions of scholarship about criminality. Be it the life
of a young man struggling against the serrated edges of the narco-
economy in South Central Los Angeles, an orphan of war ensconced
in Africa's illicit economy, Puerto Rican drug dealers in New York, or
the deportations of gang members to—and their policing in—Central
America, criminalized or delinquent points of view, to use the classic
vocabulary of anthropology, tell us much about emerging social processes.[24] They challenge long-standing normative theoretical perspectives. In this respect, the refusal of Barrio Libre to submit to the new
frontier necessitates a dizzying reorientation away from the normative
subjects of social science of the US-Mexico border. Barrio Libre reveals the original proximity of the police to the criminal.[25]

And *Barrio Libre* reveals how the pathological ends of life can be rendered a collective rite of refusal. The youths render themselves beyond academic discourses of victimhood or subalternity. The formation of Barrio Libre does not resonate with Chicano borderland scholarship nor the eloquent scholarly traditions on social banditry and subaltern studies. There is no necessarily oppositional criminal subjectivity at this juncture of Mexico-US borderlands, nor innocent standpoints.[26] That is, *Barrio Libre* contaminates certain stagnant positions in particular traditions of ethnic studies and anthropology. Moreover, the youths' delinquent undermining of the US-Mexico border through the sewer tunnels, and their participation in criminal economies, resonates with anxious talk in Mexican and southward-looking US legal circles about so-called organized delinquencies or *delinquencias organizadas* in Mexico.[27] *Barrio Libre*, that is, demands a critical interrogation of what scholars consider to be the political. Neither this book nor the youth themselves seek their redemption. Rather, Barrio Libre is a high-intensity refusal of the low-intensity warfare of the United States and, increasingly, Mexico occurring at the new frontier.

In this respect, the book plumbs the depths of state power and what I have called elsewhere its multiple "managed violences"[28]— those multiple forms of subjugation that are taken as sovereignty at this moment of vast global flows. The current rhetoric of the opposition against the exercise of low-intensity warfare at the border by the United States needs to recognize that the undocumented are subjugated well before they cross or attempt to cross the new frontier. In this respect, undocumented workers, we are repeatedly told, are "good workers." And while this position holds validity and the majority of them certainly are, it likewise lends itself to a multiscalar neoliberal governmentality, specifically, the Mexican state's—and particularly its elite's—investments in undocumented migrant remittances. Thus I write against a reified notion of Mexico as necessarily oppositional to the United States while I plumb certain university discourses that foreground the US state and the law as foundational to the social relation of immigrant illegality and deportability, as well as against the related scholarly fixation on the militarization of the border.[29] I thus distinguish the fields of discourse about delinquency and criminality from "illegality" and more-vile terminology with respect to the politics of citizenship and anticitizenship in the United States.

In this respect, this book follows calls to generate knowledge from the eroding hegemonies of privileged centers,[30] or, more precisely, from the new frontier. The book charts the criminal depths of states and the delinquent refusals of the population living within the exclusions produced by competing, daily projects of sovereignty within fields of neoliberal governmentality. Their living on the borders of the normative economy and criminal enterprises tells of the daily lives of those on the precipice of the new exercises of sovereignty amid the instabilities of neoliberal transnational flows—including techniques of policing, racialization, and criminalization—the taken-for-grantedness of transnational migration by certain progressive scholars, and other problematic conventions in the age of asymmetrically organized neoliberal globalization, new or better renewed security concerns, and their accompanying social entrenchments.

The traditional academic bogeyman of an omnipotent neoliberalism is too often taken as shorthand for the repudiation of the Keynesian welfare state, the ascendance of the Chicago School of political economy, or the trappings of empire. Its presumed characteristics include a radically free market; the rise of libertarianism and maximized competition; free trade achieved through economic deregulation and the elimination of tariffs; a range of monetary and social policies favorable to business; and the privatization of formerly public resources and services, together with their subsequent revaluation as private matters. Socially, it includes indifference to poverty, deracination, cultural decimation, long-term resource depletion, and environmental destruction, as well as new politics of recognition along ethnic and racial lines.

But the new liberalism is far more than the institution of the market principle throughout a given society. It is far more than a bundle of economic policies that return a nation-state to the tenets of laissez-faire capitalism, the gutting of the welfare state, and the accompanying new forms of cultural governance. Neoliberals are not neo–Adam Smithians. Rather, neoliberalism warrants a social analysis. In these terms, neoliberalism involves extending and disseminating market values to all institutions and social actions, even as the market itself remains distinctive.[31] And such formulations all too often portray criminal practices as extensions of neoliberal logics on the ground, "down there," "from below"—or, in this case, from way, way, below.

Indeed, the massive economic restructuring that occurred in Mexico and other parts of Latin America set the stage for unprecedented human, commodity, and cultural flows among Mexico, other parts of the Americas, and the United States. The pressurized effects of neoliberalism on bodies and subjectivities also includes bodies writ large. That is, the social and cultural relations of neoliberal globalization generated radical mutations of sovereignty in an age of neoliberal globalization, involving the subjugation of certain bodies and populations to substantiate and legitimate rule, and that increasingly take a warlike form. Radically reconfigured sovereignty shows how states, stripped to their core in the age of neoliberal global flows, grapple with the fragile nexus between territory and state through racial subjugations, cast as the delinquency of yesterday, the illegal immigrants of today, or the contemporary nightmares about drug wars of the future.

Mexico, in this respect, is instrumental in the coproduction of the new frontier. Although asymmetrically positioned vis-à-vis other dominant powers, the Mexican state, as part of a higher-order network of sovereign states and global governmentalities, exercises historically produced technologies of violence and warfare in its regulation of the neoliberal border or what I call the new frontier, epitomized in its surging militarized policing practices and its own racial politics of migration. It likewise relies on certain ideologies and certain mentalities that erase the processes that prepare a population for political and economic exile to the United States. The gradual deployment of these knowledges and practices has proven integral to the rise of Barrio Libre, since well before September 11.

I must underline that with respect to Mexico, my argument is not a sophisticated iteration of the so-called failed-state thesis now making its rounds among neoconservatives in the US foreign policy establishment. One recent director of the Central Intelligence Agency and a separate Pentagon report both declared Mexico, because of its political instability, to be on a par with Pakistan and Iran as top-ranking threats to US national security. Odious though such comparisons are, such anxieties make me turn to long-standing nightmares of insecurity that have plagued both the border and Mexico historically, and that have intensified following the implementation of NAFTA and again following September 11 through the subsequent War on Terror and the contemporary drug wars.

Nor is my framework a sophisticated reiteration of the state's putative retreat. Indeed, it is useful to contemplate the dramatic shift in anxious, insecure geographies that has occurred in Mexico over the past ten years. When I began this project, Mexico City was pathologized as the center of crime and urban warfare in Mexico. It was the site of mass kidnappings, ransom demands with threats of dismemberments, and muggings. Anyone who spent a significant amount of

time there seemed to have been mugged themselves or known someone else who had been mugged. Today, as criminalities are forged
along Mexico's new frontier, embodied in drug traffickers and their
armies of a "darker" ilk, Mexico City has become hailed as relatively
stable. It was during this transformation that Barrio Libre took form.
The youths' pathological and criminal practices tell us about the shifting criminalizing currents that configure race, nation, and sovereignty
in the context of a submission to a globalizing war as governance.

Consequently, an analysis of the new frontier brings into focus how
sovereignty constitutes a daily project of rule.[32] It is an attribute both
of higher-order sovereign networks and everyday forms of state formation,[33] and one of its principal means is warfare of varying scales,
from invasions to policing and the warfare of containment occurring
at the new frontier. And such exercises of policing or warfare as sovereignty on "alien" bodies inaugurate migrants to the new power relations, or to the fields of knowledges, ideologies, and governing practices that together bring unity to what they experience as "the state"
of the United States.

New frontiers typically, but not necessarily, correspond to actual
international boundaries. The human way stations of Ciudad Juárez,
Mexico, and Ciudad Tecún Umán, Guatemala; detention centers
in France; and Ambos Nogales (both Nogaleses) are where the uncharted, economically vital, multiethnic populations steel themselves
and await resources, as they prepare to cross international borders
without documentation, or to seep over, around, or in this case, under
violent exercises of statehood, where the undocumented are made
painfully aware of the precariousness of their lives in the often "dark,"
undocumented boundary crossings and accompanying illicit economies.[34]

The concept of the new frontier disrupts the macropolitical givens
of globalization. It likewise disrupts abrupt dismissals of what is taken
to be sovereign power. In this respect, neither the militarized policing
of the US state nor the special Mexican policing of their shared international boundary constitutes anachronisms; rather, they both exemplify new legitimations forged on politically differentiated bodies, on
bodies popularly and often scientifically taken as objectively different.
Indeed, it is noteworthy that the term "frontera" in Spanish connotes
both borders and frontiers. Such violent exercises of sovereignty draw
on historically constituted forms of subjugation and organized state
violence to produce the ordered disorder of the new frontier. That

is, they rely on two central concepts; biopower, or how power takes charge of life, and biopolitics, the subjugating and controlling techniques used for biopower's exercise, or the expertise, intervention, and subjectivity with respect to vitality, variously construed and linked to sovereign power and to state racism in state socialisms, Western liberal capitalisms, and fascisms.[35]

Certain populations have long been characterized as perpetually suspect, punishable, guilty, bad, and subject to policing and normative sanctions. It is here that racism and its product, race, are taken as exemplifying the myriad technologies of biopolitical states. Race becomes in this formulation the material trace of biopower; it is often lived as the submission to power within global relations of inequity, and the material constitution of politically differentiated, subjugated bodies. Racism likewise allows for the imagining of the "inhumanity and rule over foreign people"[36] and the sovereign right to exterminate — or, in this context, render killable, disposable, and exploitable — certain populations. Aside from challenging ideas of global racial formation,[37] such subjugations of Others inaugurate them to their new orders. Differences are concretized in these fields of incomplete sovereignty that brutally inaugurate other bodies to new orders, crystallized at contemporary borders that in turn have become new frontiers.

That said, it must be underscored that contemporary policing practices throughout much of the globe increasingly rely on military knowledge, tactics, and weaponry. This peculiar and particular conjunction of the military's power to kill and the police's power to regulate is doubled in the case of undocumented migrants crossing the border and the youths of Barrio Libre. Both migrants generally and the youth of Barrio Libre specifically confront the boundary-policing practices of the United States and Mexico. Although many scholars have insisted on the centrality of the law in such questions, it is in the law's exercise — the militarized policing of the new frontier and its inevitable failures — that power relations such as racialized and gendered nationalisms license the abandonment, or punishment, incarceration, and subjugation, of Others.

These conditions animate the twinned and intertwined geneses of the new frontier and Barrio Libre. In seeping under the new frontier, the denizens of Barrio Libre dramatize the perverse effects of often violent, dramatic exercises of sovereignty on the part of both Mexico and the United States. The specific history of Barrio Libre thus captures the brutal, orchestrated use of force in the creation and the governance of Others and reveals the politicization of death and violence — even criminal violence — as new tactics of neoliberal governance and rule. The pressures of neoliberal sovereignty manifested in the illicit human flow across, through, and, in this case, under contemporary borders express the necessarily incomplete nature of neoliberal sovereignty. And these conditions birth new resistances, new criminalities, delinquencies, and pathologies, and new refusals occurring in this case at the level of the body.

Finally, too often analyses of race remain one-dimensional. Thus, I appreciate calls for greater complexity, for intersectionality — that is, an examination of how multiple axes of inequalities are mutually constitutive, always dynamic, and irreducible to one another — following the pioneering works of Third World feminists.[38] The value of such scholarship is irrefutable. I draw particularly on those currents vested in anticapitalist critique.[39] The politically organized subjection that I take as race, and its gendered and sexualized underpinnings, must always be anchored in globalizing struggles over inequity and rule, and the multiple licit and illicit struggles over resources. That is, the gendered experiences of race and the racial experiences of gender are entangled with questions about power and resources. Nevertheless, all universal categories are fraught, historical, and contradictory.

The Borders of Scholarship

Barrio Libre signifies a move away from a doctrinaire, affirming vision of academic identity politics, and it rejects deracinated approaches to political economy. Criminality and delinquency constitute subjugated realms of knowledge and antinormative practices that suffer erasure in those academic formulations that privilege a politics of affirmation. Similarly, in its emphasis on the making of the criminal and delinquent, the book contests the utopian hybrid spaces so celebrated in border theory and postcolonial theory.[40] That said, border theorists, particularly those in anthropology, have provided the foundation for my analysis. Renato Rosaldo's *Culture and Truth: The Remaking of Social Analysis*, for example, incorporates border theory into anthropology and calls for new subjects of analysis. Rosaldo echoes Gloria Anzaldúa's critique of Chicano homonationalism in his critique of anthropology's structural functionalist residues and its search for autonomously developed, deep, coherent patterns of a uniformly shared culture that are unaffected by hierarchical divisions and quotidian practices. José Limón's poetic *Dancing with the Devil* remains a deep influence on my thinking, and to this day I still excavate its intertextual complexities and elegant prose. But many devils live at the new frontier; social wars and internal contradictions run all too deep.[41]

Similarly, the analytical framework of transnationalism and globalization that rose to prominence in the 1990s radically foregrounds how new technologies of transportation and communication, often in concert with macroeconomic and state-commandeered processes, have generated a new range of sociocultural phenomena. Indeed, some scholars saw transnational activism and other activities as the end of nation-states, if not of empire.[42] Although I remain indebted to such bodies of scholarship, they all too often ignore borders and other violent reactions to global forces. Indeed, it is notable that one of the chief proponents of the new possibilities of globalization has since significantly revised his position.[43]

The meanings and social attributes of "youths" vary tremendously across space and time. Preindustrial Europe, for example, lacked a distinct transitional phase between childhood and adulthood. Lower-class juveniles in nineteenth-century Britain were termed "nomads"; they were situated in their terrain of the internal colonies called the "Jungles."[44] White middle-class young people have been taken as the invisible norm by which impoverished youths of color are judged.[45] Scholarship on "youth culture" or "subculture" has tracked youth agency as a way to validate young people's cultural productions across much of the globe.[46] Such approaches tend to draw on structural conceptions of culture as an ordered series of meanings, values, and symbols. They underscore how young people, as differentially positioned subjects, may exercise agency by strategically recoding dominant social and cultural practices. Indeed, scholars in the Centre for Contemporary Cultural Studies (CCCS) at the University of Birmingham, England, suggested long ago that youths express their agency in creative reorderings of the signs and symbols of the dominant culture through their use of particular commodities. Those scholars who broached criminality and delinquency in this tradition — such as Stuart Hall and the other authors of *Policing the Crisis*, with their innovative conceptualization of "moral panics," or Paul Gilroy, in *"There Ain't No Black in the Union Jack"* — addressed the politics of race and nation with respect to black muggings in late-twentieth-century Great Britain, echoing my emphasis on the contemporary nightmares of insecurity. Nevertheless, they did not address the actual practice of mugging itself.

Youths around the globe prompt social anxiety, whether we speak of sexual transactions in Madagascar, the culture of violence in inner-city US schools, or street youths in Brazil.[47] Today, commentators bracket undocumented youths and border youths within rhetorics of delinquency and gangs, although many scholars challenge these conflations.[48] Pathologizing discourses about gangs and the dark sociology of social control crystallize anxieties about out-of-control youths of color in the United States and increasingly elsewhere in the Americas. Surprisingly, scholars have paid little attention to the relationship between immigration policing and undocumented youths, although there have been some exceptions.[49]

That said, the residents of Barrio Libre and their movements below the new frontier straddle certain disciplinary boundaries between Latin American and Latina/o studies. Román, one of my key interlocutors in Barrio Libre, once commented that, in the darkness below the international boundary, "sometimes, you don't know where you are." His remark illustrates how multiple, competing, and asymmetrical sovereignties haunt the spaces through which bodies flow and subjectivities are made, even these pathological, criminal, and delinquent ones. I thus draw on competing regional, disciplinary, and ultimately political literatures, on both the insurrectionary and decolonizing orientations of Latino-Chicano studies and the more ambivalently positioned Latin American studies. While the former are invested in the emancipatory potential of academic knowledge production, sometimes effected in collaboration with community members, the latter remain complexly positioned in relation to US geopolitical concerns. Activist methods used in both bodies of scholarship complicate such binaries, as does the border-crossing scholarship of Ruth Behar, María Josefina Saldaña-Portillo, and Rosalinda Fregoso among the many Latino and Latina scholars who have conducted research in Mexico.[50] My research likewise furthers calls from inside and outside the discipline of anthropology for transborder studies and for considering the Americas as a totality, as well as related debates on the categorization of space and peoples.[51]

Barrio Libre similarly enters into entangled long-standing scholarship on borderlands criminality, culture, and capitalism across what is known as Greater Mexico, as well as with certain calls for a materialist turn in border studies.[52] A new generation of border scholars has investigated ethnic, racial, and gendered social relations in Juárez, Chihuahua, a major Mexican border community, critiquing the privileging of the US spaces of the border.[53] Historical anthropologists of Mexico's northern borderlands have primarily studied the relations between indigenous people and settlers in terms of state formation.[54] Meanwhile, certain bodies of scholarship that privilege "illegality," "the undocumented," and similar terms often fail to question the very premises of state control of territory and population.

Other scholars in ethnic studies have called for a critical reevaluation of "deviancy" as a category of analysis. They contrast it with a largely masculine, orthodox politics discussed in academic circles, and viewing it as potentially, but not necessarily, generative of new spaces of political intervention and affiliation.[55]

Of course, the young people who territorialized Barrio Libre and terrorized migrants are more than just delinquents or criminals. The ethnographic writing of this text shows where their individual experiences —including a young woman's pending motherhood, the deportation of a young man's family, the gradual evisceration of Mexico's public welfare programs, and the persistent search of some of the youths for dignified labor—surpass my emphasis on their grappling with the new criminal depths of sovereignty. Moreover, the project also emerges from certain concerns about the traps of ideology in representation. Often the move to humanize, a dominant effort in anthropology, or the suggestion that after all, we are all humans, disavows power relations and hierarchies, which ultimately are reproduced in practice nonetheless.[56]

My writerly sensibilities depart from the "experimental moment in the human sciences."[57] Although this tradition draws on theoretical, methodological, and representational innovations in anthropology, the indefinable, disruptive, and disorienting forms of subjugated ideas and "dark" subject matter of this project challenge the normative theoretical vocabulary of the discipline. Moreover, ethnography—as both the signature and the all-too-often extractive and unequal method of knowledge production, and as a mode of scholarly representation— has a troubled history. Postdisciplinary formations such as ethnic studies view it and its practitioners with suspicion.[58] Nevertheless, I draw on the long-standing practice in anthropology and certain postdisciplinary formations of using certain literary devices—namely first-person vignettes, which are set off by section devices. They allow me to imbed myself in the research process and represent my grappling with the descent of the youths into Barrio Libre, while textually depicting certain moments of participant observation, a primary method of sociocultural anthropology. Such conceits also allow me to underscore the agency—contaminated, criminalized, circumscribed, pathological, limited, and vexing—of *los delincuentes* of the Free 'Hood as they struggle to survive and embrace imminent death, while undermining the radically reconfigured social relations that constitute the new frontier.

Mapping *Barrio Libre*

The first chapter of the book offers a history of the new frontier between the United States and Mexico. It underscores the complexities of political economy and sovereignty in the border region's transnational history and shows how both governments ideologically and discursively mobilize race and criminality. The chapter posits three epochs: the old frontier, or the settler colonialist projects of sovereignty of both countries in what was becoming the southwestern United States and northwestern Mexico in the late nineteenth century, when race and criminality began to emerge as stratagems central to rule; the modern border of approximately 1920 through the mid-1990s, when the racial alchemy of US immigration law was embodied and ultimately practiced in the institutional violence of law enforcement; and, finally, the consolidation of neoliberalism in Mexico and in the accompanying, respective, violent assertions of sovereignty, as well as the emergence of the Free 'Hood at what I called the new frontier.

Chapter 2 begins my discussion of the birth of Barrio Libre with respect to the Mexican state and specifically to new security regimes. The youths at first were mere nuisances, working in the informal economy along the border and panhandling. Eventually, they were transformed into living nightmares, concurrent with the consolidation of neoliberalism in Mexico and the rise of the Mexican policing apparatuses at the new frontier. These apparatuses remain inextricably linked to the government's investment in projects of neoliberal globalization, specifically the facilitation of undocumented transnational migration.

Chapter 3 foregrounds two prominent border figures, cholos and chúntaros. Many of Barrio Libre's inhabitants identify themselves as cholos; the term also denotes a romanticized figure in Latino/a studies. Here, ethnographically, I underscore how these self-identified cholos prey on chúntaros—hicks, in border parlance—who are typically taken as the undocumented. I situate these figures within the debates on race and *mestizaje* in Mexico, charting how such discourses configure the targeting of chúntaros by the cholos of Barrio Libre, and transnational anxieties about cholos in the Americas and in anthropology.

"Post–September 11 at the New Frontier" is an extended, ethnographic interlude. It is a series of vignettes, beginning with a moment when some of the youths in Barrio Libre and I watch footage of the attacks in New York on September 11, 2001, in their immediate aftermath through a few days afterward. It reiterates a linkage between race and sovereignty, but one again heavily mediated by liberal capitalist underpinnings.

Chapter 4 ethnographically charts militarized policing practices of the United States as part and parcel of the new frontier and as instrumental in the birth of Barrio Libre. It narrates the tragic death of one of the youths of Barrio Libre, the regimes of surveillance and the militarization of the border, and their perverse proximity to the emergence of Barrio Libre. The chapter likewise intervenes in the debates on sovereignty, distancing the new frontier from influential debates in the academy, while showing how the exceptions at the new frontier prove inextricable to neoliberal capitalist logics and the coproduction of Barrio Libre.

Chapter 5 grapples with questions of representation, the culture of poverty, and the complexities of writing about those seen as nightmares and the ideological screens projected on the pathological, criminal, or delinquent agencies. It underscores the necessity for nuanced empirical research in order to grapple with the complexities of "pathology," particularly substance abuse and criminal violence in which certain young people are mired. The chapter draws on ethnographic interviews and vignettes of young men and women of Barrio Libre, as well as on certain theories of ambivalence. The youths speak of "choosing" Barrio Libre—in effect, contradicting the established view in social science that dominant values and discourses "penetrate" subordinated communities. This chapter refuses to situate the youths either as victims or as subaltern heroes. Rather, it argues that the youth of Barrio Libre embrace their imminent death as a final strategy of refusal to the order of the new frontier.

"Nervous Cocks at the New Frontier" is a second, nervous, extended ethnographic interlude about a cockfight organized by one of the youths of Barrio Libre. It harkens back to Clifford Geertz's famous essay on his encounter with police at a Balinese cockfight, a narrative that has become a convention in interpretive anthropology.[59] In contrast, this interlude stresses how the dynamics of militarized policing, again taken as the necessary complement of sovereignty in an age of neoliberal globalization, charge such moments.

The conclusion of the book, "The New Frontier Thickens," ethnographically charts how the youths' maturation into young adults corresponds to the latest intensification of border enforcement and its incompleteness in new drugs in the Mexican borderlands and the latest intensification of the war against migrants in the United States. The conclusion segues into a discussion of the conditions of the new frontier and the struggle for immigrant rights.

Notes on Methods

Without entering the tortured debates regarding facticity, positionality, and empiricism, my work occupies an ambivalent position in relation to theoretical commitments to Enlightenment notions of reason, truth, and transparency. I practice ethnography as an empirical researcher, but not as an empiricist or a positivist. Ethnographic research methods such as participant observation and informal interviews were central tools in my documentation of this subterranean, criminalized population's vexing undermining of the dominant sovereignties of Mexico and the United States at the new frontier and the youths' participations in criminal economies. I do not use such methods naively. Again, I am not attempting to grasp an actual delinquency or criminality, but the articulations of social and power relations, knowledges, and ideologies that give Barrio Libre form, hail it, and render it a central attribute of the daily lives of its inhabitants at, or actually below, the new frontier. Although I "witness" its daily effects,[60] ranging from subterranean erosions of the international boundary and provocative claims of territory to violent racialized expropriations, I situate its genesis in relation to that of the new frontier. I illustrate the complex, intertwined productions of criminality and pervasive militarized policing practices of both the United States and Mexico and their overlapping, competing technologies of rule, their circulations, contingencies, and the depths of their respective crystallized power relations, which give the new frontier its form.

Moreover, the materiality of firsthand ethnographic research — actually talking to and interacting with complex, speaking subjects — checks certain prevailing notions in the academy. Ethnographic methods can become the basis for new knowledge production. That is, ethnographic methods decenter knowledge production, moving it beyond the ivory walls of academia, and acknowledge the decolonizing premise of certain traditions of scholarship: that all humans have the capacity to be intellectuals, but only some are privileged to be recognized as such.

My commitment to the inhabitants of Barrio Libre predates my arrival in the academy. I am the former director of a small nongovernmental organization (NGO) that intervened in the lives of at-risk young people. The organization, Mi Nueva Casa, was established in 1995 and was administered by members of the local county attorney's office. Its board of directors consisted of well-meaning law-enforcement officials, including representatives from the local sheriff's office, the police department, the public health department, and the county government.

Often, however, my activities as an ethnographer revolved around helping the young people with health issues and trying to make their lives easier. Most NGOs in Nogales, Sonora, refused to engage with this population; they were too violent and "contaminated," and they were considered to be the irredeemable human waste — the shit — of the new frontier. Only Mi Nueva Casa addressed the problem. It was funded largely by the Arizona Supreme Court Juvenile Crime Prevention Fund, whose mission was to contain this population, keeping them in Mexico. On the other side of the border, local politicians, generally of the rightist Partido Acción National (PAN), and certain policing bodies participated in the organization, as did staff members of social service agencies of the Mexican government. Thus, my ethnography of the descent of the youth into the Free 'Hood and the rise of the new frontier was not a new, exciting, exotic field site for me, nor a traditional anthropological research project.

Frequently, the youths' homelessness forced me to adopt ad hoc research methods. The youths missed meetings and sometimes disappeared for days or even weeks, while they were incarcerated or traveling through the vast transnational terrain of Barrio Libre. Alternatively, I would find them at the orifices of the underground sewer system; at the offices of the Mexican youth penitentiary; at Mi Nueva Casa; and on the streets of Nogales, Sonora, hustling for money. When I did find them, I would invite them to eat a meal with me or to have a (nonalcoholic) drink. I would sometimes audiotape an interview. I would ask them about what was going on in their lives and, frequently, follow up with a question linking their response to Barrio Libre. Sometimes, I would ask, "¿Qué significa Barrio Libre?" (What does Barrio Libre mean to you?) At other times, the youths would immediately begin to tell stories that explained their activities or responded to my general question. I rarely conducted formal interviews.

Extensive note taking and audiotaped ethnographic interviews were central to this project. They allowed me to develop partial, situated knowledge about particular individuals in Barrio Libre. The recordings were complemented by historical analyses and other ethnographic data.

That said, much of this research occurred at Mi Nueva Casa. It was housed in a small duplex one block from the international boundary, where one of the entrances to the transnational sewer system lay. It had a television, a place to eat and wash, computers, foosball tables, and a noble staff who were themselves wrestling with the regimes of neoliberal impoverishment and self-sufficiency. Indeed, much of what happened between the youths and me was informal, taking place over games of foosball, at meals, while we played basketball at the public schools, or while the youths worked in the streets, selling packets of gum to the tourists or washing the windshields of northward-bound vehicles. Occasionally I interviewed youths in the ditches at the moist, dark, putrid entrances of the tunnel.

Throughout my research, I was careful to adhere to professional standards. I introduced myself as someone who was "writing a book." I made use of consent statements and signature pages or recorded their consent if they preferred. Moreover, I explained to each subject the option to participate or to stop participating without any consequence. Although occasionally I was able to interview agents of the US Border Patrol and other policing forces, more often the authorities refused to work with me. My association with los delincuentes of Barrio Libre, it seemed, had contaminated me. Finally, the sensitive subject matter of this book required that I follow the convention in anthropology of using pseudonyms, unless otherwise authorized. Also, many of the young people of Barrio Libre expressed deep concerns about reprisals, as certain publications have included their photographs. Therefore, I agreed not to publish any photographs that would jeopardize them. Moreover, my writing and reportage was discussed with them at length.

Finally, I end this introduction by underscoring the following point: The vast majority of the dispossessed and marginalized populations of the Mexico-US borderlands refuse the regimes of criminalization generated in the vast exercises of sovereignty and their necessary incompleteness in the borderlands. They do not inhabit, nor do they participate in, criminal or criminalized spaces. My hometown of El Paso, Texas, for example, recently won the distinction of the safest city in the United States. And a recent article in the *New York Times* reports that "the rate of violent crime at the border, and indeed across Arizona, has been declining, according to the Federal Bureau of Investigation, as has illegal immigration, according to the Border Patrol."[61] Nevertheless, the passage of the draconian anti-immigration measure SB 1070 in Arizona and similar vicious measures in other states across the United States, the deployment by the US federal government of more National Guard troops to the border, the ongoing violence of the narco war in Mexico, and other exercises of the new security regimes in both Mexico and the United States bring more theory to flesh and crystallize the haunting effects of more nightmares to bear.

CHAPTER 1

Other Nightmares and
the Rise of the New Frontier

And so it was with the Major Sheriff of the county of El Carmen. Just as the words "Gringo Sanavabiche" come out of Román's mouth, the sheriff whipped out his pistol and shot Román. He shot Román as he stood there with his head thrown back, laughing at his joke. The sheriff shot him in the face, right in the open mouth, and Román fell away from the door, at the Major Sheriff's feet.
—AMÉRICO PAREDES, *With His Pistol in His Hand*

Be they the barbarous Apache or other native people, "illegal aliens," cholos oozing under the international boundary, or terrorists, nightmares or dense anxieties about porous boundaries and Other bodies weigh on the Mexico-US border region and its latest permutation as the new frontier. They involve a certain political utility that global mechanisms and economic systems colonize and exploit, always dialectically and in relation to local, historically constructed power relations.[1] These "dark" iterations—today's "wetbacks," "anchor babies," terrorists, and drug traffickers—speak to anxieties among race, nation, and punitive governance, and to the fictions of state sovereignty in a zone of international flows and movements. That is, the history of this particular international boundary highlights the multiple contingencies of and competitions over sovereignty, its shifting configurations, fragility, and historical contingencies. Questions of bodies oozing between Mexico and the United States, be they migrants generally or the specificity of Barrio Libre, attest to how nation-states, in the words of Ramón Gutiérrez, render "a virtuous body from a sinful one, a monogamous conjugal body regulated by the law of marriage from a criminal body given to fornication, adultery, prostitution, bestiality, and sodomy."[2]

What I call old and new frontiers bracket the history of the modern international boundary between the United States and Mexico. I situate the old frontier in the settler colonialisms and their projects of sovereignty of what was to become the southwestern United States and northwestern Mexico, late in the nineteenth century, and questions of race and criminality began to emerge as key strategems of rule. This period is followed by the consolidation of the modern border (1920 to the mid-1990s) and its paramount expression in the creeping militarization of border law enforcement, as is evident in the development of the US Border Patrol; this section also highlights the centrality of Mexico in organizing documented and undocumented migrant flows. The chapter then turns to the third epoch of the new frontier (1990 to the present). This period consists of the consolidation of neoliberalism in Mexico and its amplification in certain managements of migration in the United States and warlike exercises of an incomplete sovereignty characterizing this period's Border Patrol campaigns.

These three moments are not meant to constitute an exhaustive, totalizing, teleological account that affirms the history of the international boundary, much less the new frontier. On the contrary, the old and new frontiers accentuate the warlike signification of sovereignty at these moments in comparison to the relative stability of the epoch of the institution of the modern border. Thus this history looks at the jagged ends of state formations, how governments and people mutually constitute borders in the complexities of daily life in a region where the extreme wealth of the United States confronts the extreme and intensifying poverty of the Global South.

The chapter likewise complicates certain traditions of scholarship. It disrupts those that frequently monumentalize the Border Patrol or the US empire or those that privilege the machinations of US agribusiness with respect to undocumented crossings and border enforcement. Instead, it foregrounds the imprints of Mexico's political economy. Certain policy decisions and relations of power affect the distribution of resources and multiple accompanying relations that are foundational to rendering Mexican nationals as migrants. Moreover, the chapter necessitates drawing on bodies of scholarship rarely put into conversation: histories of the border, which largely emphasize the US Southwest; the history and historical ethnography of northern Mexico; and the history of migration between the two countries. The chapter ends with the rise of new frontier and certain origin narratives about Barrio Libre.

The Old Frontier

Mexican and US projects of colonization constitute what I refer to as the old frontier. Nightmares of native savagery were mobilized in both the United States and Mexico to justify genocidal regimes of the respective settler colonialist projects. Moreover, as I will retrace in this section, Mexican colonial communities in the country's north would adopt the pathologized tactics and practices of the native warfare during the eighteenth and nineteenth centuries. Similarly, in Texas in the nineteenth century, a settler colonialist project, and accompanying techniques of racialization and criminalization, was used to justify violent rule in Texas, and later across the southwestern United States. Of course, these projects were vastly different. They were complicated by a political economy that desired others to be deeply subjugated but ultimately living people.

Long-standing conventions and attitudes in Mexican historiography consider the inhabitants of Mexico's northern states as marginal to the formation of the national consciousness. Sonorans and other *norteños* have been regarded with suspicion and skepticism given their proximity to and presumed domination by the United States. They have been paradoxically cast as both semi-American and semi-Mexican.³

Yet, the country's northern states — those along what was then becoming the international boundary between the United States and Mexico — played a crucial role in the assertion of Mexican sovereignty and the colonization of the northern territory at the expense of the barbarian Apache and other native peoples. These colonizer communities in the north of Mexico were positioned as *gente de razon* (civilized people). Indeed, the complex relations between *serranos* — a term that denotes the community of peasant warriors in nineteenth-century Chihuahua — and the then largely centralized Mexican state reverberates here. As Ana Alonso has argued, the colonial Mexican state drew on codes of masculine honor to award land titles in order to advance projects of territorial conquest and subjugation of indigenous peoples, whom it characterized as barbarous, pathological, or criminal in comparison with the white patriarchs on the jagged edge of Mexico's colonies.⁴ The Indians of northern Mexico fought tenaciously and with some success against these projects. Yet warfare is a cultural process: a reciprocal specialization in violence was established between the settler colonialists and the indigenous peoples, particularly the Apache.

And said specialization played a significant role. Nevertheless, the relations of power shifted late in the nineteenth century. The serranos' privileging of local forms of solidarity or community identity positioned them as unruly. They were cast as threatening, and ultimately pathological, during the rule of the strongman Porfirio Diaz. They were effectively criminalized and transposed into antimodern savages, resonating with the colonialist nightmares about the savage natives. Their "natural" masculinity had to be socialized and violently tamed through the technologies of order and progress.[5] Notably, during the Mexican Revolution (1910–20), some Mexicans claimed that the famed Mexican outlaw and revolutionary Pancho Villa was part Apache and that his brutal practices were part of this nightmarish legacy.

Similar dynamics can be found in the conquest of what is today's southwestern United States. The general outline of this history has been largely well rehearsed by now: Following the "annexation" of Texas in 1836, the Mexican-American War of 1846–48, and the eventual occupation of Mexico City by US troops in the middle of the nineteenth century, Mexico ceded to the United States over a million square miles, roughly half of its national territory. Approximately eighty thousand Mexicans summarily became US citizens. The Treaty of Guadalupe Hidalgo, the Gadsden Purchase, and other agreements eventually coerced Mexico into relinquishing what is now the southwestern United States to the dominion of the United States.

Then, as now, projects of asserting sovereignty in Texas and the rest of the newly acquired southwestern United States involved criminalizing or pathologizing lives. But at this juncture it served to legitimate colonial violence.[6] There were numerous and largely discounted lynchings of Mexicans, cast as outlaws. Indeed, according to some revisionist histories, Mexicans were more likely than African Americans to be lynched in Texas.[7] Land expropriations occurred alongside low-grade, localized nightmares of what Américo Paredes termed the "Texas Legend," which held Mexicans to be a ghastly lot. They were cruel by nature, cowardly thieves who supposedly recognized Texans as superior.[8] They were simultaneously envisioned as racially impure: an unholy, unsanctioned, pathological hybridity of Indian, African American, and "blackened" Spanish. Although the newly conquered Mexicans were legally considered white, socially and politically they were radically marginalized—lives situated in the collapsing of punishment and death, what Alan Gómez refers to as "living death."[9]

Folklore, oral traditions, and related cultural forms sought to disrupt the emerging stratagems of racialization, dispossession, and criminalization. For Paredes, the *corrido*—a culturally specific oral tradition of the "people who worked the land" put to song—documented US-Mexico border conflict. In his seminal *With His Pistol in His Hand*, Paredes documented and analyzed the corrido of Gregorio Cortez. This wrongfully outlawed character challenged Anglo cultural, social, and political domination and, it must be underlined, Anglo law enforcement.[10] Other corridos documented the folk hero, Joaquin Murrieta. He was initially full of pro-US idealism, but he became a Robin Hood figure—a border bandit—avenging the racist murders of his wife and brother.[11] These and other criminalized challenges to the emerging order of the late nineteenth century became memorialized as acts of resistance, both in the corridos, which were recounted in stories, and later in scholarly works.

In contrast to Texas, sustained contact, much less conflict, between Mexicans and Anglo-Americans was rare in the Arizona-Sonora settler colonialist context of the old frontier. A small number of Anglo-Americans trickled into the Arizona-Sonora region to pursue mining opportunities following the Gadsden Purchase in the nineteenth century. These initial encounters did assume the characteristics of a "race war," as some scholars have put it.[12] The nightmares of the Other did not haunt the Arizona-Sonoran borderlands to the same extent as those of Texas, at least not with respect to the Mexican population. Yet, Sonora holds a long history of anti-indigenous as well as anti-Asian violence.[13]

Following the brutal containment of the Apache late in the nineteenth century by the United States and Mexico, a large migration of Mexicans came to southern Arizona.[14] They found themselves in a community with increasingly pronounced residential segregation. Prior to the Gadsden Purchase, most of Tucson's population clustered within or around the walls of the colonial presidio. The constant threat of Apache attack rendered Mexican Tucson a small and compact settlement, not much more than a military garrison on the east bank of the Santa Cruz River. It was there and at that time that the Barrio Libre of Tucson emerged.

Meanwhile the US Civil War and Chinese immigration to the United States brought a groundswell of support for the Chinese Exclusion Act of 1882 and the so-called Gentlemen's Agreement of 1907 between the United States and Japan.[15] These measures restricted the immigration of laborers from Asian and certain European countries, which in turn allowed Mexican immigrants to meet the steadily increasing demand for low-wage jobs in the emerging Southwestern economy.[16]

Locally, in Arizona, dark associations were soon cast on Tucson's emerging Barrio Libre. It developed a criminal reputation that varied over time—from a haven for bootleggers in the 1920s and the site of a vibrant but rather dangerous nightlife to the home of ordinary hard-working Mexican families. Moreover, Barrio Libre had a significant indigenous component. Both Tohono O'odam and Yaquis from Pascua lived on its western and northern edges, and there was significant intermarriage between Mexicans and the indigenous peoples, both of whom were at the fringes socially of polite Mexican society.[17] Urban renewal wiped out many of the old adobe structures built in the late nineteenth century.

As the twentieth century unfolded, the international boundary between Arizona and Sonora was largely a space of goodwill. The establishment of the railroad and new border towns increased commerce between respective border communities. No official barrier separated Nogales, Sonora, from Nogales, Arizona; only a stone marker in the middle of what was called Calle Camou (on the Mexican side) and International Street (on the American side) delineated their limits. Spanish was commonly spoken on both sides of the then transparent international boundary.

People on the American side recognized the importance of maintaining good relations with Mexico and its people. Both communities' relative remoteness from the centers of respective national governments prompted elites of Arizona and Sonora to develop a working consensus. US citizens in Nogales spoke of growing relationships with the Mexican town, and some business establishments "crossed" the border. For example, one saloon allowed its customers to circumvent the laws of both countries by moving from one end of the bar to another.

Law enforcement involved complex relations between Nogales, Sonora, and Nogales, Arizona. For example, in one instance, Sonoran officials—including the governor and a Mexican official based in the United States—conspired to transfer a mentally impaired individual from southern Sonora, which had no medical facilities, to Phoenix. The operation involved an elaborate ruse with the assistance of a local policeman in Nogales, Arizona. Meanwhile, at the level of the US government, there was virtually no restriction on immigration from Mexico until 1929.[18] Eventually, a rapid expansion of agriculture and the accompanying market relations in the newly minted US south-western states resulted in an ever-increasing dependence on migrant workers for seasonal planting and harvesting of crops.

The demand for migrant labor, however, must be seen in relation to the nineteenth-century genocidal and related settler-colonialist campaigns against California Indians and related instantiations of sovereignty. Anti-Chinese violence in California had been bolstered by the passage of the aforementioned Chinese Exclusion Act, which severely limited the availability of Chinese laborers. Landowners sought to replace these workers with African American migrants from the Southern states, but there was significant popular resistance to their presence. Agribusiness likewise experimented with Japanese labor, recruiting slightly more than twenty-seven thousand Japanese to the United States between 1891 and 1900. Those efforts proved too successful. Labor organizing, together with an anti-Japanese campaign in San Francisco, led to the Gentlemen's Agreement, under which the Japanese government agreed to significantly curtail Japanese immigration to the United States. Similarly, the end of the Spanish-American War in 1898 rendered Filipinos a desirable working population, until an act of Congress effectively ended Filipino migration to the United States. This process and the continuing quest for the least expensive marginalized workers eventuated in the US dependence on Mexican nationals migrating across the border, a dependency formed in relation to the potential sovereignty-signifying violence of the emerging international boundary-cum-frontier, typically embodied in law enforcement and those acting on its behalf.[19]

Meanwhile in Mexico, a significant amount of US capital had penetrated northern Mexico during Diaz's iron-fisted regime (1876–1910). That part of Mexico was soon showcased as exemplifying Mexico's modernization. An impressive network of railroads was built, linking Mexican cities and mining and industrial sites, as well as agricultural sites in the United States, to central Mexico.[20] These processes shifted the economic center of Mexico northward, toward the then newly made frontier with the United States. Porfirio Diaz, Mexico's strongman president, began insisting on growing crops for export and privatizing communal lands, leaving many rural people landless and hungry and inaugurating migrant flows. A dramatic population boom exacerbated these conditions. Indeed, according to some estimates, some 98 percent of Mexico's farmers had no land at this time. And with the newly developed and US-financed railway system, the painful reality of declining wages, the rapidly rising cost of staples, and landlessness, many Mexicans adopted the strategy of journeying northward.[21]

Notably, deepening capitalist relations in Mexico's north and the region's integration into a centralized political system created the conditions that provoked elements in the region to support the Mexican Revolution of 1910–20. Tellingly, several scholars have detected a nationalist or anti-imperialist ethos underlying the revolution. According to one prominent historian, in rebelling against the Diaz regime, Mexican peasants were also revolting against US imperial interests.[22] John Mason Hart also maintains that the defense of Mexico's sovereignty and of the economy of Mexico's national, state, and local regimes was the underlying cause of the social revolution of 1910 and the nineteenth-century provincial uprisings that preceded it. This perhaps explains the pattern of popular assaults on US property that occurred, as well as a series of conflicts between the US government and a host of Mexican Revolution–era figures.[23]

Indeed, in June 1906, workers at a mine in Cananea, Sonora, not far from the international boundary, who were paid half as much as their US counterparts in the same mine and who were forced to purchase goods in company stores and to live in undesirable conditions, went on strike under the leadership of the Partido Liberal Mexicano (PLM) and US anarchists.[24]

It is at this moment that a certain exercise of violence at the old frontier must be foregrounded. A posse of 270 cowboys and miners, along with a unit of Mexican paramilitary forces, aided the Arizona Rangers in suppressing the strike. The Territorial Legislature of Arizona had created the Rangers in 1901.[25] They were modeled after the Texas Rangers, who were known for their practices of racial terror against Mexicans, Native Americans, and African Americans, specifically escaped slaves. As representatives of the emerging political economic and racial orders, the Texas Rangers were an early manifestation of the perverse relationship between criminality and policing in the southwestern United States. They were intimately tied with the settler colonialist projects of the old frontier and frequently called the "rinches de la Kineña or Rangers of King ranch, in accordance with the Borderer's belief that the Rangers were the personal strong-arm men of Richard King and the other 'cattle barons.'"[26]

The Mexican Revolution underscores how frontiers historically signal instability and the violent tactics taken by nation-states in order to rule them. In this historical context, from one to one and one-half million Mexicans immigrated to the United States between 1890 and 1929. In other words, because of the violence and social instability of the Mexican Revolution, approximately one-eighth of Mexico's population moved north of the border. Initial channels for this migratory flow had been provided by the California Gold Rush and by the movement of people in Sonora, Sinaloa, and other northern Mexican states to and from the former Mexican territories of the US Southwest after 1848.[27]

Moreover, the southwestern United States served as a crucial site in the organization and recruitment of, and support for, Mexican revolutionaries. The Partido Liberal Mexico (PLM), a key player in the 1910 revolution, recruited many of its members or sympathizers from among migrant workers and Mexican communities in the United States. For example, Catarino Garza, a Mexican journalist, guerrilla leader, and intellectual, attempted to undermine the Diaz regime from a base in south Texas.[28] Notably, the US government criminalized militant organizers in the United States as illegal aliens, and they were beaten and imprisoned.[29] And during this period the Mexican state was instrumental in policing and surveilling expatriates in the United States, with significant support from the US government.

Pancho Villa's infamous rampage of a small town in southern New Mexico similarly underscores the volatility of the old frontier. Villa and his men's actions incited further mobilizations of US troops, rangers, and National Guard units to the region. Thousands of troops amassed along the frontier as both a warning and a deterrent to Mexican border crossings, literalizing warfare as sovereignty signification. Shortly thereafter, US President Taft agreed to the federal financing of the Texas Rangers.[30] And US troops entered Mexico in 1914 and 1916.[31]

Meanwhile, the shared memories of the earlier Mexican-American War (1846–48), the campaigns of racial terror, and the expropriations of lands by the Mexican population through sometimes vicious, other times subtle means, and often in the form of legal chicanery, inflamed the Southwest.[32] Several well-chronicled examples of Mexican popular insurgency occurred; these include the El Paso Salt War, the Cortina War, and the Plan San Diego.[33] In Del Rio, Texas, officials conducted more than thirty-two thousand interviews to make a meager 108 arrests of undocumented subjects. Elsewhere in the Southwest there were attempted lynchings, frequent shootings, and racist threats against Mexicans—all demonstrating the contours of sovereignty that signify violence tied to policing and warfare, and the subjugations of certain populations.

The Modern Border

The photograph *The Littlest Catch* (fig. 2), taken in 1929, gestures at a transformation in rule that occurred in the border region. In the image two US Border Patrol officers, armed and garbed in the agency's fatigue uniforms, tower over a child. The youth reaches only up to their waists. The little boy, presumably an undocumented youth, carries two bottles of water. One officer gazes into the camera. The other looks down on the boy. Taken at El Paso, Texas, the image signals a gradual shift from late-nineteenth-century settler colonialist exercises of sovereignty to its twentieth-century articulations and new ways of managing the border and migration between the United States and Mexico.

Evoked in this picture is a benevolent patriarchy that is inextricably tied to the consolidation of the modern border. Questions of asserting rule shift to governance and the daily managements of populations. Diminished were the tactics of racial terror central to the settler colonialist project of the nineteenth century. US and Mexican control of their respective regions of the borderlands had been established. Nightmares about the Apache and other native peoples, as well as revolutionary Mexico and its border bandits, ended. New nightmares began. They would coalesce around what was becoming the preeminent figure of immigrant illegality, the Mexican immigrant.[34] A distinction is important; these nightmarish figures were imagined as interlopers. They were not feared as invading forces nor were they revolutionaries, but they were nightmarish criminalized Others.

On May 28, 1924, the US Congress inaugurated the Border Patrol. Its consciously constructed military uniform stressed its continuity with long-standing sensibilities of domination in the southwestern United States. The inauguration of this new police force in the United States marked a new era of immigration regulation. It includes exclusions of whole groups from entry into the country, solely on the basis of race or nationality. The Johnson-Reed Act of 1924 restricted migration according to a formula that led to countries receiving unequal numbers of immigrant visas. It codified popular prejudices about

2. Courtesy of the National Border Patrol Museum, El Paso, Texas.

"greater and lesser inherent degrees of 'assimilability' among variously racialized and stigmatized or perhaps more precisely contaminating, migrant populations" and foregrounded the avowed preoccupation with maintaining the white or Caucasian racial purity of American national identity that fills the *Congressional Record*. Remarkably, migration from the countries of the Western Hemisphere—Mexico foremost among them—remained unrestricted by any numerical quotas.[35] Here, the centrality of policing begins to emerge. Activities such as "repatriation drives" encouraged Mexican immigrants to leave the United States during the Great Depression, and the Mexican-born population in Texas plummeted by 40 percent, which signified how management rather than assertions of territorial control was the new governing rationale.[36]

That said, the centrality of Mexico to the flows of power and bodies at the modern border and policing efforts there must be underlined with the dawn of the epoch of the modern border. More specifically, the *bracero* agreements—which allowed Mexico to officially export agricultural laborers to the United States—foregrounded the inability of the Mexican state to sustain the well-being of its population. Although initiated as an emergency measure to solve a World War II labor shortage in the United States, the bracero agreements were periodically reenacted, while increasingly coming under the control of agribusiness. Braceros—those Mexicans rendered exportable under the agreements—became subject to widespread abuse, as the calculus shifted from controlling territory to subjugating immigrant bodies. The bracero program underscores the influence of Mexican officials in the transnational power relations and regimes of border enforcement. The Mexican government made commitments to prevent Mexican laborers from surreptitiously crossing into the United States.

In turn, the US government committed to detecting and deporting those who had successfully effected illegal entry, rendering the Mexican government a critical partner in the design and implementation of migration-control strategies.[37] Unless the workers broke the terms of their contracts, the US Border Patrol had little to do with the management of braceros and subsequently with border enforcement. Eventually, organized labor and other interests in the United States managed to bring about the end of the program in 1964.

And this ushered in the radical illegalization of undocumented labor. Undocumented migration became the norm. It is notable that the INS apprehended an annual average of only 7,023 undocumented migrants between 1940 and 1943. The numbers increased from approximately 29,000 in 1944 to 69,000 in 1945, and to almost 200,000 in 1947.[38] Migration that is from Mexico became increasingly undocumented, marking the gradual transition of what was at first a low-grade, largely local problem to today's nightmare of illegality sweeping through much of the United States. New regimes of border enforcement appeared. They were tied to US laws, but were implemented in terms of policing and were inextricably linked to questions of sovereignty and illicit transnational flows.

Yet a residue of state violence and the region's colonization remained prescient. A recently retired US Army officer was soon appointed as commissioner of the INS, foregrounding the consolidation of militarism in border enforcement. He guided the Border Patrol's professionalization, transforming the agency from a group of nativist vigilantes, often with ties to powerful interests in local border communities, to a quasi-military professional organization. Indeed, he characterized the actions of his agents in military terms in his first annual reports. Several original members of the Border Patrol had been Texas Rangers. They animated the legacy of brutal sovereignty making.[39]

The residues of occupation, specifically militarism, were particularly evident in the tactics of 1954's Operation Wetback. The operation—whose name was derived from a racial slur—marked the first large-scale, systematic implementation of military strategy and tactics by the INS against the undocumented. Some four hundred Border Patrol personnel were concentrated in designated sectors of the southwestern United States with high populations of the undocumented. The agents worked in concentric, widening circles to push the undocumented across the border. Then other Border Patrol agents, who were supported by aircraft, conducted mop-ups. Estimates vary on the effectiveness of this operation. Suffice it to say that there were from 107,000 to 164,000 apprehensions; the INS claims 1.3 million were deported.[40] The attorney general sought initially to have US Army troops conduct the massive roundup. He also advocated allowing the Border Patrol agents to shoot some "wetbacks."[41] Operation Wetback underscored that the border had been consolidated; the logics of settler colonialist violence had subsided to one of regulation about the then low-intensity nightmares of "illegal aliens."

Meanwhile, Mexican sovereignty mutated under the weight of global capital. New dynamics crystallized at the then modern border. The end of the bracero program and the increased emphasis on enforcement spawned immense pools of cheap labor in northern Mexico, particularly along the border. In 1964–65, in part to absorb the shock of increased unemployment caused by the return of the braceros and so-called dried-out wetbacks, the Border Industrialization Program (BIP) began.[42] The government essentially codified foreign ownership of factories and other forms of production at the border, acknowledging the pressures on its population and, again, the asymmetries of the increasingly global economy by allowing US- and eventually other foreign-owned assembly plants on Mexican soil at the border and introducing maquiladoras as novel stratagems of global capital on the border region.

These assembly plants were the only firms exempt from the nation's laws requiring majority-Mexican ownership, signifying further the mutations of Mexican sovereignty. Labor was less organized in Mexican border cities than in either central Mexico or the United States. Moreover, in contrast to other global locations, the border allowed managers to live on the US side and take advantage of US schools, healthcare, and other services. Although the program developed slowly at first, by 1972 nearly one-third of the value of all US components sent abroad for assembly migrated through the border plants. After 1972, maquiladoras were no longer legally limited in the border region, though their spread to other areas was slow. By 1979, production by maquiladoras accounted for one-quarter of Mexico's manufacturing exports. Although the average wage in a maquiladora is 25 percent higher than in other industries, maquiladora managers have routinely engaged in underhanded practices to prevent labor organizing.[43]

The rise of the maquiladoras, to return to the intersectional component of the larger framework I laid out in the introduction, greatly affected gendered relations of power in the region surrounding the international boundary. The bracero program had primarily recruited male workers. Yet the implementation of the maquiladora assembly plants in the Mexican borderlands involved the active recruitment of female migrants to the region, drawing on gender ideologies of docility and the widespread belief that women were better suited to the grueling demands of assembly-line labor.[44]

Mexico's capitulation to the realities of the global market signaled the end of its experiment with what had been a relatively successful state-directed capitalism. Over several decades the country had modernized, changing from a mainly rural and agricultural nation to an

industrializing and increasingly urban society. This period is often referred to as *la epoca de oro* (literally the era of gold, or the country's
miracle years). The economy expanded at a brisk pace, and Mexico
was able to meet a large part of its consumers' demands with domestic manufacturing. During this time, the government worked closely
with the country's financial elite and gave a high priority to keeping
domestic prices and foreign exchange rates stable. Early in the period,
subaltern Indians and peasants increased their production of agricultural products at a rate higher than the growth of the population, re-
ducing the cost of living and requiring only minimal agricultural imports.

Nevertheless, over time the interests of the majority of Mexicans
suffered as farm products were largely reserved for export markets. In
1964, Mexico shipped 334 million pounds of vegetables north; thir-
teen years later, the flow had increased to 1,018 million pounds —
amounting, in some seasons, to 60 percent of the fresh vegetables sold
in the United States. By the 1970s, there was a crisis in the countryside — a site, it must be emphasized, of significant unrest during the
revolution. Meanwhile, public services were being reduced, and the
government was mired in debt. There was a major deficiency in con-
sumer goods, and agricultural products had to be bought at high prices
in the international market. The mechanization of agriculture, again
under state direction, had helped eliminate many subsistence farmers
while increasing the division of labor.[45]

Indigenous *campesinos* began to experience not a miracle, but a
nightmare in these conditions. Discourses of indigenismo and mestizaje celebrated the ancestral past of Indians and their cultural fusion
with the modern Spanish colonizers, but their material conditions
were grave.[46] It should be noted that these processes invited mobilizations and initiated political actions over pricing, democratic institutions, and land tenure across the country, including Chiapas, Coahuila,
Sonora, Guerrero, and Sinaloa. In the second half of the twentieth
century, these actions rocked the national government.[47]

The unrest in rural Mexico was accompanied by unprecedented
waves of political oppression, which has belatedly come to be recognized as Mexico's own dirty war. Infamously in October 1968, somewhere between five thousand and fifteen thousand demonstrators
gathered at the Tlatelolco housing complex to protest recent government repression of the Mexico City student movement. Between five
thousand and ten thousand soldiers brutalized the demonstrators, and

there was official involvement in "systematic beatings, near drowning and electric shocks."[48]

This constellation of social and political relations exacerbated migrant flows. By 1974, one-third of the Mexican border population consisted of migrants. The expanded labor pool in turn spurred the economic transformation of industry that made the Southwest the region of the United States with the fastest economic growth for the period 1960–75.[49] A new era of massive immigration—both legal and undocumented—occurred, including a greater share of women and entire families than in the past. Between 1960 and 1980, more than a million Mexicans legally immigrated to the United States, but the biggest statistical increases were seen in the records of apprehensions of the undocumented: in the 1960s, the INS recorded more than one million arrests; in the 1970s, the figure was more than seven million.[50]

Meanwhile, anticolonial currents rippled across the world. Notably, new political actors emerged at this time in the United States in the context of the civil rights movement. To the credit of the migrant farmworkers in California and their politicized Mexican American supporters, creative tactics—like marches to the state capital, fasts, folk church services, public theater, and a long-term, largely successful boycott of the grape industry—resonated across the United States. "Mexican Blowouts" in Los Angeles schools, youth conferences across the southwestern United States, and similar civil protests in Texas and New Mexico, along with other strategies—from Reyes Tijerina's storming of the courthouse in Taos, New Mexico, to the rise of the Raza Unida Party in Texas and the creation of the Brown Berets as a barrio defense network—represented a sort of decolonization movement among the ten million Mexicans then in the United States.

Many of these tactics did produce tension between undocumented Mexican nationals and US-born Chicanos.[51] Yet the appropriation of an array of elite indigenous groups and symbols from the Mexican Revolution mobilized the Mexican American community despite a diverse array of political agendas, ranging from ethnic separatism to assimilation in the 1960s and 1970s.

The lethal nature of warfare as sovereignty making began to intensify in both official and unofficial channels. Border Patrol officers were receiving military training in counterinsurgency techniques. In addition, paramilitary units of the Ku Klux Klan in the 1970s roamed the border, attacking Mexican immigrants and exercising a popular version of sovereignty lethally and criminally, but also logically. Moreover, during the late 1960s and early 1970s, individuals' lives and organizations were devastated by state terror organized through the National Security Agency and the six initiatives of the counterintelligence program (COINTELPRO) of the Federal Bureau of Investigation (FBI). In addition to surveilling relatively conservative Mexican American organizations like the League of United Latin American Citizens and the GI Forum, COINTELPRO included the Border Coverage Program, which began in the late 1950s and continued until at least 1971. Although less is known about this program than about any other COINTELPRO initiative, it is clear that it focused on the political links between organizations in the US-Mexico borderlands. It involved regional government agencies in the borderlands—including some of those in San Diego, San Antonio, Albuquerque, El Paso, and Phoenix—and had offices in Mexico City and Monterrey, Nuevo Leon, Mexico. In addition to using a variety of defamatory and disruptive tactics, FBI offices in El Paso and San Diego came up with the incredibly deceptive tactic of having FBI agents pose as INS agents and interview applicants for border-crossing cards. Potential informants, infiltrators, and saboteurs were recruited during interviews in exchange for a card.[52] New nightmares of insecurity began to materialize new tactics of rule.

In late 1979, the first criminal indictment ever filed against INS agents was handed down by a federal grand jury. It came only weeks after the Border Patrol had announced a policy of diverting illegal aliens from Mexico into the deserts and mountains east of San Diego, which would probably cause their deaths. This was an early instantiation of the linkages of death and migration governance in the borderlands that demonstrated how certain bodies are imagined as contaminating, ultimately killable, and nightmares.

Early in the 1980s, Mexico suffered another severe political and economic crisis. Dynamics of capital flight occurred; Mexican bankers and industrialists began withdrawing up to $100 million a day. In response, the government slashed oil export prices and broke its promises by announcing that the state-owned oil company had signed a five-year deal to sell crude oil directly to the United States. In February 1982, the government devalued the peso by 65 percent, claiming that this would prevent demands by the International Monetary Fund for an austerity program in Mexico. A full-scale financial panic erupted in 1982, when the government announced it could not make payments on its foreign debt for the next ninety days. The peso was severely devalued twice more. A large number of small businesses and farms shut down, and more than a million workers were laid off. Hunger stalked the land.[53]

Mexico's 1980s political and economic turmoil occurred as the watershed Immigration Reform and Control Act (IRCA) passed. The legalization of some two million brown bodies and the necessarily incomplete nature of the militarized policing of the border stoked certain nightmares of contaminating bodies. They drove fears of demographically driven migration through the US-Mexico "backdoor." Nightmares of insecurity and Others' medical risks, their contagion possibilities, and their so-called cultural enclavism, alongside the fiscal burdens posed by such migration, fill the congressional record. The southwestern border became a flashpoint of media scrutiny, political debate, and public outrage. Indeed, IRCA increased monies for detention facilities, ground and aerial surveillance hardware, fencing, roads, and border-policing practices under the joint control of the Departments of Justice, Treasury, and Defense. The measure included a significant infusion of resources to enhance the Border Patrol's existing approach to the detention and apprehension of illegal entrants.[54] Border Patrol appropriations nearly doubled what they had been only five years earlier. Moreover, IRCA-era policing eroded the *posse comitatus* statute, a longstanding measure which had bracketed off police from military activities. By 1989, for example, the US Department of Defense, under INS jurisdiction, was awarded direct surveillance, inspection, pursuit, and all-important construction duties in the US Southwest, including the erection of security fences and border lighting.[55]

Meanwhile, the 1980s marked the beginning of neoliberalism in Mexico. The exhaustion of Mexico's state-directed capitalism in the 1970s, the intertwined nightmarish ending of the Mexican miracle and the country's dirty war, the decline of the petroleum-based economy, and the country's skyrocketing foreign debt had set the stage for the country's entrance into the General Agreement on Tariffs and Trade (GATT) in 1986. In many ways, GATT marked the country's transition to neoliberalism, while at the same time reconfiguring the country's sovereignty. In 1988, after what many Mexicans and foreign observers believe was a fraudulent election, Carlos Salinas de Gortari assumed the presidency. The US-trained economist began and completed the negotiations leading to NAFTA, which again dramatically mutated the sovereignty of the Mexican state.

This agreement signaled the consolidation of neoliberalism in Mexico. It is in this historical context that the maquiladora labor force, central to the economy of the borderlands, nearly quadrupled, growing from 43,000 in 1993 to more than 105,000 by 2000. During this same period, foreign investment in the state of Sonora totaled $381 million, two and a half times what it was before NAFTA. As maquiladoras quickly expanded along the northern border, they increasingly employed border residents and others who had migrated to the region from elsewhere in Mexico.[56]

Mexico slid into its worst economic crisis since the Great Depression on December 19, 1994, in what Mexicans commonly refer to as *la crisis*. The peso lost 70 percent of its value between 1994 and 1995. Unemployment doubled, and many people were driven from their land or otherwise displaced from their livelihood. By 1999, six years after NAFTA's implementation, a state of economic emergency had become the norm for Mexicans. By 2000, the real income of the country's workers had declined by 84.6 percent, and the nation's once thriving middle class had been eviscerated.[57]

Nightmares of the New Frontier

On June 12, 1992, five agents of the US Border Patrol were patrolling an area near Nogales, Arizona. In a remote canyon, they encountered three men. The agents took them to be lookouts for Mexican narcotics smugglers. In violation of INS firearms policy, Agent Michael Elmer fired three shots over the head of one of the men. The three men fled toward Mexico. Elmer then shot at the men a dozen times, hitting Dario Miranda Valenzuela twice. The agents then conspired to hide the dying man in a ravine. Doctors estimate that Miranda may have been alive for thirty minutes after the shooting. Eventually, Elmer was arrested. He became the first Border Patrol agent to be charged and tried for murder. During the trial, other troubling allegations against Elmer came forth, including charges that he had sexually harassed and brutalized another Mexican male and had wounded yet another Mexican man when he shot into a group of thirty undocumented immigrants. He was also accused of sexually assaulting another "suspected illegal alien,"[58] Rene Romero. The Human Rights Watch reported:

Elmer stopped Romero while he was driving in southern Arizona. . . . According to Romero, Elmer yanked him from the car and threw him to the ground. . . . Elmer then handcuffed him, kicked him, and struck Romero on his head with his gun. . . . He then threatened to kill Romero. . . . Romero claims that Elmer then pulled Romero's pants down and told him to "bend down as if [you're] going to get fucked. . . . Then, he told him to "open up his ass. . . ." Elmer then searched him. . . . He struck Romero in the stomach and ribs. . . . Romero was taken to the Border Patrol station in Nogales. . . . Romero's ordeal was not over. . . . His repeated requests for medical treatment were ignored. . . . A Drug Enforcement agent interviewed him. . . . At this time, he again requested medical attention. . . . Approximately twenty-four hours later, Romero was treated at the Federal Correctional Institute. . . . His infected head wound needed five stitches.[59]

With respect to the Valenzuela case, Elmer's lawyer successfully depicted his client's shooting of the unarmed Valenzuela in the back as an act of self-defense. Elmer was acquitted, the jury finding that Valenzuela's murder was reasonable at the border. Eventually Elmer pleaded no contest to a charge of reckless endangerment. Because he had already served six months after the shooting, he spent little additional time in jail.[60]

Guadalupe Castillo, a community historian and an activist, told me that the Coalición de Derechos Humanos/Alianza Indígena sin fronteras (the Human Rights Coalition/Indigenous Alliance without Borders), a Tucson-based immigrants' rights group, sought to bring national attention to the Elmer case. The activists drew analogies among the murder of Valenzuela, other human rights violations occurring in the border region at that time, and the Rodney King incident in California in which certain officers in the Los Angeles Police Department brutalized an African American man and provoked national outrage. Castillo said that when she approached a *New York Times* correspondent to complain about the newspaper's lack of interest in the story, she was told that the American people did not care about the border: "It's a Third World country."

It is also notable that late in the twentieth century, the benevolent paternalism evident in figure 2 underwent a rapid transformation. A 1978 cabinet-level Task Force on Terrorism, chaired by then Vice President George H. W. Bush, profiled "terrorists" in the following manner: "Fully 60 percent of the Third World's population is under twenty years of age; 50 percent is fifteen or younger. These population pressures create a volatile mixture of youthful aspirations that, when coupled with economic and political frustrations, help form a large pool of potential terrorists."[61] The report underscores certain night-marish scenarios about out-of-control Latin American youth, cross-ing the international boundary into the United States. Youths and undocumented migration became reimagined. No longer worthy of benevolence, the undocumented were painted as dangerous, unwel-come, and all-too-brown nightmares, teeming to cross the border.

It is in this ideological and discursive context that warfare as sover-eignty making and governance begins to take fuller form. This is illus-trated by the revision of the Posse Comitas Act. The act had banned the participation of the armed forces in civilian policing, except in ex-treme and rare circumstances. Its relaxation in the Defense Authori-zation Act allowed the military to assist civilian law enforcement agen-cies in matters of law enforcement, including the training of federal, state, and local police officials in the use and maintenance of military equipment. The army likewise began conducting surveillance opera-tions using Mohawk helicopters in the Texas border region, and an army training exercise — often to be repeated — began in southern Ari-zona, followed by other collaborations between the military and Bor-der Patrol.[62]

Moreover, as warfare and policing intensified, so did the collapsing of race and national difference. Long-standing historically and politi-cally produced discourses in the borderlands — dating back to at least the old frontier of the nineteenth century — linked Mexican, Native American, and other subordinated populations to banditry, crimi-nality, and pathology. These discourses prefigure what has come to be called the new racisms or cultural racisms — in short, discourses of cul-tural fundamentalism.[63] Increasingly, such anxieties emanate from the new centers of states, their new frontiers.[64] They underscore the pro-duction of racisms tied to boundary policing practices, revealing how the legitimacy of the latter consolidates the former in sovereignty-signifying practices in the age of neoliberal governmentality. Indeed, INS policies governing the detention and release of unaccompanied minors emerged for the first time at this juncture. Some regional INS offices would release minors only to parents, while other offices would release children to any responsible adult or organization. In 1984, the INS Western Region — which consists of Washington, Oregon, Cali-fornia, Arizona, Nevada, Hawaii, and Alaska — adopted a policy stat-ing that except in unusual and extraordinary cases minors would be released only to their parents or legal guardians. In practice, this led to the detention of many more children. Few minors could locate adults who satisfied such stringent requirements. Children not released were placed in a variety of INS detention facilities, usually in state and county juvenile prisons.

But in order to grasp the significance of the descent of Román, Margarita, and others into Barrio Libre, our analysis must delve deeper. The change in US attitudes toward undocumented youths corresponded not only with Mexico's rocky political and economic conditions but also with new views of crime and race in the United States. The civil rights movement had created an aggrieved white public in the United States — one decidedly unwilling to support the welfare of others, particularly foreign Others — and contributed to the country's transformation into a neoliberal and consequently penal state.[65] This shift underscores long-standing anxieties about border insecurity, specifically drug trafficking, terrorism, and undocumented migration.

Mexico's neoliberal turn inaugurated the gradual stripping away of the country's corporatist, or liberal, state. It signified for many Mexicans the end of any hope of redressing social inequalities.[66] Indeed, Article 27 of the Mexican constitution, the revolutionary tenet of land reform, was revised in 1991. That effectively ended any hope of future land reform. It also introduced a movement toward the privatization of *ejidos*, a semicollective land-tenure structure that, since the Mexican Revolution, had served as the basis for redistribution of more than 95 million hectares to some 3.1 million beneficiaries. Moreover, the gradual evisceration of Mexico's one-time welfare state during my time in Nogales, Sonora, was palpable. The principal funding for Mi Nueva Casa — the NGO where I did much of my firsthand ethnographic research — came from a grant from the Arizona Supreme Court Juvenile Crime Prevention Fund. Meanwhile, DIF and other Mexican government programs that were designed to confront the array of issues that affect street, homeless, and problem youths faced significant constraints.

Neoliberal structural adjustments likewise occurred on other terrain within the national political economy. The government liberalized imports, controlled inflation and the balance of trade, and generated incentives to attract massive foreign investment. The 1994 signing of NAFTA (known as the Tratado Libre Comercio south of the border) — a comprehensive plan for liberalizing trade among Canada, Mexico, and the United States — and the accompanying structural transformations in Mexico mark the consolidation of neoliberalism in Mexico. Attorney General Janet Reno had claimed that once NAFTA was passed, it would help "protect our borders" and that failing to pass it would make "effective immigration control . . . impossible."[67] Yet, according to Drug Enforcement Administration studies before the passage of NAFTA, the increased entrance of Mexican trucks could "prove to be a definite boon to both the legitimate food industry and drug smugglers who conceal their illegal shipments in trucks transporting fruits and vegetables from Mexico to U.S. markets."[68]

In the last decade of the twentieth century, and with NAFTA on the horizon, the INS amplified social controls at the border. In the El Paso area, Operation Hold-the-Line commenced in September 1993, on the eve of NAFTA's passage. Some four hundred Border Patrol agents and their vehicles were positioned along a twenty-mile stretch of the border, and helicopters took off in a show of force. The dramatic success of this plan led to the eventual adoption of similar tactics in Operation Gatekeeper in California.[69] With both the San Diego–Tijuana and El Paso–Juárez corridors heavily policed, undocumented immigration increased through Nogales. Shortly thereafter, in 1995, Operation Safeguard commenced in Arizona. The Border Patrol's blurring of antinarcotic efforts with anti-immigration activities in everyday social practices at the US-Mexico border—despite a federal prohibition against military involvement in domestic law enforcement—speaks to the presence of sovereignty-signifying violence in the global era and its nightmarish reverberations.

This complex history of the US-Mexico border region, its policing and migrations, spawns the Barrio Libre. A young woman of Barrio Libre, Margarita, explained the rise of the Free 'Hood during this extended moment: "La Beti [another young woman] and some of her friends crossed the border into the United States [in the late 1980s]. They hid from the Border Patrol in trashcans by some of the restaurants, and on the roofs of banks and stores. They asked for money at the McDonalds and on International Street. They were there for a few days, hanging out, being free, do you understand? Well, the cops started to bother them and they started hiding in the tunnels."

And the stage, or an anxiety producing sewer system, is set. Rife with *agua negras* (black waters), and industrial and human waste, the tunnel begins to transform into a site of vexing freedoms and the eventual embrace of imminent death. The dark fissure of the new frontier begins to foreground the perverse proximity between the youths and low-intensity warfare as incomplete sovereignty making and the accompanying dark anxieties about increasingly vast, increasingly unregulated flows of people imagined as brown. Seeping back and forth through the sewer system, under the international boundary as it became a new frontier, and between Nogales, Sonora, and Nogales, Arizona, these first youths found freedom. They were in their 'hood: "We were in Barrio Libre."

Conclusion

This chapter proposed three epochs in order to produce a genealogy of the twin births of Barrio Libre and the new frontier: the old or colonialist frontier, the modern border, and the new or neoliberal frontier. Such epochs proved inextricably tied to regimes of sovereignty—or, better, that which is taken as sovereignty—and punitive governance of the region, mediated by political and economic processes. With respect to the latter, Mexico's political economy was foregrounded, in contrast to those studies that privilege either the US empire or the Border Patrol. Moreover, frontiers, taken as moments of challenged, deteriorating, or otherwise radically reconfigured sovereignty—which in this case reveals the violent cores of both the United States and Mexico in the border region—find their historical roots in the racialized order of things.

Such is the case with the serranos of Namiquipa, Chihuahua. Originally positioned as a community of peasant warriors on the frontier of Porfirian Mexico, and charged with annihilating the savage Apache, they later became criminalized as recalcitrant subjects of modern Mexico. Meanwhile, in nineteenth-century Texas, conquered Mexican populations were similarly positioned. They were socially excluded and criminalized, and they suffered depredations and expropriations at the influx of Anglo colonists. Indeed, it is no coincidence that the early projects of Chicano studies undid this ideological work of colonization, transforming criminalized males like Gregorio Cortez and Joaquin Murrieta into proto-revolutionary folk heroes. Nevertheless, the specific history of Ambos Nogales lacks what is traditionally viewed as race conflict with respect to Mexico and the United States.

The emergence of the Border Patrol signals a diminishment in the violent tactics rooted in settler colonialist projects of the United States and Mexico in their shared border region. Instead, it is governance, but a governance involving dynamics through the edges of two nation-states, and their necessary, if increasing, daily exercises of sovereignty.

In order to bring into focus the significance of the descent of Román, Margarita, and others into Barrio Libre, I delved into Mexico's rocky political and economic conditions and the new regimes of crime and race in the United States. From the early spawning of the Mexican Revolution by US interests to the wholesale transformation of Mexico's political and economic regime under the imposition of neoliberal forms of economy and governance, questions of sovereignty prove inextricably tied to the country's rule, particularly in that zone adjacent to the United States. Indeed, such questions are only exacerbated by the deterioration of Mexico's welfare state to an increasingly violent, militarized, and, as I will argue later, increasingly white-identified core.

Similarly, as discussed above, in the United States, the transformation of the liberal order after the civil rights movement created a public that refused to support the welfare of others and rampant nightmares about Other bodies, as the United States joined Mexico in becoming neoliberal. These mounting anxieties were epitomized in the aforementioned 1978 Task Force on Terrorism, characterizing Latin American youths as terrorists. And such nightmares of insecurity about the porous and increasingly globalized border took the form of drug traffickers, terrorists, and "illegal aliens," resonating with the savages of the old frontier while licensing new low-intensity warfare at eventually what became the new frontier.

This chapter also introduced the now anxiety-filled category of youths in border and migration scholarship. Its position in the hegemonic nightmares has varied over history and from region to region. A benevolent hetero-patriarchy could be discerned in figure 2, which is emblematic of the modern border and contrasts with the settler colonialist project of the new frontier. Later, as neoliberalism and its privileging of transnational capital took root, an accompanying politics of dispossession in Mexico conjured a nightmarish scenario of out-of-control borders and terrorist youths who exploit the necessary incompleteness of sovereignty at the Mexico-US border, turned new frontier.

CHAPTER 2

Against Mexico
Thickening Delinquency of the New Frontier

Un fantasma recorre el campo mexicano: el fantasma de la migración. . . . Se desfonda el país, pero en particular las comunidades rurales mexicanas se están vaciando. Y los primeros en agarrar para el norte son los jóvenes campesinos.

[A ghost haunts the Mexican countryside: the ghost of migration. It despoils the country, in particular the rural Mexican communities; they are becoming ghost towns. And the first to go to the north are the youths.]
—ARMANDO BARTRA, "Los nuevos nómadas"

No contemporary form of rule can be understood in its own discursive regime or autonomous repertoire of images without an appreciation of its gendered, racist, and patriarchic qualities—what Philip Abrams long ago termed "politically organized subjection," which for him was the mystification or collective misrepresentation of the modern nation-state.[1] I thus write against Mexico in its contemporary manifestations and its warlike assertions of rule. These practices permeate its institutions, economic hierarchies, privileging of certain languages, and violent management of bodies. I write against Mexico and its massacre in Tlatelolco; the police violence against the Popular Assembly of the Peoples of Oaxaca (APPO); the raped, dismembered, and disappeared of Ciudad Juárez; and the drug wars raging across Mexico. The state has reconstituted itself under neoliberal globalization. Its investment in undocumented flows of bodies, flora, and fauna, particularly at sites such as borders, requires complicity in the policing and warfare as exercises of sovereignty at the new frontier, and consequently in the coproduction of Barrio Libre.

I write against Mexico and the widespread assumption that a large proportion of its citizenry should be exiled, precariously situated as migrants, abandoned in the scorching neoliberal ovens of the killing deserts of Sonora and Arizona as they seek to cross into the United States. Their corpses and the disrobed, sunburnt remains testify to their exposure to the elements and dramatize bodies stripped of protections, while Mexico's bleached genteel class grows fat on remittances at home. I write against Mexico because nation-states in the twentieth and twenty-first centuries have increasingly adopted new post-territorial technologies of domination and rule inextricably linked to a calculus of subjugated lives situated in greater proximity to death, a state of affairs that resonates with contemporary scholarship in critical race theory.[2] I write against Mexico because it has birthed some of the wealthiest — if not the wealthiest — men in the world. Such bearers of capitals and patriarchy can for a $1 million investment now live in Texas and fly to their businesses in Guadalajara or other cities in Mexico, rather than oozing through the shit of the new frontier, be it drugs wars, militarized police and vigilantes above, or, the formation of Barrio Libre below.

Such refractions of state power require an analysis that incorporates an emphasis on the banalities of violence and power at the level of daily life and their complex intertwining with always asymmetrical transnational capital and population flows. That is to say, I write against Mexico and related calls for open borders because they are too easily appropriated for dubious purposes.

I write against Mexico from the standpoint of what some have characterized as *el derecho de no migrar* (the freedom to not migrate).[3] El derecho de no migrar recognizes that Mexico is instrumental in the production of displaced bodies situated as porous and exposed to the vicissitudes of crossing borders in becoming undocumented. The right not to migrate highlights the complexities of the subjugation of undocumented migrants and the management of such populations. It calls for the recognition of certain strategies of population management legitimated by the Mexican state, its embrace of neoliberal globalizing governmentality, in terms of the regime's economic policies and governing stratagems, including its negotiation with higher-order networks of sovereign powers represented in the regimes of free trade such as GATT and NAFTA. A right to not immigrate would prevent migrants from passing through the necessarily incomplete regimes of security warfare such as Plan Merida, and derivatives such as Plan Chihuahua. To write against Mexico in the current moment begins to stitch together "the open wound" of the contemporary border,[4] or what I term the new frontier. It continues to hemorrhage.

I write against Mexico to disrupt, challenge, and complicate those often top-down academic formulations that foreground the US state, its imperial legacy and the law as foundational to the social relation of immigrant illegality and border violence, at the expense of critically confronting the instrumentalities and historical specifics of Mexican political and economic asymmetries. Such a position contrasts with the fetish of movement, characterized by certain naive calls for open borders or concomitant calls for an elementary freedom of human movement. These positions are too readily appropriated by global interests and certain longstanding contradictions between capitalist needs for abstract labor and national desires for abstract citizens.[5]

I write against Mexico because I regularly witnessed the Mexican authorities arresting people who could be called potential immigrants, those who appeared to be about to attempt to cross the border through irregular means, in the late 1990s and early 2000s. The authorities simply yanked the would-be migrants off the border fence that separates Nogales, Sonora, from Nogales, Arizona. Such practices exemplify how undocumented migrants, well before crossing the border, encounter a constellation of dehumanizing practices.

Certain sensibilities and discourses in Mexico are inextricably related to the logics of warfare as sovereignty making and situate the migrants as prey to government officials or criminal formations. Violence—in this particular scenario, criminal violence—becomes integral to governance, affirming the migrants' departure, their exposures to the environment, to the authorities, and to criminal and pathological formations as undocumented bodies.

I write against Mexico because too much of an emphasis on the liberal empire of the United States risks mischaracterizing the specific exercises of power and subjugation that configure the northward flow of undocumented bodies from Mexico and other parts of the Americas across international boundaries. Thus, my positioning against Mexico raises methodological, theoretical, and ultimately political warnings against recent efforts by scholars of Latin America and Latino studies to remap these distinct scholarly agendas. Such innovations risk blurring important distinctions and theoretical as well as political questions, divisions, and approaches between the distinct genealogical traditions of ethnic and area studies, particularly given the latter's structural posi-

tion between the respective nation-states and as a historically positioned oppositional check on dominant knowledge productions. I likewise write against Mexico because the post-territorial stratagems of the
Mexican state complicate projects in Chicano and Latino studies and
other state-sanctioned projects that embrace prefigured, historically
and politically specific, oppositional identity categories.

I also write against Mexico because of the country's recent and all-
too-convenient embrace of its émigrés at the turn of the century. Indeed, migration to the United States has long been subject to political
manipulations. I write against Mexico because in the bloody aftermath
of the Mexican Revolution and the rise of the modern Mexican state
early in the twentieth century, new thinking about migration focused
on the threat to peace and prosperity configured by a mass of highly
mobile and politically volatile worker-soldiers in Mexico's north. Their
potential for rebellion preoccupied many business leaders and government officials.[6] Indeed, early in the twentieth century, migration
studies such as those funded by the Social Science Research Coun-
cil emerged as an intellectual, political, and to some extent eugenicist
response to the unprecedented flows of people across the borders of
nation-states.[7] Public intellectuals such as Manuel Gamio, the father
of Mexican anthropology, sought a new, enlightened, progressive
Mexico that could take its place among Western nations. For Gamio
and other Mexican intellectuals, emigration to the United States
marked one way to improve a racially inferior provincial "Mexican-
ness."[8]

Although asymmetrically positioned vis-à-vis the United States,
specifically, and other dominant nation-states, the Mexican state is
linked to new, anxiety-ridden configurations of sovereignty, and to
certain pressurized subjectivities, produced in spaces rife with the perverse proximity of law enforcement and lawlessness. I write against
the Mexican nation-state's intensified policing turned warfare at the
border turned the new frontier. I write against this radical mutation in
exercises of rule and its dark influences in the making of Barrio Libre
and in positioning migrants as vulnerable life, be it in the deserts, in
the sewers, in vigilante crosshairs, or in the radar of drones.

A brawny young man has a swollen purple welt under his left eye.
He looks down, and spews venom: "They pistol-whipped me. I was
going up [out of the tunnel] into Nogales, Arizona, and the motherfucker from Grupo Beta [a special Mexican police force] came up
behind me. He grabbed me by the hair and pulled me back down.

He pulled me back in [to the tunnel]. I thought they wanted us out of there. He took my earnings for the day and beat me up pretty bad. He kicked me in the ribs." His illicit gains — brutally extorted from an unlucky, displaced, impoverished, and terrorized undocumented border crosser who sought to undermine the contemporary border — had been confiscated and this special Mexican police force had pulled him back into darkness.

Stories of the Mexican police infiltrated the Free 'Hood. They were their Others. Another youth of Barrio Libre tells of having his ribs broken by this same militarized police force. A young woman broke her arm as she fled them. The youths were regularly stopped, searched, harassed, and sometimes beaten and arrested by Mexican police forces. The youths of Barrio Libre both terrorized and were terrorized.

Mexico's New Frontiers

As I noted in chapter 1, the 1980s marked the beginning of neoliberalism in Mexico. Here I turn to some more specifics. Mexico's wholesale investment in neoliberal policies of decentralization and structural adjustment lead to a mammoth economic crisis. The regime also marked the end of the Mexican state as a regulator of society and as a provider of welfare provisions. Returning to the characteristics of neoliberalism discussed in the introduction, the new state privileged global interests, effectively privatizing and gutting formerly government-provided social services. Order was to rule the day and it was to be guaranteed through a militarization and policing of society, ensuring smooth and orderly global transactions.[9] Multiple "quasi-governmental" or "state-like" institutions became the articulating body of government through a politics of self-regulation.[10] This consolidation of neoliberalism in Mexico reconfigured the border.

It, like other adept and asymmetrically positioned neoliberal nation-states, develops, legitimates, and enacts national policies designed to exploit global economic opportunities. They manage and they exploit the profitable flow of information, capital, and — of utmost importance for this book — people.[11] Programs such as Tres por Uno, in which the Mexican federal government contributes additional funding to migrants' remittances to local communities, and certain official hailings of migrants as heroes underline Mexico's economic and social reliance on migration.[12]

The Policia Federal Preventiva, Grupo Beta, and other national as well as local police forces, secure and cultivate the undocumented passage of profitable lives. Militarized policing practices by Mexican officials at the new frontier introduce an economic dimension in my emphasis on and policing and warfare as sovereignty. Certain Mexican police forces are charged with safeguarding those bodies about to expose themselves to the temporality of crossing the new frontier and its risks, such as the criminal violence of Barrio Libre.

These new police practices articulated with certain logics of whiteness embedded in the particularities of Mexico's racial dynamics must likewise be factored into this configuration of criminal violence and reconfiguration of state and non-state violence and economics. As recounted in chapter 1, the defeat of the indigenous, brought about by the privileging of a culture of masculinist warrior violence in certain frontier communities, marked the region's transformation from what anthropologists and historians in the eighteenth and the nineteenth centuries had characterized as a frontier to the border as the modern state stabilized. Ana Alonso, for example, showed how a largely autonomous warrior peasant community in northern Chihuahua served as the state's "gatekeepers of civilization" through "an invented tradition of origins" that stressed the whiteness of northerners. Eventually the state turned on this colonial community, criminalizing its members as obstacles to "order" and "progress," and they became leaders in Mexico's bloody civil war.[13] Similarly, at the juncture of the new frontier, the "whiteness" of the north and *fronterizos* (Mexicans of the border) is often juxtaposed with the "brownness" of central Mexico and the *indios* of southern Mexico.[14] The racial power relations specific to the region, and to Mexico more generally, turn on this logic of unrecognized whiteness, privileged Mestizo brownness, idealized or ghettoized indigenousness, and repressed blackness, which play out in the securing of migrants' lives and the concomitant criminalizing of cholos—a term for rebellious urban young people of Mexican descent—and other threatening types.

The term "cholos" in Latin America has long been reserved for people situated somewhere in the racial mix between Indian and mestizo.[15] In the United States and in the border region, the word "cholos" refers to rebellious urban Mexican and Mexican American youths.[16] But the term has garnered a new potency in an era of neoliberal flows and new stratagems of rule. It is a synonym for "gang member" or "thug" across much of the Americas, signifying a historically constructed racial, social, and criminal anxiety. *They* are the unauthorized, unsanctioned, and pathologized hybrid Others. They embody the nightmares of "modernizing" youths who are engaged in urban and border warfare.

The young men of Barrio Libre went out of their way to don the criminalized fashions of cholos. They wore baggy pants, sometimes a hairnet, tattoos, and T-shirts proclaiming "mi vida loca" or showing representations of marijuana leaves or la Virgen de Guadalupe, the patron saint of Mexico. Such emblems pointed to their participation in or identification with undocumented networks of marginalized youths in the United States and transnational circuits with Mexican Americans in the United States.

For the young women of Barrio Libre, gendered power relations reinforced similar identifications. As young impoverished women on the serrated edges of the neoliberal economy, they were often cast off, pushed out, or exorcised from the normative world of conventional labor. Their baggy clothes and dark lipstick, central features of chola aesthetics and emblematic of their participation in undocumented networks, often precluded their acceptance in the docile female labor force of maquiladoras.[17] One young woman, for example, explained that when she was working in a maquiladora, managers demanded that she and her coworkers dress *como gente decente* (like decent people), a neoliberal incarnation of a much older colonialist discourse — specifically, a phrase that refers to the supposed savagery and inhumanity of indigenous peoples. Local businesses refuse to hire youths wearing cholo clothes. To be a cholo or chola was to be seen as a pariah, a menacing criminal thug, intimately linked to undocumented transnational, criminal networks and their underground workings.

The Borders of Legitimacy

I can make out the lyrics of Los Tres Deliquentes (The Three Delinquents), a Los Angeles hip-hop band, from the headphone of Javi's beat-up Walkman. "El Chicano gave me the tape when I was in Barrio Libre," he says, referring to a young man in the Barrio Libre of Tucson, Arizona, discussed in chapter 1. I am trying to interview Javi at the *Mono Biche* (Naked Doll), while he and the other youth are hard at work on this day in 1999. The *Mono Biche* is a towering statue of an Adonis-like, muscular Benito Juarez, a nineteenth-century president of Mexico, made of glistening black stone, who is flexing his tremendous biceps, donning curly hair, and spearing an eagle. It is located about a mile or two south of the international boundary and where this already cast off population could find work, toiling on the edge of legitimacy. Close to the *Mono Biche* is another statue, this one of Father Kino, a Spanish priest who was a missionary to the Tohono O'odham, who once dominated the region. There is no statue to Native Americans. Close by is also a business that produces bottled water—the latest fashionable commodity in Nogales. Trucks circulate in and out; they deliver water in large containers to clients around the city. Streams of water flow from the plant into a drainage ditch and then into the darkness of the underground gray cement sewer.

But the imperative to hustle, to approach cars and wipe their windshields for money, repeatedly interferes. Javi approaches a light purple Oldsmobile. The man behind the wheel frantically signals no. Javi ignores him, the driver relents, and Javi wipes the windshield with a squeegee. The driver lowers his window and offers a couple of pesos— about twenty cents—as the young man smiles. He moves to another car. Other youths also hustle. Many drivers yield and offer a peso or two. It was common knowledge that young women were rewarded more highly than men in this menial labor. It was also common knowledge that much more could be earned in the shadowy, underground world of contraband smuggling and mugging the undocumented in the dark subterranean economy of Barrio Libre.

I wait as Javi approaches a black sedan. The woman behind the wheel agrees reluctantly. He cleans the windshield with the squeegee and earns a few more pesos. His next client speeds off rather than paying him, after he wipes his window. It takes ten minutes for him to find a driver that again gives a few more pesos. He has probably made the equivalent of eighty cents over the half hour. Román had told me long before that to be in Barrio Libre was to "not work." It was to survive on a life of petty crime in the tunnel or on the streets. But many of the youths did work. They navigated the increasingly blurring borders between the legitimate and the "dark" criminal economies. Indeed, those who dwelled in the Free 'Hood distinguished illicit from licit practices in their vernacular. Terms like *bajar*, *tumbar*, and others that translate roughly as "taking down" signal the dark mugging practices, integral to Barrio Libre.

Some of them used false documents or lied about their age to gain employment in maquiladoras. Mexico has strict laws about child labor. But the youth managed to find ways to seep through them. Margarita, for example, was a teenage mother who would work from midnight to 10:00 AM at a maquiladora after taking care of her children all day and following her mother's ten-hour shift at the same factory. Margarita was uncertain what product she was making, but told me that her work involved soldering and circuitry. After work, Margarita would collapse on the couch at the Mi Nueva, a halfway house, where she sometimes came for breakfast.

Every few months, Margarita would quit her job in frustrated exhaustion. She would then indulge in Barrio Libre, living free off of violent earnings that she and others made mugging migrants and embracing its more pathological ends, specifically the abuse of spray paint and other industrial substances for a few days, often with her children in tow. But her maternal responsibilities would eventually compel her to return to the realm of the legitimate economy. She would then spend days sobering out and trying to find enough money so that she could buy clothes so as not to look like a chola. She repeatedly told me that she wanted her children to lead a better life. Other youths would similarly manage to find work in the maquiladoras, only to eventually either quit or be forced out because of their threatening style.

Another youth in the Free 'Hood had been a chimney sweep in a tile factory. Several others worked as *pinches* (bus boys) in restaurants, and a few sold tacos on the street. Other inhabitants of Barrio Libre earned money doing odd jobs, such as mixing cement on construction sites, laboring in small businesses, selling small packets of gum, washing car windshields (fig. 3), or sweeping chimneys.

Many of the young people moved throughout Mexico and the United States to find work. Román explained to me for much of 1998 he had left Nogales, Sonora, to live in Guadalajara, and through family connections had gotten work as a security guard for the transportation system. Jesus had worked for several months at a farm in Imuris, Sonora. He had quit in disgust because the pay was too low for the backbreaking work, which included lifting one-hundred-pound bags of soil. But they tended to come back to Nogales, Sonora, and Barrio Libre.

Indeed, Román, despite his previously mentioned assertion to the contrary, did work. By day he and some of the others were *taqueros*; they sold tacos at a small neighborhood taco stand. But by night they ran drugs, which in Román's mind was a masculine enterprise. Indeed, one night, he and his accomplices had wandered east of the border fence, miles beyond the militarized exercises of law enforcements, into the deserts and headed north, where eventually he hid the drugs. In

3. Washing windshields. Photo by author.

short, they practiced their vicious freedoms of the Free 'Hood to supplement the collapsing of their options and brutal exorcism from public space amid the gradually intensifying securitization of migration at
the new frontier.

Román's complex experiences on this new frontier are telling. He
took odd jobs; he trafficked in contraband and mugged people as an
inhabitant of Barrio Libre. He was the father of one of Margarita's
children. Both he and Margarita expressed a desire that these children would not be "free"—that is, they did not want the children to
become inhabitants of Barrio Libre. His experiences as the son of a
migrant laborer speak to the inflections of migrations and the social
relations of illegality and deportability in the birth of Barrio Libre. He
learned English when he went to school in the state of Washington, in
the United States, and improved it during one of his numerous incarcerations in the prisons of the new frontier, before his father's naturalization status was revoked for having allegedly sold cocaine. Once
Román, his father, mother, and his brother were deported, the family
went to Guadalajara. Román's father returned to the United States *por
chúntaro* (illegal alien, colloquially), and his mother stayed in Guadalajara. Román eventually ended up in Nogales, Sonora, however.

Barrio Libre hailed him, and he accepted it. It short-circuited the cycle of wealth production. It took him about a week of factory work or other legitimate forms of economic activity to earn the equivalent of what he could make in one night in the untaxed subterranean expropriations that occurred in the tunnels. And, as we will see later in this book, Barrio Libre brought with it other pleasures.

The Gonzalez brothers' experiences were also inflected by transnational migration. The eldest of the brothers, Güero (Blondie) — so named for his light skin and freckles — had spent many years in the Free 'Hood. He hadn't seen his father, a migrant, for six years. Güero told me that he had attended school until the sixth grade. Those who knew him before he got into "trouble" — before he became a cholo — described him as a very bright young man who excelled in school. Güero explained to me that his father had been working in construction, but "times got rough" in the economic downturn of the 1990s. According to one of Güero's brothers, the father and his young family had moved to Nogales, Sonora. The mother quickly found a job in a maquiladora, and the father worked at one for a while, too. Güero explains: "But he hated it. People were telling him about life in the north, about the opportunities. He left with three other men in 1992. He came back in 1993 for two weeks. That's the last time I saw him. He still sends us money, but it's not very much."

"Why do you think he hasn't come back?" I ask Güero.

"People say it's hard to come back now. It's too hot to cross. . . . When my dad left, I was the eldest, and I thought I needed to help provide. My mom was working in the factory, and my brothers, they needed supervision and more things."

Güero began working in a small store, to help out his mom while going to school. He soon met other youths from Barrio Libre. He began to undermine the border by traveling to the Barrio Libre of Tucson. "I made some money in Barrio Libre," he said, but he would not tell me how.

Before 1994, Mexico's welfare programs would probably have provided assistance to such "troubled" youths, but its post-1994 skeletal social services could not address their myriad social problems. They could not address inadequate housing and urban infrastructure, displaced and fragmenting families, inadequate schools, and the punitive bend of the authorities on both sides of the new frontier.

A few nonprofit organizations struggled to assist them. And certain agents of the government who worked in law enforcement would occasionally offer them shelter, but this was done informally. On the whole, the youths were expected to be self-reliant. And such demands sucked them into the shit of the subterranean economy and its vicious means of production.

Securing Lives and Thickening Delinquency

In the late 1990s, the Mexican state began actively to facilitate undocumented migration to the United States. It is in this context that the gradual "securitization" of migrants' lives has occurred. This conjunction of forces has augmented, or thickened, the delinquency of the inhabitants of Barrio Libre.

Güero explained: "The police [in the late 1990s] started asking us for credentials to work on the streets. We never needed them before." Other young people reported the same circumstances. Javi said: "[The authorities] came and started to demand that los cholos get *credenciales* to wash windows." Before then, the youths could panhandle or perform menial jobs in the tourist zone. Homeless, broke, and increasingly marginalized, they could not acquire the now-necessary documentation, further excluding them from avenues of legal employment.

Gabriel told me: "[The authorities] came and chased us out of tourist zones where we used to ask the gringos for money and where we used to wash the windows on the cars going to the other side [of the border]." The tourist zone was far more lucrative than where they were situated, pushed almost a mile further south. And Victor noted: "[The Mexican authorities] came and started to demand that we get credenciales to wash windshields."

Here the presence of policing and its increasing militarization pressed on the youths, pushing them further into the unrecognized labor of panhandling and hustling for money, as well as sucking them deeper into the illicit, underground practices of selling and transporting drugs and other street and tunnel crimes. Indeed, a government official in the Mexican youth authority who worked with young people was convinced that those who lived in Barrio Libre were selling drugs as they washed the windshields of northbound cars. On the heels of the demands for credenciales, such practices became far more common among the youths.

When I asked one of the young people of Barrio Libre why he thought that policing had intensified, he told me: "They wanted to clean up the *desmadre* [chaos] of the border for the tourists." Another youth, Juan, explained: "The border was where people got their first impressions of Mexico and the authorities didn't want to give your fucking *paisas* [countrymen] a bad impression."

Aside from securing the lives of migrants, the campaign to cleanse the border-turned-new-frontier marked an effort to portray the country as a stable, democratic nation on the verge of membership in the First World. *Vagancia* (the status of being a vagrant) suddenly garnered greater potency in the late 1990s. It became grounds for policing and related processes of marginalization.

Such policing amplified the conditions that drove the youths into the criminal economy. During this moment, "cholos" increasingly began to refer to thugs. Denigrating, dehumanizing narratives about the cholos of Barrio Libre pervaded Nogales, Sonora. They were seen as the brown hordes of the border, the unsanctioned, vulgar hybrids who preyed on people about to become undocumented migrants in an increasingly amoral, blurred economy of licit and illicit labor, and of course amplified by the increasing knowledge of their practices in the sewers and its associations with feces, toxins, and the like. Stigmatized as sewer dwellers and cholos, they were sucked deeper underground and deeper into its "dark" criminal economy. Violence became one of the few ways they could make a living.

Indeed, Javi's statement below foregrounds the perverse proximity of Mexican policing practices at the new frontier and the thickening of the young people's delinquency. Javi said: "If they [the police] don't let me clean windshields, I will go to the tunnel and mug. . . . What do the police want? . . . For us to be mugging?"

Such dynamics amplified as Mexico increasingly invested in an economy that necessitated the secure passage of living and laboring bodies to the United States, who could then send remittances back home. In this context, Grupo Beta and other national and local police forces began to regularly use oppressive, if not criminal, tactics, targeting, harassing, threatening, and arresting the youths, particularly the young men. They were transformed from mere public nuisances into hypervisible menaces. An excerpt from a conversation with Franco provides some insights:

> Yesterday I was walking down Heroes Street when two from Beta stopped me. They thought that I had *broncas* [petty fines] that I needed to pay. They always say that about us, when they want to stop us. They hand-

cuffed me and started kicking me pretty hard. I told them I didn't have any broncas. They didn't believe me. They wanted to take me to jail. I was just about to get to where I sell gum when this happened. They let me out at 2:00, since I had no broncas to pay, but they still hit me. I got hit with the gun. They would push me down to the floor even harder. Over here, policemen are very mean. You have money . . . they take it away from you.

Bolillo told me about a time when an officer from this police force arrested him: "They painted me like a woman. They put on lipstick, eye shadow, and they put me in a dress." In a space pathologized in the United States as overwrought with machismo, a problematic, racist discourse mapped on Mexican and Latin American masculinities, Bolillo was put in drag and sexually humiliated, underscoring his vulnerability as a socially exorcised youth.

Margarita recounted a similarly harrowing encounter with an officer of Grupo Beta. It too had gendered dimensions. She came out of the tunnel in Nogales, Sonora, with another youth of the Free 'Hood, and describes what happened:

[The officer] put his gun to my head and told me not to move. Negro [the other youth] ran. . . . [The officer] was going to hit me, and I told him, if you're going to hit me, don't hit my stomach because I'm pregnant. . . . He then handcuffed me and took me to the office. There they told me they were going to send me to the *correccional* [youth detention facility]. He asked me, if I send you to there, will you stop? I told him . . . send me . . . I'm here already . . . there's nothing I can do about it.

Her comment that "I'm here already" captures the density of police power in her life and the lives of other young people at this moment in Nogales, Sonora.

Margarita's deft, defiant use of the ideologies of motherhood show how these new policing apparatuses at the border integrate gendered power relations in the exercises of sovereignty at the new frontier. Indeed, this narrative captures how the neofrontier relations reify normative power and, again, the necessity of racial analysis to incorporate questions of interlocking oppressions of gender and hetero-patriarchy within global relations of inequity. Moreover, her experiences as an active member of the Free 'Hood disrupt notions of gang violence as necessarily masculinist.[18]

Nevertheless, the youths' perverse proximity with policing and low-intensity warfare as governance was characterized by a degree of intimacy, despite the acts of repression. They knew some of the officers on a first-name basis and, in some cases, officers would reduce the charges when arresting them. Their proximity to policing suggests a vexed relationship between it and delinquency:

> *Gilberto*: Tell me something . . . you said something about a Beta officer.
> *Margarita*: They call him "the Blade."
> *Gilberto*: Why?
> *Margarita*: Because he carries a big knife, it's scary. Then there's Arce, Sabula, Victor, Cabeza de Borrego, Adrian.

The youths suggested that such a knife was often used for criminal practices by this figure.

When I asked several of the youth in Barrio Libre which of the multiple police forces patrolling the border and forging sovereignty they would rather encounter, all of them replied the US Border Patrol. Both Román and a friend described this particular agency — in a point that must be highlighted here — as their bus service back to Mexico: "When we want to go back to Nogales . . . we let them catch us."

Moreover, during my fieldwork in the late 1990s — and to a lesser degree in the early 2000s — Mexican police forces regularly harassed and rounded up displaced, nomadic subjects, the potential immigrants, those banished to exile. They would target those who appeared to be about to attempt to cross the border through irregular means, yanking them from the border fence that separates Nogales, Sonora, from Nogales, Arizona, and then arresting them. Officers would also target people marked by weathered skin, wearing tacky western shirts and tight jeans, and speaking Spanish with an indigenous accent — an official, violent concretization of difference on certain subordinated bodies that suggests racialization. This convergence of the mugging practices in Barrio Libre and corrupt policing practices captures the perverse transnational effects of discourses of illegality, promulgated by representatives of the United States and other exercisers of sovereignty.

Moreover, rumors emerged in Nogales, Sonora, in the late 1990s and early 2000s that certain Mexican police officers were working as mid-level players in the "black" market. Stories of their involvement in the traffic of bodies and contraband across — and under — the Mexico–US neofrontier further destabilized the legitimate order of things: the young people's criminal violence was problematic for the officers' illicit trade. Thus the police, better armed and ensconced in the emerging criminal realms of undocumented migration and the smuggling of contraband, further marginalized the inhabitants of Barrio Libre and aggravated their delinquency.

The same could be said for *polleros,* those who infamously traffic in human cargo. They emerged as another group involved in the darkening new racial and criminal economy of the neofrontier. They too exploited the fissures found in the incomplete exercises of state sovereignty in the age of neoliberal governmentality. Román explains: "We would fight the polleros. We were bad for their business. We wanted to mug the chúntaros and they [the polleros] wanted them to pass with ease. So we would fight. They started carrying guns. Some of them would shoot at us."

Stories of pollero violence against young people circulated among the inhabitants of Barrio Libre. Jesús told me: "One time I was asleep in the tunnel. *El pelón* [the one with a shaved head, a pollero] came around the corner with a group [of migrants]. He and two other men started hitting me with their flashlights. I wasn't going to do anything. Margarita started to scream. Then they took off."

Román gave the following account of another incident:

> There were like fifteen chúntaros and a pollero, and then the . . . pollero . . . came out . . . over here, all bad ass and buff, the dude, and he starting telling us right away, "don't get near" and supposedly that we wanted . . . that we were going to mug them and no, well, we took no guns, knives, or at least sticks to hit them . . . and El Tortas got near him . . . and the pollero smacks him . . . El Tortas was crying that the smack he had received was hurting. And then they got us and they called me . . . called him first and then called me, and then they called me again and "Get back down, motherfucker."

Conclusion

With respect to neoliberal Mexico, certain profitable lives versus those deemed human waste have proved central in the emergence of new criminal subjectivities that comprise Barrio Libre and other criminal formations. The youths of Barrio Libre worked on the blurring borders between the collapsing informal economy on the streets of Nogales, Sonora, and the dark criminal practice of the underground economy. As the established international divide between the United States and

Mexico transformed into a site of vast, undocumented flows of bodies and contraband and blurring the licit and illicit modes of survival, new configurations of policing taken as sovereignty emerged, intimately linked to the securitization of vulnerable migrant life. They subsequently transformed the youths transformed from nuisances into cholos, a new form of criminal hybrid. More specifically, as new regimes of policing that secured migrant lives developed, the young people consolidated into Barrio Libre. The youth of Barrio Libre became the subject of intensified state violence, and they likewise adopted and simultaneously exercised violence as a vicious means of production in a criminal distortion of the legitimate order.

Although the exercise of legitimate official violence—policing—perpetuates sovereignty, as Giorgio Agamben notes, or the law, according to Walter Benjamin,[19] policing in this and other liberal orders also serves to protect life and maintain the well being of populations. In the case of a radically liberalized Mexico, where undocumented migration became a way of life for a broad swath of the citizenry, such regimes protect the well-being of economically vital, remittance-producing, undocumented migrants. That is, neoliberal governmentality, legitimated by the state, has proven instrumental in the management of migrants. Such lives, however, already find themselves in regimes of economic globalization and long-standing racializing discourses, which similarly coproduce the furious delinquency of Barrio Libre.

Such processes must be linked to the dark networks of shadowed power and the Mexican state, its "kin network of elite entrepreneurial families,"[20] and their ties to the powers in the drug trade at the new frontier. The authorities, much like the youths, were positioned in various ways by the new economies. They targeted those who dwelled in Barrio Libre in an effort to secure the border and remittance-producing migrants' lives, wiping away the blight that threatened the nomadic bearers of remittances, both products of the neoliberal age and again underscoring a perverse proximity of policing and criminality. But elements of the Mexican police forces of the new frontier were also pressed upon. They became players in emergent criminal economies.

The intensified policing of Mexico's new frontier coalesced what had been a loose solidarity of street youths engaged in petty crime into a hardened group of delinquents who identified themselves as cholos. Those who dwelled in Barrio Libre exercised a degree of intensely circumscribed agency as neoliberal mutations of sovereignty transformed Mexico's northern border into a new frontier. Moreover, ethnographic methods and theoretical precepts emphasizing the formation of subjectivities capture how such interlocking oppressions become sites of vexing exercises of power, even among extremely marginalized populations—giving them a sense of freedom.

Positioned on a border that was fraying under the pressures of Mexico's neoliberal-induced economic crisis, they were transformed from public nuisances to criminal. The border between their criminal and legitimate lives was likewise fraying, as the former became more and more central under the pressures of new and increasingly militarized policing tactics. This conjunction culminated in the concretization of Barrio Libre. They coalesced first on the streets. Then, they solidified in the sewers amid their associated meanings of waste and the wasting, crystallizing the gutting of Mexico's former liberal welfare state.

CHAPTER 3

Low-Intensity Reinforcements

Cholos, Chúntaros, and the "Criminal" Abandonments

of the New Frontier

> Soy libre y sobrerano. Soy Mexicano.
>
> [I'm free and I'm sovereign. I'm Mexican.]
> —ROMÁN

Cholos loom large in the Americas at the opening of the twenty-first century, where the specter is not revolution but dark, criminal menace. Cholos and cholas speak to criminal desires and delinquent possibilities, to pathological immigrations, to urbanizing criminalized youth, to migrations gone astray and immigrant dreams turned into dark nightmares as they collide with an encroaching border and immigration archipelago. With Latinos now the largest ethnic or racial population in the US federal penal system, cholas and cholos conjure up renewed demonizations.[1] They evoke nightmarish insecurity; they bear signs of unauthorized, unsanctioned, and unchecked cultural and racial flows.[2]

Cholos embody delinquency and criminality across much of the Americas. They disrupt discourses of the emergent Latino upward mobility, of the Hispanic middle class north of the US-Mexico border.[3] Once limited to certain regions of the US Southwest and major cities such as Los Angeles and Chicago, cholos—and the nightmares about them—now reach New York, Mexico City and Puebla, and Central America.

Although hardly new, cholo sightings now pervade contemporary ethnographies about Mexican migration to the United States, and about the international boundary and border crossings. One of "the undocumented" in an influential ethnography of Mexicans in Chicago explains: "All along the border!—[cholos] rob us, they fuck up

... the women."[4] In Lynn Stephen's influential ethnography, Mariano explains that, on the weekends, cholos would come and "assault, rob, and kill people."[5] Hector, in a recent ethnography of Ciudad Juárez, Chihuahua, written by Alejandro Lugo, remarks: "'Si no son los polis, son los cholos' [if the cops don't get you, the *gang* members will]."[6] From Guatemala, Charles Hale maintains that, despite "the widespread postmodern skepticism of bounded identities and claims to authenticity" that problematically infuse the discipline, Latin Americanist anthropologists often exhibit "a residual aversion to poor neighborhoods where youth wear baggy clothing and listen to hip-hop, and cinderblock walls feature graffiti that mark 'gang' territories."[7] Octavio Paz once condemned the wretched *pachucos*, precursors of cholos, as "instinctive rebels, and North American racism has vented its wrath on them more than once. But the pachucos do not attempt to vindicate their race or the nationality of their forebears. Their attitude reveals an obstinate, almost fanatical will-to-be, but this will affirms nothing specific except their determination ... not to be like those around them. ... His whole being is sheer negative impulse, a tangle of contradictions, an enigma."[8] Rudolf Giuliani padded his presidential résumé by working on the draconian policing policies of *mano dura* (iron fist) in Mexico City against these nightmarish figures. Intensifying images and discourses about their criminal fashion — including tattoos and baggy clothes — their alternative argots, and their transgressive, seemingly unfettered criminalized transnationality increase anxieties about unchecked and undocumented migrations.

Cholos and cholas call forth those far too common, uncomfortable, affective economies on both sides of the US-Mexico divide. They are the barbarians at the gate — the return of the repressed hordes — whether they come from the global South to the United States or, increasingly, from the United States to the rest of the Americas. Their delinquent points of view capture the perverse relationship among militaristic policing practices and pervasive, if unacknowledged, racial discourses in Mexico and in the United States, which the abandonments and intense policing at the new frontier between the United States and Mexico solidify. That is, the cholos generally, and in this case Barrio Libre, lived as criminalized reflection of US and Mexican dynamics of low-intensity sovereignty-making warfare and high-intensity policing at the new frontier.

Contrast the cholo — or, better yet, the pervasive nightmares about him — with a second far more reticent figure of the new frontier: the marginalized, scoffed at, and summarily dismissed chúntaro. His dream of a rural life has been rendered a nightmare. While the cholo claims space, brandishing his barrio on his body, proclaiming it and his connections to his transnational kin network on tattoos and in verbal art, chúntaros struggle frantically to fit in the new frontiers between Mexico and the United States or, further south, between Guatemala and Mexico. He (or she) has already replaced his sombrero with a baseball cap and put on tight jeans. His weathered skin, clothing, and indigenous accent—if he speaks Spanish at all—betray his unsuccessful efforts to fit in at a place designed to officially reveal national— biologized as racial—differences. His provincial characteristics symbolize his impoverished, rural backwardness and his crushed hopes. Even the daily banter of the border presumes chúntaros as emasculated, castrated, disempowered, and all too vulnerable. There is no feminine chúntara in border discourse, but there are in practice.[9]

Chúntaros clutch their rosaries to their bodies and carry tote bags or backpacks. They hide their savings in the dark crevices of their bodies, trying to protect the money from marauding bands of cholos and unscrupulous government officials alike. They hope to make it big in the United States, if only they can get there, safely. Public discourses about chúntaros in newspapers and in the everyday life of the borderlands focus on their perceived darker skin and backwardness.

But Latin American racism marries to these socially ingrained prejudices strong class connotations: chúntaros are the *maleducados* (poorly mannered), the *nacos* of the new frontier. The latter term is a malicious, *denigrating* term heard in Mexico City and elsewhere in Mexico for the rural hicks. The dislocations and discomfort of the chúntaro captures his impermanence; his marked, outsider status; and his entrance—or his anticipation of abandonment. His awareness that he is putting his life at risk, when he—or, of course, she—crosses the new frontier.

Cholos and chúntaros merge the histories of long-standing, unacknowledged racism in Mexico with the new nightmares about Latino border crossers in the United States, a mixture that coagulates in the sovereign abandonments and respective militarized exercises of law enforcement at the new frontier. The lived experiences of cholos and chúntaros speak to the implosion of borders, their transformations into new frontiers, bracketed by neoliberal arrangements and security concerns after September 11, the accompanying entanglements of sovereignties rendered fraught, and historically and politically rendered aliens. New frontiers are their way stations for these uncharted, economically vital, multiethnic alien populations of the Global South. New frontiers are where they steel themselves to cross increasingly militarized international borders without documentation.

The low-intensity warfare of contemporary policing dramatizes migrant bodies rendered inhuman, deemed illegal aliens in popular discourse, and positioned as conditional subjects outside the boundaries of their own nation-state and the United States. Indeed, much of the scholarship on this international boundary has highlighted the effects of the militarization of law enforcement in the border region.[10] But, rather than proving domination, the militarization of the border proves the incomplete, tenuous, and unstable nature of US dominion. It needs to be exercised each day in repeated performances of a violent will to rule.[11]

Following September 11 and the subsequent War on Terror, theories of sovereignty and biopower garnered great influence in anthropology and other disciplines. But international boundaries, where sovereignties are dramatically exercised, have long been central in the state management of the biological lives of the population, signaling how the jagged edges of sovereignty do indeed produce the biopolitical body.[12] Indeed, much of the debate over the crisis of the state in the age of globalization hinges on the assertion of "sovereign failures" to control borders: governments fail to control the flow of commercial instruments, currencies, flora and fauna, commodities, labor, and alien bodies. But sovereignty is diffused at the new frontier between the United States and Mexico. Moreover, the neoliberal economy relies upon certain informal, disorganized, and irregular exceptions, the contradictions central to the maintenance of illicit flows, illegal bodies, and dark desires. Sovereignty, that is, is necessarily incomplete.

And this incompleteness is mediated bodily, forged through historical and political hierarchies that disrupt the emphasis on the legal dimensions of exceptions that are so prominent in contemporary theories of sovereignty and certain renditions of biopower. Cholos, cholas, and chúntaros reveal how certain bodies are the first to be tortured, imprisoned, criminalized, and, in this case, subject to criminal or delinquent violence when engaging in unauthorized, undocumented border crossings. And in this case, modern forms of sovereignty exceed the rational, bureaucratic managements of bodies and populations: police, cholos, and other criminalized populations hold the power over life. Bodies in such scenarios are intensified, intimacies ignited, and

long-standing conflicts re-instantiated in forms that are all too haunt-
ingly familiar.[13]

Although I am certainly not minimizing the more than five thousand deaths of undocumented border crossers that have occurred in
what I have elsewhere termed the "killing deserts,"[14] too often analyses of border policing fixate on the militarization of the border by
the US authorities. Mexican authorities also engage in the militarization of the border and similar exercises of sovereignty. Importantly,
new policing apparatuses such as Grupo Beta and, later, the Policia
Federal Prevenil (PFP) have consolidated along Mexico's new frontier. The mission of such new policing apparatuses included securing
the lives and safe passage of those who were about to cross the border
without authorization. Those trafficking in bodies and contraband and
those preying on migrants similarly coalesce in the tenuous, fleeting,
synthetic incompleteness of neoliberal sovereignties, and the accompanying nightmares it generates.

That is to say that cholos cannot be taken as objects of positivist
study. Rather, they are birthed in the sense of Foucault; chúntaros
are produced in the sense of Marx; and the criminal violence of the
former against the latter is forged in the criminal abandonments of the
new frontier. I thus again look south to Mexico and the daily effects
of mestizaje as a racial formation to analyze the mugging practices of
Barrio Libre in relation to the insidious racial powers of biopolitical
states and the white supremacist residues of empire infusing contemporary discourses of mestizaje in the political and economic necessity
of abandonments of the new frontier.

The Delinquent Fashions of Mestizaje

What has been called the cult of the mestizo (mestizaje) emerged
from the ashes of the Mexican Revolution in a remarkably successful
attempt to exorcise its legacy. Scholars like Dave Theo Goldberg have
maintained that *blanqueamiento* (whitening), or an unstated, veiled
racial politics that situates whiteness at the pinnacle of modern Latin
American nation-states, undergirds mestizaje as certain logics of rule
vested in racial mixture.[15] Mestizaje effectively bleaches its subjects. It
makes the national and, by extension, regional Latin American populations phenotypically lighter through a politics of incorporation. In

short, whitening becomes a state project of proliferation through the ingestion of the indigenous, the devouring of the different as much as the ravaging of resources.[16] An unspeakable whiteness represents the culmination of the process of "normalization" that Arlene Torres and Norman Whitten characterize as "becoming increasingly acceptable to those already made, perceived, or having standing as 'white.'"[17]

Mestizaje was forged in power relations to an external Other — the imperialist United States — as well as to internal Others — the European-oriented, prerevolutionary elite and the Indians. A cadre of postrevolutionary intellectuals, ranging from Manuel Gamio — trained at Columbia University, and a disciple of the famed anthropologist Franz Boas — to the Hispanophile scholar of letters José Vasconcelos, imposed a new politics about life: a state-organized aesthetic of mestizaje. Gamio was a major force in legitimating and promulgating the discourse of mestizaje. The idea of an immutable hierarchy running from savage to civilized that characterized European evolutionary anthropology repulsed Gamio, as it did his mentor.[18] Boas's well-known anti-racist views, his early support of the National Association for the Advancement of Colored People, his stature as public intellectual extraordinaire, and his experiences of anti-Semitism are well documented, if subject to debate.[19]

Postrevolutionary discourses of mestizaje situated the beginnings of Mexican history firmly in the Aztec past. Consequently, Indians formed a part of the romanticized, distant past and contributed to the current racial mix in what José Vasconcelos, a child of the border, famously termed *La Raza Cosmica* (The Cosmic Race). The natives of Mexico were presumed to be a dead or dying culture; they were romanticized as Mexico's vital origins, but living ones were seen as backward after centuries of colonialism and oppression. Indians, then, had to be redeemed by the postrevolutionary biopolitics, a modern science of racial fusion between the Spanish and the indigenous peoples, marshaled by the Mexican state. This new mythic revolutionary history considered racial mixture to be positive and became the cornerstone of a new state-driven cultural and aesthetic project that was explicitly anti-imperialist and anticolonial, and that permeated state institutions such as schools and the mass media.

This regime has been identified as one of the most important attributes of Mexican culture of the 1920s and 1930s. It is manifest in popular culture and art throughout the twentieth century — including films, theater, and murals—and speaks the taken-for-granted racial order, exclusions, injunctions, and similar exhibitions of power relations in Mexico.

This project of postcolonial hybridity lent itself to state racism. Scientific expertise was used in the name of sovereign power to subjugate and subordinate, if not also to produce and rationalize native Mexico's political subjection.[20] In this respect, Manuel Gamio represented Mexico in the International Congress of Eugenics in New York—where, according to an account in *Ethnos*, he actively participated in a discussion of the betterment of human races and was named vice president of the meeting.[21] The migration of Mexicans to the United States, Gamio maintained, would effectively whiten Indians. They would be converted into deracinated modern workers and improve Mexico on their return.[22]

Mestizaje thus provides an enduring map of social relations in Mexico, as well as throughout much of Latin America. Its sensibilities circulate in government statistics and in public schools. Mestizaje flows among the blondes of the elite barrio of Santé Fe, in Mexico City—who, sheathed in black, tell themselves that there is no racism in Mexico. It flows northward between those in Mexico and those in the Mexican diaspora who celebrate the Sambo-like characters of *la India Maria* or the *Memín Pinguín*, and who express bewilderment at the outrage toward the latter in the United States. The northward flows endure among elderly grandmothers in Mexico's north and the US Southwest who insist that their grandchildren remained covered in the sun, so as not to get too dark. Mestizaje dissolves black and brown into white in a national space thick with the dialectics of racial formation.

Mestizaje and its fantasies of an antiracist imagined community prohibits public discussion of how nightmares about other bodies haunt everyday social relations in Mexico. They are evident in commonplace nicknames found across the country and among the cholos of Barrio Libre: Guero (blondie), Negro (the black one), and Moreno (the brown one). Notably, in addition to being taller, more hard working, and more progressive than their southern counterparts, authentic fronterizos (Mexicans from the border regions) are held to be whiter.[23]

In the mid-1990s, under pressure from indigenous movements and international organizations, the Mexican state grudgingly shifted to a politics of multiculturalism. Yet, as seen on the ground and underground in Ambos Nogales, despite the state's relinquishing of its role as mediating mestizaje, its intensifying neoliberalism accentuates cultural difference as race in Mexico. The newly liberalized indigenous peoples, recognized as culturally different, largely remain segregated as primordial primitives and idealized for such backwardness—fodder for the emerging tourism industry. When they decide to migrate, they are translated from migrants into chúntaros in the criminal abandonments of the new frontier.

Cholos, however, complicate a structural reading. "Cholos" refers to both gang members and a certain sense of marked transgression, a fashion that identifies with the illegalities of undocumented migrations. The hip-hop artists Tres Delinquentes, Control Machete, and other favorites of the inhabitants of Barrio Libre donned this style. And, as the new frontier coalesced, the inhabitants of Barrio Libre seized on the nightmares it evoked. It was an aestheticized but transgressive, unsanctioned, hybrid fashion of undocumented border crossings and Latino criminality. To wear cholo fashion was a radically conditioned choice to be visibly and self-consciously identified with a criminalized class, signified by a marijuana leaf sewn on a hat or a T-shirt celebrating "Chicano style" or "la vida loca." There was an excitement, particularly early on, among the youths of Barrio Libre. To be a cholo proved that they were on track for membership in *la M*, or the Mexican Mafia. To be a cholo was to perform a criminalized masculinity that was ideal for intimidating the displaced and, consequently, emasculated chúntaro and the vulnerable (and discursively unregistered) chúntara.

Popular discourses about cholos mobilize latent, historically constructed racial and social meanings of the contamination of a disorganized, unwieldy, and increasingly global mestizaje; and pulsating anxieties about unauthorized, pathologized hybridities of the impoverished across the Americas. Ideologues and commentators immersed in neoliberalism muster vile images and imaginaries of cholos in their attacks on impoverished, undocumented border crossers. Intensifying nightmares about cholos capture a mass-mediated, insidious, anxiety toward these dangerous, yet seductive, hybridized lumpen figures, showing how nightmares can become fashionable.

Of course, counterdiscourses about cholos circulate in transnational, alternative public spheres. Cholo style developed in the 1930s and 1940s, when pachuchos, again precursors of today's cholos, appropriated their style from the hip African American entertainer Cab

Calloway. By the 1960s, Chicano youths had adopted the term "cholo." In a provocative article, Richard Rodriguez writes of a cholo sensibility in queer communities of southern California: when it is "evoked, [this] homeboy aesthetic routinely represents aspects of *la vida loca*, a lifestyle commonly attributed to gangs."[24] Yet, unlike queer "homeboys" in Los Angeles or those figures celebrated in much of Latino studies, performed in hip-hop artistry, and opposed by middle-class fantasies of Mexico's bleached wealthy classes, the cholos of Barrio Libre illustrate that—although race, gender, and sexuality may be experienced intersectionally—certain deep contradictions prohibit such categories from being experienced transhistorically, or universally, for that matter. Global relations of inequality penetrate their lived experiences of the dispossessed, criminal position of the cholos or cholas.

Those lived experiences of being nightmares on such new frontiers—which ethnography, as flawed an enterprise as it is, remains adept at capturing—contrast with the often seductive imaginings and dangerous sensibilities found in the mass media, certain traditions of scholarship, and appropriations by hipster youths on both sides of the new frontier. The flaw in the literature on cholos and related youth cultures is that it tends to fall back on scripted positions of adolescent resistance. Such analyses restore agency to the structurally oppressed. But they repress the painful realities of deprivation and the street—or, in this case, subterranean—violence of emerging economies forged in abandonments and in new exclusions, particularly in the current moment of intensification of and perverse proximity between war and policing and the widespread exiling of migrants.

At a moment of the neoliberal augmentation of undocumented migration and the simultaneous intensification of policing and low-intensity warfare, the youths' cooptation of this impoverished, transgressive, criminalizing youth culture and its strong associations with those living illegally in the United States effectively darkened the youths of Barrio Libre. They were pariahs in the field suffused by unnamed white privilege in northern Mexico.

The cholas of Barrio Libre wore their hair long. They wore long white T-shirts and baggy jeans. The young women spiked their bangs and wore dark, heavy eyeliner as well as dark lipstick and lip liner, effectively blackening their lips. They consequently exhibited a radically criminalized femininity, situating them in the purview of official and unofficial policing as well as legal and extralegal sanctions.

Nevertheless, the young women did not usually call themselves cholas, and the young men of Barrio Libre frowned on its use. When the young women wore criminalized, yet pervasive, chola fashion in Nogales, Sonora, it proved transgressive in the normative, conservative order, bringing them a degree of freedom and pleasure. But the chola stereotype lacked the same menace. Circulating discourses about cholas did not crystallize the same nightmares about them as discourses about cholos—discourses the young men drew on in their practices of violence as wealth production. But "chola" did have more room to challenge certain gendered expectations hoisted on them. That said, heteronormative, maternal responsibilities vastly mediated the young women's experiences of being cholas, particularly as the young women matured. As many of them became mothers, they felt compelled to enter the normative world of wage labor, typically in US-owned maquiladoras. To work in them, the young woman had to change their attire to "normal" wear. The managers in such global factories tended to rely on stereotyped imaginings of docile, heteronormative, Third World femininity—which, as some scholars have argued, maquiladoras have actually actively inculcated.[25]

Still, many of the youths, regardless of gender, who sought normative wage work in maquiladoras or other venues, reported demands made to give up their delinquent fashions. Louie explained how this criminal aesthetic kept him from getting a job: "[Someone in personnel at a maquiladora] said that she didn't let workers dress like cholos because then it was more common for fights to happen. You start having your little groups, and that's how fights start. And for women not to wear short dresses. Because, you know. She said that she had no problem with cholos. That they work well. But she would not let them go to work dressed like that."

Similarly, Rubio had to leave a job at a small grocery store to remain libre in Barrio Libre. The manager told him that he dressed "like a cholo." Rubio responded, "Well, that's who I am. I wear cholo clothes." Negro recounted how he had to quit his job at a market, where he used to sweep floors and stock the aisles. The owner had demanded that he stop dressing "like a cholo." And much of the tension between the young people and organizations that tried to assist them revolved around their attire—such organizations did not want to help hoodlums, and such sensibilities were augmented by the knowledge that the youth mugged and consumed street drugs in the shit of the sewer.

Meanwhile, the criminalized fashion marked a key resource for the youth in the northern expanses of Barrio Libre. In the United States, it often allowed them to pass as US citizens. While criminalizing them and bringing them pleasure in Nogales, Sonora, it also brought these delinquentes a degree of what some scholars have termed "cultural citizenship" in the United States, although in this case heavily mediated by criminality.[26]

Moreover, certain tensions among the youths of Barrio Libre reveal how they struggled with the knowledge of being criminalized and racialized as cholos, as the following excerpt from a conversation reveals. To contextualize it, I should note that Román felt that Tortas was "conceited" because he was trying to leave Barrio Libre and no longer wearing cholo clothes. Tortas said: "One can't wear normal clothes because you say that one's conceited. What do you want . . . you want me to dress all baggy so that the police take me to jail?" As Tortas and many of the other youths knew, donning cholo or chola attire attracted the wrong kind of attention.

The tension evident in Román and Tortas's discussion about their clothing tells of the youths' asymmetrical positioning and the intensifications of interlocking global inequities that neoliberal economic policies amplify. Tortas and his family lived on the edge of desperate poverty, created by neoliberal structural adjustments; Román, as a displaced neoliberal denizen, was already situated in poverty. Although pleasurable, cholo attire for him was far more of a necessity. It was the clothing that was available to him, and it situated him in realms of nightmares that criminalize, racialize, and marginalize lower-class Mexican Americans in the United States, émigrés in Mexico, and impoverished youth at the new frontier. The incomplete reverberations of US law enforcement and Mexican policing practices reinforce the fragmentary nightmares of abject criminal difference.

Chúntaros and State Racisms

At the new frontier, the term "chúntaro," along with all its indexes, is marshaled against the uncultured and uncouth, the retrograde Indian, or anyone else who stands for the rural backwardness that Mexico was trying so hard to shed in the 1990s. Mexico's salvation was postmodern, international culture and neoliberal economic restructuring.[27] Those who embody the term tend to be the dislocated: the displaced, the deterritorialized, and often those en route from economically restructured Mexico or countries south of it to the United States. To be a chúntaro marked people's status as the displaced, their discomfort and dislocations at the new frontier, and their already alien status as they prepared to cross without authorization into the United States.

According to certain popular accounts, "chúntaro" is a corruption of "chutaro," a word in Otomí, an indigenous language of central Mexico. The word was used first in the states in the north of Mexico, such as Sinaloa and Sonora. It can also be found in states in the center of the country, such as Michoacán, which has Otomí groups. Chúntaro denigrates multilingual, indigenous peoples whose first language is not Spanish.[28] This is of particular import given that in Mexico one feature ascribed to indigeneity is language.[29]

That is, well before crossing the border, would-be undocumented migrants—imagined as rural people, indigenous, or provincial hicks—face a constellation of dehumanizing discourses and practices that exemplify the particular racializing arrangements and mentalities promulgated by the mestizaje and legitimated by the Mexican state. Imaginaries about the chúntaros prevailed among the youths of Barrio Libre as well as across sectors of the civil and state societies of Nogales, Sonora, in the late 1990s and early 2000s. References to chúntaros pervaded the everyday speech of those in Barrio Libre and heralded the arrival of the newly exiled to Nogales, Sonora. The young people of Barrio Libre boasted of being *tumbadores total* (total muggers) and spoke of *bajando chúntaros* (taking down the hicks). Such phrases were painted on the cement walls of the ditch leading to the below-border sewer system. The cholos of Barrio Libre described chúntaros in the following manner: "Well, they're not just from around here. They're short. And they don't speak Spanish too well. They're dark [*prietos*]. They dress funny, like cowboys." It should be noted that many chúntaros, particularly those migrants coming from Central America, were not phenotypically "darker" than many of the cholos of Barrio Libre. That is, I did not perceive their skin color as darker. They were sometimes noticeably lighter. Postrevolutionary ethnic and racial power relations rendered chúntaros as bodies subject to the youths' violence in the criminal abandonments of the new frontier, and positioned them—or rendered them imaginable—as dark.

An alternative genealogy of chúntaros, according to certain informants in Tucson, is that it means black bird, and when "illegals come to Tucson . . . [and] those who were of darker skin were called chúntaros." The provincial fashion of chúntaros typically consisted of cowboy hats and tight jeans. The youth of Barrio Libre imagined that the chúntaros were bearing large sums of money to pay the polleros and set up homes in the United States.[30]

From the delinquent's point of view, low-intensity warfare as sovereignty making amplified these relations. The militarized policing practices served to reify the category. The cholos of Barrio Libre would explain matter of factly that the chúntaros were those crossing the international boundary illegally, as *pollos* (chickens), to try to make it in the United States. The cholos did not see any contradiction in the fact that they did this too, in their regular undermining of the border. When I tried to persuade them otherwise, the youths would laugh and dismiss their criminal violence as being bad or, more precisely, being part of Barrio Libre. Or they would claim that they were exacting a toll on the chúntaros, demanding what they called a *cuota*, a fee for using the tunnel. Notably, this assertion returns me to the Mexican state. Some youths reported that the Mexican authorities, particularly Grupo Beta, would demand a cuota to let them be "free," which again suggests the perverse proximity between violent exercises of sovereignty and this emerging criminality, revealing the reach of exclusionary discourses about illegal aliens' power in the United States that solidified these transnationally inflected, transgressive, and mestizaje-derived identities.

Moreover, the chúntaros' pursuits of undocumented labor ignited latent frustrations among the inhabitants of Barrio Libre. They opted for the "dark," criminal mode of production, and they subsequently refused to enter those relations of illegality as many of their parents had. The inhabitants of Barrio Libre performed thus their frustration with chúntaros in their spectacular and collective violence against those whom they perceived as blind to the exploitation of the undocumented in the United States. In this respect, Román explained, "chúntaros were suckers." "If we don't steal from them, your countrymen will."

Fashions of Race

Although many of the youths in Barrio Libre were the sons and daughters of local impoverished maquiladora workers, others were the children of those exiled from rural communities and sent to the new frontier or beyond. Indeed, in the early days of my research on Barrio Libre, members of this latter subgroup of the Free 'Hood would ask for *una milpa* (a cornfield) when panhandling. Others described working in the fields with their parents. After assimilating into, or inhabiting, Barrio Libre, such provincially laden practices diminished. They quickly took on the pathologized, seductive cholo or chola aesthetic. Gone were the button-down western shirts, sombreros, and tight jeans of *los ranchos*. In their place were the backward baseball caps, loose jeans, tattoos, and T-shirts signifying their membership in the subterranean Free 'Hood.

Moreover, the youths' calculated, collective violence, exercised against chúntaros in concert with the donning of such criminal fashions, negated their proximity to those experiencing exile—the dislocated and irredeemably backward rural chúntaros. That is, their Barrio Libre does not render them chúntaros, although some have rural backgrounds. It was an opting out from the taken-for-granted given of life as the undocumented, while keeping enmeshed in the related ideologies of Mexico as a postracial imagined community. They were instead cholos, seeping under the new frontier between Mexico and the United States and mugging the already subjugated people of Mexico's neoliberal turn, the newly displaced, marginalized, and parochial, uncouth peasant who frantically sought to become part of the border and Mexico's transnational ethnoscape.

Nevertheless, slippages between chúntaro and cholo identities allowed those who dwelled in Barrio Libre a degree of empathy. Their encounters with official violence, personified in warlike policing, led to some personal transformations and critical reflections by some of the inhabitants of the Free 'Hood. After a year away from Barrio Libre, visiting his parents in central Mexico, Louie returned and explained to me that, as he was returning to the drainage ditches, empathy seeped into him. "To tell you the truth," he explained:

> I was one of the last ones that would go into the tunnel by myself. During those days, no one would go down there. I remember that the last time I came to Nogales, no one would go down there. Everybody would tell me that things were pretty bad. I got myself a jacket and a lamp, and a marker . . . and started mugging chúntaros. Then I started thinking that these people are as poor or poorer than me; and us taking away their money—it's kind of not fair. Ever since then I stopped doing it. I was also having nightmares. I kept dreaming that I was going to get killed in the tunnel.

As Louie's story suggests, cholos and chúntaros, as mestizaje-derived categories and amid the pressurized managements of bodies and the violent significations of sovereignty, may seep into one another if situated in global relations of inequity. Indeed, a version of the term "chúntaro" can now be found north of the border in the United States, where the categories of chúntaro and cholo interpenetrate. The term seems to be garnering some cachet in undocumented and Mexican American youth cultures. Indeed, the term is now widespread, circulating through songs like "Chúntaros Style" by El Gran Silencio in the contemporary, transnational music scene.

Conclusion

The pathological points of view of those who inhabit Barrio Libre capture the perverse proximity of militarized policing practices, pervasive racial discourses in Mexico, and new managements of territory and populations along the new frontier. To be a cholo or chola in Nogales, Sonora, is to be immersed in the pleasures and dangers of being criminalized and also to be positioned as impoverished, urbanizing youths involved in transnational circulations of desires and commodities. To be recognized as a cholo or chola in Nogales, Sonora, by virtue of a certain criminal sense of fashion such as a shaved head, bandanna, and baggy jeans for the young men, or baggy clothes and thick eyeliner and lip liner for the young women, was to invite a range of official and unofficial sanctions. The radically conditioned adoption of cholo or chola fashion was a way to refuse the abject position of vulnerability that the hick chúntaros inhabited, and to adopt an aesthetic of criminal menace, ideal for an underground economy involving expropriations and violence.

To be officially or unofficially recognized as a chúntaro invited marginalization and occasional extra-official or downright illicit violent expropriations. In the delinquent's point of view, the chúntaros' fashion positioned them as impermanent and displaced. It likewise signaled money-bearing, parochial outsiders without ties to the community. These long-standing meanings resonated with the imperial reach of the antimigrant policing practices and discourses of the US immigration apparatus. Moreover, for the youth of Barrio Libre, these individuals were proverbial suckers, heading to the United States to be exploited. The youths targeted the newly liberalized campesino turned migrant. They thus became the criminal reinforcements of the low-intensity exercises of sovereignty at the new frontier and drew on the long history of the Mexican state's scientifically validated ideologies of marginality toward the indigenous. Chúntaros were the latest victims of such biopolitics. They were always alien bodies to the Mexican state. Their experiences show that the state of exception is not the fundamental paradigm of rule today, at least in neoliberal Western democracies. Rather, certain bodies—be they indigenous or black in Latin America, or Muslim and migrant in other contexts—become subject to state-mediated violence not necessarily through legal exceptions, but through long-standing distributed knowledges that are validated by experts. In other words, what the criminal abandonments of the new frontier reveal is not a state of exception but a racialized status quo, intimately tied to the deep state racism of Mexico's postrevolutionary biopolitical order.

Nevertheless, the criminal fashions of the cholos of Barrio Libre and the rural fashions of the chúntaros allowed seepage between these new border subjects. When stripped to the core and denuded of their respective criminal and rural fashions, recognitions of similar circumstances, in terms of global inequity, brought one youth—and one can imagine others—empathy. Louie chose not to mug.

Post–September 11
at the New Frontier

Mexicans call the sixteenth of September el deciseis —*that is when they celebrate their country's independence from colonial Spain. In honor of this holiday, Román has welcomed me to what he calls his "penthouse." This two-room cinder-block shack, with a sheet-metal roof and holes for windows and doors, sits precariously on a hill in a* colonia *(neighborhood) of Nogales, Sonora, Mexico.*

From the penthouse, Román can see Nogales, Arizona, and at the moment two green and white Suburbans of the US Border Patrol. The odds are 30 percent that the agents inside the vehicle are Latinos. As of 2001, the Border Patrol holds the distinction of the federal agency with the largest Hispanic representation.

Beto, another of the youth who borders adulthood in Barrio Libre, turns the dial of the 1970s-era television. All the channels are devoted to news of the September 11 tragedy. Franco makes a casserole of Doritos and tuna, a dish he calls una torta. *He learned to make it while imprisoned in Arizona for his repeated attempts at unauthorized entry and burglary in the United States. The lived experiences of Franco and other youth of Barrio Libre, their subterranean movements and perverse proximity to policing and war making as sovereignty building, and the immobilizations and other tensions that such phenomena have birthed underscore how the border-turned–new frontier has long been the site of security warfare. It is mediated if not corrupted by the historical specifics of neoliberal globalization, generating nightmares.*

Román gestures at the televised images of Ground Zero. Despite being thousands of miles away from the border and separated by the jagged edges of the new frontier, New York is the center of our conversation.

"They know who has done it. Right?" Guero asks.

"They say," I reply.

Osama bin Laden materializes on the screen.

"He looks like the devil," says Beto, whose nickname is Chamuco, a term for the devil. "I hate those fuckers," Willi remarks: "The ones I hate are those white people. . . . There were a lot of Mexican people working there."

Images of the imploding buildings appear over and over again. So does the outraged, stunned commentary.

Román seethes: "He [bin Laden] wanted to fuck up the white people and he fucked my raza. There were about fifty Mexicans that worked in the cleaning maintenance. They had just arrived. . . . I'll kick this man. . . . That fucker killed fifty of my paisanos . . . fifty Mexicans. . . . They worked in the two towers." Flaco (a nickname meaning "the skinny one") jumps into the conversation: "He [bin Laden] killed ilegales." Again, the long reach of this term is worth noting.

On September 11, 2001, the number of Border Patrol agents in Brownsville, Texas, surpassed the number across the entire US-Canadian border.[1] Since then, new draconian police powers of the homeland security state have had profound consequences for all migrations. These include the approximately eight thousand Muslim immigrants or visitors sought for questioning by the FBI, and the five thousand who have been detained.[2] September 11 likewise amplified the long-standing nightmares of the United States and Mexico, as well as the multiple subjugations that constitute US sovereignty both domestically and internationally. Normative imaginings of citizenship and of homeland have intensified and become expressed in capillary forms. They range from vigilante groups to the horrendous practices that occurred at Abu Ghraib. The paramilitary death squads of the new frontier include The American Border Patrol (not the actual US Border Patrol), Civilian Homeland Defense, Ranch Rescue, the Arizona Guard, and the Minutemen, and they terrorize and hunt undocumented immigrants. They have detained groups of them at gunpoint, and shot at them. One of the leaders, Gary Spenser, claims that Mexican immigrants dilute American culture, an instantiation at the new frontier of ideas and that Samuel Huntington espoused after September 11. Their Spanish language, their forms of dress, their Catholicism, and deep Western "knowledge" of race—namely, colonialist proto-racisms and nineteenth-century racial "science"[3]—render Mexicans and presumably other Latin American populations irreconcilable with the "cultural core" of the United States.[4]

I try to argue with Román. I begin explaining about the support of Israel from the United States, the latter's unquenchable thirst for oil, and its multiple and complex histories of imperialism, and about how with the collapse of the Soviet Union there is no country to check US influence. I move to immigration and the militarization of the US-Mexico border. I am about to tell them of my analysis of the new frontier and how they—los del Barrio Libre—fit into it.

Román and the other youths ignore me. Román finishes his analysis: "They worked in cleaning. Janitors. That what I heard."

Román exclaimed: "Look at the people. Look at them!"

We remain glued to the screen. The men and women crying, the people praying, the firefighters and police frantically clawing through the rubble silence us. On the television, New York firefighters dig through smoldering rubble, atop what I imagine are the dismembered, melting corpses. The ash of burned human flesh cakes passersby and clouds the televised air.

Previously, official and sometimes extra-official violence alongside the vast political economic reorganization of Mexico created the conditions that led these young men to opt into the dark, vicious mode of production. Now, intensified mass-mediated nightmares and invocations of the carnage of September 11 have reaffirmed the imagined horizontal fraternity of nationhood, once articulated by Benedict Anderson, even at these depths.[5] Beyond the fury of the fantastic autonomy of Barrio Libre, these youths demonstrate love and sympathy for their countrymen, those who were situated in relations of illegality and deportability and were caught in the brutal blazes of September 11.

Román recalls a conversation he had with a correction officer in one of his recent incarcerations in the border archipelago: "A guard over there [he gestures northward] told me that I could fight for the United States. They would give me papers, and pay me. And he told me that I would have all the women I wanted." *I shudder at the circulation of hetero-patriarchic violence and its legitimation by an officer of a higher-order sovereignty.*

The booty of war can also be found here at the post-NAFTA frontier. As bodies are increasingly and oppressively managed by Mexico and the United States along their shared frontier, the thumping pulse of discothèques echoes through the streets of Nogales, Juárez, Tijuana, and other Mexican border communities. Over the past several years, I have noted an increasing number of strip clubs in Nogales, Sonora. Young women come to the border from the interior of Mexico, hoping to make it to the United States, and find their efforts thwarted. Hotels that used to teem with bodies yearning to go northward are now inhabited by scantily clad young females. As drug traffickers have gotten involved in other subsidiaries, so they traffic in undocumented bodies and economies of sadistic pleasure. Indeed, unlike the majority of the young men of Barrio Libre, who at this moment were increasingly incarcerated either in the United States or Mexico, a few of the young women—in addition to working in the service sector of the Nogales, Sonora, economy—prostitute themselves, underscoring the retrenchments of gendered power relations at the new frontier.

SEPTEMBER 21, 2001

A police car cruises down the dusty road toward us, as two of the young men of the Barrio Libre and I walk through the street of the Buenos Aires colonia in Nogales, Sonora. I believe I can see a rifle butt in the back seat. The two youths that I am with tense.

"What are you doing?" the officers demand of the youths.

Suddenly, the officers scrutinize me. Reaching for his holster, the one in the passenger seat says, "He's Arab."

I blurt out: "I'm a US citizen."

After I explain most of my research and show my passport, they leave us alone. Now more than ever, my dark skin color, shaved head, and goatee provoke suspicion south of the border.

Reflecting on this scene, Román remarks: "Had you not had your passport . . . they would have taken you to jail and you would wish you were dead." His comment captures one example of the vicious racial-cum-criminal foundations—the warlike relations—that undergird sovereignty at the new frontier.

NOVEMBER 25, 2001

I sit, facing north, on a wall outside of Román's penthouse. About two miles away, on the other side of the border, I see the familiar green and white trucks of the US Border Patrol on a hill. Today as I crossed into Nogales, Sonora, from Nogales, Arizona, I passed members of the US National Guard and multiple border patrol agents, in addition to the several US customs agents and Nogales, Arizona, police officers.

Román's "wife," Ofelia, washes the clothing of Román and their two children, alternating between two pails, one with clean water and one with dirty water and a little soap. Román dusts the patio, clearing off debris. Felix, Román and Ofelia's five-year-old, busies himself with a green crayon and a torn Mickey Mouse coloring book. Ofelia does not claim to belong to Barrio Libre. She became Román's partner after he broke up with Margarita, who had left Nogales. In not claiming Barrio Libre, Ofelia is following far more normative notions of Mexican gender and sexuality. She works part time in a maquiladora, while Román pivots between his positions in the licit economy aboveground and the dark, illicit economy below in the borderlands. He sells tacos by day and runs drugs across the new frontier by night, exploiting its designed failures and the accompanying necessity of the daily reinstitutions of sovereignty.

Indeed, Román tells me that he went to look for a job this week at a maquiladora. But the border economy continues to hemorrhage. I tell Román and the others that commentators are warning of recession in the United States due to the September 11 tragedy, and that I have been told that several maquiladoras in the area are closing. They will probably move further southward or even to China. "I even wore my best shirt" for the trip to the maquiladora, Román jokes, pointing to a clean white T-shirt. No longer subterranean, the inhabitants of the Free 'Hood increasingly find that the border between the illegitimate and legitimate economies of the new frontier has narrowed.

It has been a little over a week since Mi Nueva Casa—the nonprofit that provided minimal services to the youth, that I once directed, and that served as a base for my research—shut down. For the past year, Román had been an employee of the agency. Having become a father, he has left the violence of Barrio Libre. He remarks that his place is the new Mi Nueva Casa.

Hearing a mechanical roar, I turn and look down from my perch. Two Mexican military jeeps and a truck full of Mexican soldiers pass us. Román encourages me to take a photograph. I refuse, recalling an incident from a couple of years before when I took a photo of Mexican police arresting several potential immigrants attempting to climb over the wall separating Nogales, Sonora, from Nogales, Arizona. I was questioned and then released with a stern warning not to photograph the activities of the authorities.

The soldiers in the jeep look our way. I slowly walk out of view.

"Are you afraid?" asks Flaco.

He laughs and recounts my recent experience of being questioned about my citizenship by the authorities. This has become a frequent topic of conversation among the young men of Barrio Libre. Flaco tells me: "You should shave your beard. You look Arab." The retrenchments of race, sovereignty, and policing at the new frontier run all too deep, pressing on bodies, seizing the young people's imaginations, and hailing vast, dark nightmares in Mexico and the United States.

CHAPTER 4

Against the United States

The Violent Inaugurations and Delinquent

Exceptions of the New Frontier

> Increasingly, wars, the practices of war, and the institutions of war tended to
> exist, so to speak, only on the frontiers, on the outer limits of the great State
> units, and only as a violent relationship—that actually existed or threatened
> to exist—between States.—MICHEL FOUCAULT,
> *"Society Must Be Defended"*

*I look up as Román points toward the rolling hills that brush up
against the fence of the international boundary. It is the Día de los
Muertos (Day of the Dead)—a popular Mexican holiday that honors
the deceased. A US Border Patrol vehicle parks not far from a tower
where a video camera is aimed at Nogales, Sonora. Its occupant exits
the vehicle and scrutinizes this cultural veneration of death through
binoculars. Román, a sixteen-year-old rock of a man-child with a
goatee and square shoulders, makes an obscene gesture in the agent's
direction. He laughs.*

*Román had lived in Chicago and Seattle before his family's deporta-
tion landed him in Nogales, Sonora, and he began his descent into Barrio Libre. Román had since worked on the borders of the Nogales economy, selling tacos and packets of gum or panhandling, washing the
windshields of northward-bound vehicles stuck in traffic, and smoldering in the scorching heat of the Sonoran desert, and, as part of Barrio
Libre, he mugged those attempting to undermine the militarized enforcement of the border, underscoring to the undocumented migrants-
to-be their vulnerability, their abandonment to the temporality of undocumented border crossing.*

*Helicopters buzz in the sky above us. Surveillance cameras mounted
on towers shoot southward, filming the terrain below (see fig. 4). Bor-*

4. Shooting southward. Photo by author.

der Patrol officers in SUVs and other all-terrain vehicles move up and down the dusty streets of Nogales, Arizona. Infrared sensors report intrusions into US territory.

But statistics indicate that the campaigns of warfare as policing are incomplete. Although some undocumented migrants are stymied, delayed in human way stations such as Nogales, Sonora, on the Mexican side of the new frontier, and thousands of others have been imprisoned or died crossing the new frontier, the undocumented population in the United States has grown robustly throughout the 1990s and continues to expand in the new millennium.[1] The vast majority of immigrants who attempt to circumvent militarized border enforcement ultimately succeed.[2]

Indeed, miles east and west from Nogales, Arizona, the incompleteness of sovereignty and its violent if not criminal effects become crystallized. *The border fence ends. And the rolling hills of the beautiful Sonoran Desert, with its mesquite trees and saguaro cacti, belie its centrality in a new politics of subordinated life and death. Warfare and policing have transformed it into a neoliberal oven, a killing desert, in a terrain where the temperature routinely exceeds one hundred degrees.*

I tell Román of a University of Houston study I had read. The study estimated that approximately sixteen hundred immigrants had died from dehydration and hypothermia as they tried to cross the border illegally between 1993 and 1997, attempting to avoid the militarized exercises of sovereignty.[3]

The number later grew to two thousand.[4] *Today, there are several thousand documented deaths and countless partial human remains. People who have survived the criminal abandonments of the Mexican frontier become violently inaugurated to the economic and social order of the United States.*

Román replies: "And that does not count for the violence. I bet you Beto's death doesn't count."

He then recounts the story of his friend's death. The young man had left his home in central Mexico in 1996 when he was fourteen. The country was still suffering from the repercussions of its worst economic crisis since the Great Depression — a crisis that began in late 1994 as NAFTA took effect. Along with the tearing asunder of Mexico's corporate state, the imposition of neoliberal globalizing logics wreaked havoc on the finances of Beto's family. What remained of Mexico's starved welfare programs did not help him. Beto and his parents decided that he would go to the United States and send money back home. He would find work in Los Angeles, probably busing tables at the same restaurant where his aunt worked. He would send money home when he could. Yet, as with many of the young people of the Free 'Hood, he could not make history as he pleased.

Beto learned that los chiles verdes (the green chilies) — what some of the young people of Barrio Libre called the Border Patrol because of their green uniforms and because "they make the border hot" — were making crossing difficult in El Paso and San Diego, two cities that had been primary destinations for migrants as they passed through the border. He thus headed to what was then a new clandestine route through Sonora, where he hoped to slip through the border at Nogales. He arrived during one of the highpoints of the aforementioned Operation Safeguard. When he tried to cross, he was quickly apprehended.

Román explains that "the Border Patrol told Beto they had seen him on the cameras . . . they sent him to [the youth authority of Nogales, Arizona]."

More than a hundred young immigrants were then overwhelming the small facility. Some of them later coalesced into Barrio Libre. Eventually, Beto and the others were sent to the juvenile authority of Nogales, Sonora. Yet Mexico's eviscerated public welfare programs, such as the Sistema Nacional para el Desarrollo Integral de la Familia (commonly referred to as DIF) and others designed to manage "problem" youths, lacked sufficient resources to grapple with the complex problems of the young people of Barrio Libre. The understaffed and underfinanced youth authority was exploding with young people who, like Beto, had traveled from elsewhere in Mexico looking for work. Some had even come from Central America. And, DIF's principal agent in Nogales, Sonora, lived under a cloud of suspicion. He often had to take young people into his own home.

Beto met several youths who claimed to be part of the Free 'Hood. Their promises of freedom and open defiance of the authorities impressed him. Beto soon was released, sent to live on the streets with no family, only a few pesos in his pocket, and fewer options — but also with new friends and a developing contaminated knowledge of subverting the international boundary, the authorities, and social conventions.

Some two weeks after his original attempt to cross the border, and while the Nogales region was still "hot," Beto tried to cross again. Román explains that this time Beto chose the preferred route of the young people of the Free 'Hood. He literally undermined the border through the moist underground world of the transnational sewer system. As luck would have it, when Beto exited the sewer system via a large drainage ditch in Nogales, Arizona, the local police were there, and he was quickly handed over to the Border Patrol.

Román explains that Beto's new knowledge had prepared him. He had grown bristly stubble on his face, like many young men of Barrio Libre. Beto's not-quite-five-o'clock shadow aided him in claiming adulthood. He thus avoided being returned to either of the youth authorities. Instead he entered "voluntary departure," a daily exception that unfolds at the border whereby deportable aliens, particularly Mexicans, who are apprehended are permitted — indeed, encouraged — to waive their rights to a deportation hearing and return to Mexico without lengthy detention, expensive bonding, or trial.[5]

Released near the border, Beto tried again. On his third attempt to cross the border, and his second navigating through the subterranean terrain of Barrio Libre, or the sewer tunnel, he was successful. He exited the tunnel into a drainage ditch and climbed up into the United States. He then stowed away on a train to reach the northern terrain of Barrio Libre, the "real" Barrio Libre of Tucson, Arizona. As he jumped from one boxcar to another, probably trying to hide from the Union Pacific police force that was on high alert for immigrants, he slipped and fell onto the track.

"Lo cortaron así" (it cut him like this), Román reports, making a chopping motion across my waistline. The train had severed Beto's body into two.

The grainy shots of the gray cement drainage ditch capture the sinewy subterranean scatological connection between Nogales, Arizona, and Nogales, Sonora. The scene is being filmed by an officer of the Nogales, Arizona, police department, who stands on an overpass almost directly over them. The footage shows police officers and Border Patrol agents (most of whom are Hispanic), hands on their holsters, asking the youths what they are doing, telling them to go back to Mexico, to stop abusing spray paint.

On the ground of the ditch, sleeping bags, once-white T-shirts and blue jeans growing brown, fast-food wrappers, and soda cans stained with spray paint gesture at their darker practices and reveal that this dark orifice is the sometime home of Barrio Libre. They mill about on camera, tirando libre (throwing freedom) in the shadows of the sewer system: they form first a "B" and then an "L" with their fingers, seeing not a sewer but a passageway to their freedom, the terrain of Barrio Libre.

The grainy footage then shifts to the flash of a light cutting through the darkness of the sewer tunnel behind the youths. A group of the undocumented materializes on the screen as they make their way toward the bright sunlight of Nogales, Arizona. El Enano (the dwarf, a nickname for one of the youths) wields a metal pipe. He repeatedly strikes one of the migrants in the leg. A child in the group screams. Another of the young men of Barrio Libre seizes a migrant by his lapel. With his other hand, he rips a chain from the neck of the unlucky man, who is wearing a cowboy hat—a telltale sign of a chúntaro. The officers above, once again on the screen, order the youths to stop. They don't.

But suddenly, this violent inauguration of "the undocumented" into what will be their new lives as undocumented laborers in the United

States ends. The bloodied, terrorized migrants—now scarred from their undocumented but filmed border crossing—have survived the criminal depths of the new frontiers of Mexico and the United States. They hurry toward the bright desert sunlight of Nogales, Arizona. They scamper up the walls of the ditch, spurting into the United States, over the gold and silver spray-painted graffiti that reads "BL" or "Barrio Libre" or nicknames such as "el guero" (the blond one), "el chamuco" (the devil), and "la negra" (the dark or black woman). They head to where the Border Patrol officers are probably waiting for them. Those who are caught are likely to opt for voluntary departure. They will be escorted to the border and be observed crossing back into Mexico, from where they will only try again to cross. A few of the inhabitants of Barrio Libre are probably arrested, off-screen. The rest ooze back into the fetid shadows of the underground passageway, an indirect consequence of warfare as neoliberal sovereignty making.

And there are similar manifestations. A few blocks to the north, at the entrance to the highway, Border Patrol officers stop a small bus carrying brown bodies to Tucson and other close-by communities. They question the bus's occupants. Down another street, a manhole opens, and several presumably undocumented migrants emerge. They sprint away toward the documented noncitizens and Mexican American citizens moving through the rundown shopping district of this Arizona border town, hoping to dissolve into the crowd.

Close by, a group of Border Patrol agents and police officers, wearing military fatigues, lord over several suspected undocumented migrants who lie on their stomachs on the scorching black pavement. Not far away, a would-be migrant resists and runs from officers. An authoritative voice commands "Stop! Alto!" The officer tackles the brown body running north, driving it into the steaming pavement with a sickening thud, thus reaffirming US sovereignty at the new frontier through the subjugation of this brown body.

~~I watch as two men climb over the border fence. An INS agent and~~ *a police officer soon arrive on the scene. One of the immigrants flees. Neither of the officers gives chase. The police officer pulls his radio from his belt and talks, presumably with other officers in the area. A police car arrives and pursues the fugitive. Resigned, the first immigrant waits. He seems to get on his knees without orders from either officer. The INS agent binds him in handcuffs made of thick, durable plastic.*

Later that day, like on most days, another immigrant peers over the fence that represents the international boundary between Nogales, Sonora, and Nogales, Arizona. Suddenly, he signals to a group waiting behind him. A mad scramble ensues. Approximately seven men climb to the top of the fence and jump onto the steaming pavement of the United States. Three sprint for the neighborhoods of Nogales, Arizona. They will probably have been seen on video cameras connected to the local Border Patrol station, which will dispatch agents to hunt them down. Yet some have a chance. They run toward the brown mass of "documented" Mexicans and Mexican Americans who move through the shopping districts of the dollar and secondhand stores of Nogales, Arizona.

A few who jumped the fence appear to have made it. I later learned that a truck hit one of them, crushing his ribs and severely injuring him, as he ran through an intersection. Later that day, more people peer over the border fence and the process begins again.

Nightmares of insecurity are effects of the necessarily incomplete exercises of sovereignty at the new frontier. They underwrite the low-intensity warfare at the new frontier. Indeed, this kind of warfare is designed far more to regulate bodies than to conquer populations. Media spectacles of undocumented border crossings and processes of illegality more generally have been widely equated with the US nation-state's loss of control of its borders. Nightmares of drug traffickers, terrorists, and illegal immigrants weigh down on the new frontier; these dark fantasies legitimate the continuing and ongoing amplification of militarized regimes of social control and a perverse birthing of criminal types in its necessary fissures.[6]

Undocumented *Sacer*

"The production of a biopolitical body," writes the political philosopher Giorgio Agamben, "is the original activity of sovereign power."[7] Drawing on Carl Schmitt's ideas about the "state of exception," Walter Benjamin's works, and Foucault's concept of biopower, Agamben holds that modern politics "knows no value . . . other than life."[8] He further holds that the very persistence of exception defines the political in Western democracies. His genealogy of exception originates in an ancient ritual Roman legal declaration of *homo sacer* and renders the individual as bare life, or a human being stripped of the sovereign protections of citizenship. For Agamben, this exception remains prescient in the capacity of the sovereign state to establish a state of exception, to commit those stripped of citizens' rights to zones deemed exceptional, and to torture or kill those reduced to the status of bare life without legal protection. Moreover, such sovereign power extends beyond those who are explicitly agents of the state, covering all those who have authority over aspects of human vitality, including "the jurist[,] . . . the doctor, the scientist, the expert, the priest"[9] and their tacit alliance with sovereignty. Agamben holds that the state of exception is actually the rule of contemporary liberal democracies, revealing that concepts such as biopolitics can uncover linkages between totalitarian states and liberal democracies. Bare life is epitomized in his concept of the camp, a space in which "power confronts nothing other than pure biological life without any mediation";[10] a space where human life reaches a point where any crime committed against it proves defensible.

Indeed, concepts advanced by Agamben have aided scholars in theorizing the relationship between violence and sovereignty in events as diverse as September 11, Abu Ghraib, and Guantánamo Bay.[11] With respect to the US-Mexico borderlands, one scholar has drawn on Agamben's notion of the state of exception in his analysis of US Supreme Court decisions to suggest that Border Patrol policing practices exemplify a "permanent state of racial emergency, or the permanent legal racial exception."[12] Another scholar examines the morbid, tragic femicide occurring in Ciudad Juárez, Chihuahua.[13] Ana Alonso maintains that homo sacer illuminates the political dynamics of the colonization of native peoples, who bared their lives in their refusals to confirm to colonists' notions of what it meant to be civilized as the Spanish exploited their labor, sacked their homes, and reformed and sometimes raped their bodies in northern Mexico and southwestern United States.[14]

In contrast, Michel Foucault maintains that biopower or certain power and knowledge relations about biological life, such as healthcare, welfare, the birth rate, and sexuality, "make" certain populations governable. It situates them on certain grids of intelligibility, where they eventually become complicit in their own subjection. Biopower's negative referent, however, is of particular import to this chapter. For Foucault, "letting" a particular population or subset of a population die constitutes state racism. It requires an appearance of biological difference between those who must live and those who must die, and racism for Foucault is a crux. It produces that appearance of biological difference. Death in this formulation is the residual effect of histories of invasion, the bloody founding of states, the ongoing wars, and brutal subjugation of bodies taking place below the peace, where subjects to new sovereignties are made.[15] Achille Mbembe has observed in this respect that terror formations, such as those occurring in the conflicts of the Middle East and the subjugation of bodies in the plantation economy, anticipate the state of exception.[16] Ann Laura Stoler charts such race wars and the limitations of this concept in the African colonies.[17]

Foucault, however, falls prey to what he elsewhere has termed "the disappearance of torture as spectacle."[18] It haunts his formulation of racism. It erases the ongoing exercises of invasive techniques of power on living bodies, all too often on nightmarish Others. In this respect, the undocumented enter a lacuna between warfare and policing as sovereignty making and neoliberal governmentality, crystallized at the border. Experiences of the undocumented thus signal how certain subjects are violently inaugurated, either directly or indirectly, through the racist political violence of the state. Thousands die, but the vast majority of the undocumented live and indeed succeed in crossing.

This lesson reiterates what has long been the case in the US-Mexico borderlands: militarized policing practices affirm the sovereignty of the United States, one that risks unraveling under the weight of transnational migrations and commodity flows that challenge the US border order. Notably, the aforementioned conquest and colonization of over half of Mexico—the contemporary southwestern United States in the nineteenth century that I discussed in chapter 1—was organized discursively and ideologically in racial terms. Although formally outlawed in the United States, similar exercises of state racism are exemplified in contemporary anti-immigrant discourse and gendered around noncitizen fertility. They have been obscured in the new liberal disorder of the contemporary borderlands and its accompanying blurring of race and nation.

In this respect, the *Border Patrol Strategic Action Plan: 1994 and Beyond, National Strategy* is instructive. Authored by experts from the Department of Defense Center for Low Intensity Conflict (CLIC) and Chief Patrol Agents from all regions and selected Headquarters staff, it advances a strategy of border and migration controls called "prevention through deterrence."[19] It expects that with the militarized campaigns of the Border Patrol in the 1990s, such as Operation Hold-the-Line in the El Paso region and Operation Gatekeeper in the San

Diego region, "violence will increase as effects of strategy are felt."[20] The document describes the strategy in the following manner: "The Border Patrol will achieve the goals of its strategy by bringing a decisive number of enforcement resources to bear in each major entry corridor." It continues: "The prediction is that with traditional entry and smuggling routes disrupted, illegal traffic will be deterred, or forced over more hostile terrain, less suited for crossing and more suited for enforcement."[21]

Similarly, consider this excerpt from a talk at a conference at the University of Arizona, given by Gustavo de la Vina, then a senior officer of the US Border Patrol:

We are dealing primarily, predominantly with people and narcotics. Where you do a lot of that would be coming in legally or attempting legal entry through the ports of entry either in containers or things of that nature. So you have that segment of criminal activity, fortunately it is not a big segment but it is a segment to deal with. It is a segment that has an impact. The problem with that is that it all blends in together. You have the good people, you have the bad guys, and they are all in one group. I wish that we had the border broken down into zones. Those that [are] entering to seek jobs, could enter from here to here. Those that are dealing narcotics should enter here and those that are dealing with gangs and auto theft enter here. It would be very very easy. Unfortunately, the bad people know that and he mixes [*sic*] with the good people. . . . The Border Patrol, they are going into these types of situations cold. We don't know what we are dealing with. We know that our mission is the border, and anything entering illegally is our responsibility. So when an agent approaches a group he doesn't know what he is dealing with. We never know. We are very fortunate that the majority, as I mentioned, are just seeking employment. Bringing this element of criminal activity into the border issue adds a dynamic to the border. That dynamic turns out to be in the form of danger and violence, unfortunately. Danger and violence normally translate into tragic incidences. Which means loss of life, injury, and not only to the migrant, also to the border patrol.[22]

"Prevention through deterrence" speaks to how neoliberal sovereignty becomes complicit with the larger dynamics of the neoliberal economy and how different orders of exclusion and exception are perversely proximate to new criminalities and related threats over life.

The noncitizens who pass through the precarious temporality of border crossings, and finally into the contemporary liberal democracy of the United States, become undocumented sacer. They are left to die. They are stripped bare, exposed to the multiple agents of sovereign power and its fissures. Undocumented migrants in the temporality of crossing the contemporary border encounter a zone of exception, but it is one of a neoliberal order. As biological lives already subjugated before crossing the border, they become inaugurated to the United States through the direct and indirect brutalities that are central to the everyday governance of contemporary neoliberalism and global capitalism, the latest iteration of the vampirish sucking of life out of labor. The vast majority of them suffer the condition of being situated as near death, which is characteristic of racialized labor.

The incomplete nature of neoliberal US sovereignty in the border region in the global age requires its violent affirmation. For this reason, nightmares weigh down, permeating the country, and organizing the subjugation of Others, channeling them into the killing deserts, and exposing them to regimes of militarized policing or the brutalities of the parallel criminal economy and its agents. And, in the late 1990s through the early 2000s, one such site was the dark underground channels of the below-border sewer system where migrants confronted the criminal and delinquent violence of those who inhabited Barrio Libre.

Moreover, the undocumented population's passage through differing national orders of racialization complicates this analysis.[23] Although I do not wish to minimize the multi-ethnic character of the Mexican immigrant population, race and racism have long functioned as a process that homogenizes groups with ethnic distinctions.[24] That is, undermining or crossing the new frontier and the multiple relations of domination that coagulate around it repositions the undocumented, aggravating their already subordinated position. In this case, it also situates them as prey: life exposed, undervalued, and in greater proximity to death. The racial position of undocumented migrants becomes forged in this process. In complex relations with their status of becoming illegal and deportable, race at this new frontier represents the cumulative effects of numerous, historically configured, and lived ideological processes that dehumanize a population to such a point that state violence, merciless disposability, and other forms of population management — including seemingly mundane accidents and seemingly unrelated criminal violence — appear appropriate or inevitable.[25]

Undocumented border crossers it is now presumed in this late neoliberal moment, should face militarized policing and other exercises of state violence. And, the now well over five thousand migrant deaths have rendered noncitizen death and subjugation as taken for granted. Despite how troubling such comparisons are, it is worth noting that for the death camps of World War II to occur, the European Jewish population had to be effectively dehumanized, rendering them radically Other, unworthy of life — or worthy of life in the banality of evil that defined the concentration camp. Indeed, many analyses of Nazi death camps have noted that in them the exercise of brutal state force and the machinery of terror once reserved exclusively for colonies were turned on a population within Europe.[26]

Moreover, the undocumented *sacer* interrupts positions that insist on the centrality of the law in the racial subjection of illegality.[27] It is the exercise of the law, in militarized policing practices and its violent fissures, that constitutes race, not the law in and of itself. On crossing the new frontier, almost all Mexicans become revalued in the organized racial formation of the United States. And popular ontological signifiers of the pathologized hybridities — such as the speaking of subordinated languages, hygienic practices, dress, and phenotype — make undocumented border crossers, and often those who resemble them, subject to official and extra-official scrutiny.[28]

NOGALES, ARIZONA

Outside the glass doors of the Nogales, Arizona, Border Patrol station, rows of shiny new green and white SUVs *and a new helicopter landing pad testify to the US investment in boundary control. Inside, a room lined with racks of high-powered rifles, pistols, and stun guns, together with rounds of ammunition, bulletproof vests, helmets, and binoculars, further testifies to this buildup, well before the War on Terror.*

An officer explains that the high-powered weaponry is to be used only out in the deserts when dealing with drug smugglers: "We would not allow you to check one out to patrol downtown Nogales." His squared shoulders and closely cropped hair tell of his military tour. A former soldier like many of his colleagues, he was a medic in the first Gulf War.

Through some windows he allows us to look into a room with cement walls, painted white, and several benches. Several men sit on a bench. Some sleep; others sit or stand. They will be in the cell for a few hours or a few days. Some will be sent to the penitentiary for having committed a felony.

In another room, several cameras peer into the everyday life of Nogales, Arizona, and Nogales, Sonora. Buenos Aires, a colonia just south of the border in Nogales, Sonora, appears on one screen. I believe I can make out figures moving down the street. On another, several young people in school uniforms wait for a bus in Nogales, Arizona. On a third, a Border Patrol SUV *cruises down a street that parallels the border. I see downtown Nogales, Arizona, near the port of entry. Two officers observe the monitors, ready to communicate with agents who are in the field and dispatch agents to sites of unauthorized crossings.*

*On one monitor, I can make out the end of the border fence in the desert outside of Nogales, Arizona. Joint Task Force 6 (*JTF-6*), a military unit that up to the 1990s trained in the southwestern United States, has built roads that give the Border Patrol access to the area. Next to the fence, multiple paths of beaten brush and compressed brown sand that crisscross the desert testify to the exposure of the undocumented to the neoliberal ovens of the killing deserts, an attribute of the necessarily incomplete sovereignty of the United States in the region.*

The officer escorts me to another room where he shows me the IDENT *system. The system, then at the cutting edge of boundary control technology, takes a digital photograph of the subject as well as electronic fingerprints of the right and left index fingers for a biometric database. It provides the subject's history, showing where and whether "the alien had been apprehended by immigration in the U.S. before at any time and anywhere."* IDENT *technology was unveiled in 1994. It is based on the US Navy's Deployable Mass Population Identification and Tracking System, and it serves as the underlying architecture of the post–September 11 tracking system known as* US-VISIT. IDENT *further details the number of* INS *apprehensions of the "subject," where he or she was caught and by whom, and whether it was for an immigration or criminal offense: "Immigrants can now give us 1,000 different names and we will find out their information," the officer explains.*

Nevertheless, daily exceptions unfold at the border, such as the process of "voluntary departure" described earlier. They speak to the neoliberal configuration of a sovereignty that is increasingly in question and that requires constant political subjugations at the level of life itself that are both dramatized in daily militarized policing and felt in struggles over language and related cultural practices. Such lived experiences indicate an order of exception, not linked solely to the deep murderous function of the state, but to the management and violent inauguration of bodies as Other in an age of global flows and new security concerns. These prove productive in the descent of youth into Barrio Libre.

Delinquent Productions

Oddly enough, undocumented juveniles, such as the youths of Barrio Libre, legally acquired sovereign protections when caught by the Border Patrol. Children who are separated from adults cannot be questioned or fingerprinted unless they have committed a felony. Following their capture by the Border Patrol, they were frequently "released" into Mexico, sent for a short stay at the county juvenile authority, or sent to the Mexican consulate. Moreover, when they turn eighteen, their records will be wiped clean. The perverse proximity of policing plays into this exception of the neoliberal age. A Border Patrol officer explained to me: "They know nothing is going to happen to them. . . . They know their record is wiped clean by the time they are eighteen, if they were treated as a juvenile and not as an adult. Sometimes we see the same kids, and there are some bad kids. . . . We see them over and over again, and we can't do anything until they are eighteen. We cannot fingerprint a juvenile unless a criminal offense is committed, and we cannot fingerprint a juvenile for immigration purposes unless the juvenile is fourteen or older."

Nevertheless, many of the inhabitants of Barrio Libre would strategically claim to be adults, as that often meant that the US authorities would hold them for shorter amounts of time. Yet the young people's frequent confrontations with the Border Patrol and other police forces, their frequent incarcerations, and their mugging of migrants who choose to enter the jagged spaces of incomplete sovereignty speak to the complex mutual complicity between militarized policing and criminality at the new frontier.

They also speak to the necessary incompleteness of the higher-order sovereignty of the United States that fed their imagination, their unbridled sense of freedom. Margarita and Juana describe the geography of the Free 'Hood in this way:

> *Margarita*: [Barrio Libre is] in Nogales, Sonora; it's in the tunnel, Phoenix, Tucson. Where else?
>
> *Juana*: Chicago, El Paso, all the way to Los Angeles. . . . It's a barrio that goes through all the cities, floating like that, and over that way [gesturing northward].
>
> *Margarita*: Through Tucson, Phoenix, here in Nogales, Arizona, over there in Nogales, Sonora. . . . It's Barrio Libre wherever you are.

Notably, many of these US cities have major immigrant populations. In this respect, claims of being totally free were common among the youths, signifying to them an autonomy beyond the dominant, if incomplete, sovereignties of the United States and Mexico. Nevertheless, Barrio Libre was more than a free-floating geography, superimposed over the dominant one. As we have seen, to belong to it was an expansive, furious refusal of normativity, an enraged subversion of the respective sovereignties of the United States and Mexico that seeped from under the new frontier into Tucson, its actual Barrio Libre, and beyond. Notably, Tucson's Barrio Libre has its own vexed relation with policing. It had developed a reputation of being a tough place. While Tucson's Barrio Libre was in formation, the local police department largely did not patrol it—one of the reasons behind its name.[29]

Moreover, upon finding their freedom by successfully seeping under the border, some of the inhabitants of Barrio Libre explained how they exploited the power in their resemblance to US citizens of Mexican descent. As they would travel farther from the underground passage, they would attempt to "blend" in with the local Mexican population, resembling delinquent iterations of what some have termed "cultural citizenship."[30]

Listen to Teporron describing one such attempt: "I had just gotten off the train in Tucson Arizona. A chile verde [Border Patrol agent] stopped me and asked, 'Hey, you Mexican?' And I said, 'Who me? I'm not Mexican. I'm American.' And the dude said, 'You're American?'" Laughing, he continues the story: "Yeah, man, I'm American. And I kept walking. And . . . he believed me. I couldn't believe it." Teporron's narrative captures the racialization of Mexican as "illegal alien" in the officer's utterance; but the narrative likewise captures how certain people can disrupt it, even grossly marginalized ones.

Román echoes this point: "If I dress right, and wear baggy clothes, the Border Patrol thinks I'm Chicano."

Such practices underscore the fact that the cholos and cholas of Barrio Libre are far more than simply tunnel kids. They navigate the complex terrain of the licit and illicit economy situated within the managed violences of the new frontier. And having undermined it through the sewer system or circumvented it by other means, they would often stow away on trains, hitch a ride, or sometimes walk the sixty miles to the ethnically Mexican neighborhood of Tucson, Arizona, also called Barrio Libre.

This Free 'Hood of Tucson was historically the first destination for many migrants from Sonora. Carlos Vélez-Ibañez, a native of the region and an anthropologist, points out that many youths from this neighborhood fought in World War II and the Korean War. It produced state senators, educators, and other professionals. Indeed, before 1880, a small class of ethnic Mexicans shared a substantial degree of political and economic power with the growing white elite. But in 1881 the Tucson city directory distinguished between classes of ethnic Mexicans and Indians, designating Barrio Libre as a "slum district" inhabited by "Papago Indians" and "lower class Mexicans."[31] Prevailing discourses and imagery about Tucson's Barrio Libre pathologized it as a free zone, where vice and poverty flourished and "where anything could happen." The neighborhood's boundaries expanded and contracted according to the needs of the larger Tucson community for Mexican workers.[32] These latter two facets strongly resonate with the youths' appropriation of the term.

Moreover, while in Tucson, the young people from the subterranean Free 'Hood often joined up with other marginalized Mexican American youths in the Free 'Hood of Tucson. According to Román, they would hang out with them, party, and live together. They also introduced several of the young people of Barrio Libre in Nogales to a community organization that provided meals to the homeless in South Tucson. One young man, through this transnational network of Barrio Libre, met up with a mother who worked in the service sector. In return for providing child care, he was allowed to stay at her house. And Margarita, a young woman whom I wrote about in an earlier chapter, developed a close friendship with a young woman from a Tucson community organization and sometimes stayed with her when she visited Tucson.

Such delinquent practices—the youths' seeping below the militarized managements of bodies and their associations with marginalized US Latinos in the "actual" Barrio Libre of Tucson—capture how the youths of Barrio Libre reconfigure and expand such exceptions. These necessary subterranean fissures of liberal sovereignty instigate new dynamics: the youths could temporarily subvert the dominant sovereignties of the new frontier. In this respect, the birth of the Free 'Hood has qualities of what some have termed "Third Space."[33] But it is largely dystopian in this case, and it garners an additional charge in that this third space occurs betwixt, between, and below two nation-states and the crosscutting, volatile, and incomplete sovereignties of the new frontier. In other words, criminalized populations as well as normative ones can carve out spaces in the new frontiers of race and identity of neoliberalism, far more space than in the totalizing spaces of death camps of Agamben's formulation. Indeed, the youth of the Free 'Hood prized clothing that signified either association or identification with a transnational circuit of US Latinos, such as baggy pants and T-shirts proclaiming "Chicano Power" and the like. Other youths would claim US citizenship in English. Such subversions of the new frontier charged their discourses of freedom and their amorphous imaginings of space of their Free 'Hood.

Nevertheless, war and policing as sovereignty still deeply inflected the youth. While some scholars would perhaps seek redemption, their biological lives proved grim despite these moments of freedom.

Several of the youths and I had just had lunch — spaghetti, corn tortillas, bottled salsa, and Coca-Cola — on this day in 1999. Victor begins the familiar chorus. He proclaims: "Soy libre. Soy libre, cabron. Voy a Barrio Libre" (I'm free. I'm free, dude. I'm going to the Free 'Hood). He has recently been diagnosed with hepatitis, probably contracted in the tunnel. Despite his yellowing skin, he continues to enter the transnational sewer system. Victor and Bolillo pantomime their experiences with the Tucson police department. Always the loudest and most animated of the youths, Bolillo forms his fingers into the shape of a pistol. He shouts at Victor in English: "You, there — on your knees, mother fucker! On your knees!" Victor falls to his knees. In broken English, Bolillo continues: "Hands behind your back!" He then pretends to handcuff Victor. Victor protests: "Soy libre, cabron!" (I'm free!). Bolillo responds with an expletive-filled diatribe. He pretends to strike Victor with the pistol.

Later, I ask Victor and Bolillo about this performance. They tell me that they were performing their memories of being in the Barrio Libre of Tucson. They had been spending time with a group of impoverished Chicanos. Notably, despite their cultural and phenotypical resemblance to this population and their adoption of Chicano dress, they still became subject to policing.

Román recounts another episode: "There we go running . . . we go running through the tunnel for the outside, to exit. And outside we run into the Border Patrol and then . . . we started walking and he [a Border Patrol agent] says, 'Hey, you American?' and then I said, 'Oh yeah, I'm an American citizen.' 'Let me see your papers,' said the officer. 'I don't have my papers, man. I'm American, I'm an American citizen.' I told him, 'Hey, wait up . . . wait for me over there, on the bridge . . . I'll see you over there so I can show you my ID.' *. . . And the motherfucker says, 'OK, come with me over there.' We had to turn ourselves in 'voluntarily' [referring to the aforementioned voluntary departure regime]."*

Román was then arrested and eventually sent to the juvenile detention center in Nogales, Sonora: "Chavo was there. When we were let out, we headed to the tunnel."

And as the following story suggests, these effects reverberate through Barrio Libre and throughout my time doing fieldwork.

As I exit the converted duplex that an organization has transformed into the makeshift halfway house called Mi Nueva Casa to provide rudimentary services to the inhabitants of Barrio Libre, I run into Román. I have not seen him for months. "They dumped me at the border," he explains. He had been caught by the Border Patrol and been released the evening before. He says: "They watched me as I crossed into Mexico, following my detention. I spent last night on the streets of Nogales, Sonora. I went by the tunnel, but it was too hot. And I couldn't find Margarita."

"Record this," Chavo demands on another occasion, pointing to my tape recorder. "I want to talk. Be sure to put this in your fucking book." He and his "wife"—inhabitants of Barrio Libre used such terms to describe their committed relationships even if, like Chavo, they were not formally married—were waiting in the parking lot of a hotel in Nogales, Arizona, having exited the sewer tunnel. But the chiles verdes caught them. Before this arrest, Chavo had gone on a trip to Guadalajara to visit his mother and extended family. There he had worked as a security guard at a small business. Yet he missed his "wife" and their children.

On his return, he and his "wife" had sought to go to the Free 'Hood of Tucson. The Border Patrol caught them in Nogales, Arizona. Chavo lied about his age. "I told them I was eighteen because I didn't want to do one year in juvenile [detention]," the seventeen-year-old explains to me. He was held for several weeks and then escorted to the international border, where he was released. In contrast, his "wife" was not arrested. She was taken to the border where she paid a small fee and was released under the voluntary departure regime explained above. Chavo tells me: "They're nicer to the girls."

Conclusion

To understand what it is like to be violently inaugurated—to be positioned as vulnerable human life, to risk crossing through the neoliberal ovens of the killing deserts and to risk confronting the death squads of the new frontier vigilantes, to be rendered prey to the inhabitants of Barrio Libre or other new frontier criminal types, or conversely to understand the descent of impoverished youth seeping into the shit of the criminal depths of the state power—requires an analysis of war as sovereignty making that is inextricably tied to neoliberalism and its production of undocumented migration. The vast militarized border policing campaigns of the 1990s and early 2000s, which signify the rise of new frontier, are necessarily incomplete. They do not stop undocumented migration. Instead, they generated conditions of vulnerability and subjugation that violently and criminally inaugurate noncitizen border crossers to the US economic and racial order, while dramatizing new configurations of what is taken to be sovereignty, economy, and criminality. Such dramatic fissures of militarized border policing likewise generate sentiments of insecurity and fears of invasion among an anxious citizenry with totalitarian proclivities at the globalizing neoliberal moment. They accept the punishment and violence against the nightmarish figure of the undocumented and support pernicious anti-immigrant legislation.

And in such neoliberal organized exceptions to the zones of episodic low-intensity policing and high-intensity forms of law enforcement, certain parallel modes of domination, expropriation, direct and indirect violence, and their radical refutations take hold. That is, the necessarily incomplete coupling of military and police power in US border enforcement practices speaks to the material operations of power on living bodies. The vast majority of the undocumented do succeed in crossing the border, and it is in such spaces of passage that criminalities and delinquencies such as Barrio Libre are born. Criminalities, delinquencies, and pathologies are spawned by the incompleteness of the militarized police power in its attempts to both kill and regulate. Notably, the soaring death rates in the killing deserts have caused the Border Patrol to add life-preserving rescue services to its roles. Special units of the Border Patrol now scour the deserts to provide food, water, and medical services to lost or injured migrants.

They preserve life, but it is life that is already violently inaugurated or rendered close to death in the new order.

The violence of what is taken as sovereign power in the United States—with its exceptions and daily subjugations and other effects—compensates for sovereignty's incompleteness, its fragmentations across space and time, and its dramatic reconfiguration under neoliberalism. Despite the more than five thousand corpses that have so far been found scorching in the killing deserts, both undocumented migrants and the youths in Barrio Libre find a radically conditioned agency in these zones of social death—whether in the neoliberal ovens of the killing deserts or the brutal, but often successful, underground crossing in the sewer system.

In choosing to risk crossing the new frontier, noncitizens become cognizant of the precariousness of their lives. They choose, in a radically conditioned sense of the term, to enter the rarified states of exception of militarized policing and abandonment, where—in certain scatological crossings of the late 1990s and to a lesser extent the early 2000s—they encountered the inhabitants of Barrio Libre and became their prey. The criminal managements of bodies at the new frontier require that the already subjugated citizens of Mexico, Central America, and elsewhere who cross the new frontier, propelled by neoliberal globalizations, self-consciously strip away their sovereign protections, to seep through the jagged fissures of the daily militarized management of bodies, borders, and territory. That is, the killing deserts, the capillary sovereignty of the Minutemen and similar vigilantes, and the intensifying exercises of militarized policing at the new frontier, together with its gaping absences, crystallized at these supposed extremities of the nation-state's ongoing relations of violence and power—the power of violence and the violence of power.

Moreover, such new stratagems of rule are instrumental in this production of delinquency. Their repeated exposure to sovereign militarized policing and its multiple, proliferating reverberations requires an underlining of the perverse proximity among it, the birth of Barrio Libre, and the violent inaugurations of Others to the barest of lives in the United States. Barrio Libre thus constitutes a "dark," distorted reflection of warfare and policing as sovereignty making at the new frontier, which the youth in their daily practices of passing as Mexican American citizens sought to transform.

CHAPTER 5

Oozing Barrio Libre and
the Pathological Ends of Life

The suicide bomber appears here once again as a symbol of the inevitable limitation and vulnerability of sovereign power; refusing to accept a life of submission.—MICHAEL HARDT AND ANTONIO NEGRI, *Multitude*

Handkerchiefs and dented, empty soda cans stained with spray paint lie on the cement ground of the ditch that leads to sewer tunnels. The tunnels are below a small, open-air restaurant in Nogales, Arizona, about a half-mile north of the international boundary. Border Patrol officers, police, and other authorities patrol the area, driving up and down the streets. Patrons of the establishment drink, smoke cigarettes, and speak slow English to the predominantly Spanish-speaking help. In the ditch, gold and silver spray-painted *placas* (graffiti tags) pronounce this *their* terrain: "Barrio Libre" and "Libre Total," along with the names of many of the youths of the Free 'Hood. The sewer tunnels that it connects to have been transformed into a site of delinquent refusal. A brown body—an undocumented migrant—emerges from the tunnel and looks around for the authorities. A few others trickle after him and they run into Nogales, Arizona. After a few minutes I see three young people whom I recognize from Barrio Libre seep out of the sewer.

They glare at me from the ditch as I look down at them. Once again, I climb down. I enter the drainage ditch. Only a few hours before, I had played foosball with Román at Mi Nueva Casa, the makeshift halfway house that could never do enough, where he had had breakfast and had told me of his work last night at a taco stand. He had made about fifty pesos, not even five dollars. Apparently after that, he decided to supplement his income in the dark underground economy.

Loco: What the . . . who the hell is that?
Román: Relax bro'; he's a friend.
Loco: Tell him he better go, or I'll take him down [*bajar*].
Román: No, it's fine. He's my friend. Don't be afraid, Gilberto.
Margarita: Look, Gilberto is here. [She beams.]
Gilberto: What do you do when you are down here?

Their spray-paint-stained hands and clothes, a Coca-Cola can dripping with paint that Román carries in his right hand, and Margarita's eyes half closed already tell me. They are back at this practice, the one I am reluctant to write and talk about and that haunts my work as a politically committed anthropologist. Román holds the aluminum can to his nose and inhales the golden vapors, deeply, holding this poison in his lungs and then exhales a golden breath toward me. Almost in unison, Loco holds the handkerchief covered in spray paint to his face, and inhales deeply. I have paid attention before to the deep sounds of breathing.

Román: We are free. We are the Free 'Hood.
Victor (interrupting): *Somos libre* [we are free].

Spray paint, that is, is far more than the medium for the youths to mark their place. The youths of Barrio Libre would "huff" spray paint, "espray," or glue, and sometimes gasoline or marker fumes, and other industrial goods found in these post-NAFTA ruins. These fumes warp the mind. Repeated "abuse" debilitates the user, corrupting the mind, corroding the lungs, as they are lined with paint particles, slowly killing the user. It is a painful, gradual, seemingly interminable suicide. "Death," as Foucault once remarked, "is outside the power relationship."[1] And Barrio Libre, ultimately, was an embrace of the pathological life well on its way to death.

Street drugs were too expensive. The burgeoning makeshift housing in Nogales, Sonora—indicative of the stymied pressure at the new frontier—rendered spray paint and other industrial toxins cheap and readily consumable. These and street drugs provide the cruel high of impoverished urbanizing people. It is an addictive pleasure that is cheaper than beer, cigarettes, and other recreational drugs. For some of the youths, inhaling these toxins remediated the harsh conditions of homelessness; for others, this pleasure was a potentially addictive practice of their freedom, which in its repeated abuse rendered them self-consciously abhorrent, repulsive, and irredeemable.

At a different moment of my research, when I asked another young man in the Free 'Hood why he inhaled paint, he replied: "Because I like it. I inhale the spray paint because I like it. I like how it makes me feel." I had expected a response along the lines that the inhalation of spray paint anesthetized pain. Indeed, dedicated social workers of Mi Nueva Casa would play on the sympathies of hand-wringing liberals, explaining that these practices helped keep the youth warm. In contrast, this young man spoke of its pleasure. But he conveyed that he knew of the repulsion such practices provoked. In this respect, Román once grew irritated by my incessant questioning and concerns about this practice: "Ah, Gilberto, always asking questions. We paint ourselves [inhale spray paint] because we want to. To be free. We're Barrio Libre. It's what we use to make us crazy." Another ethnographic intervention provides further texture. Willi at another juncture echoed this: "[I inhale paint] because I like it." He then added: "It pisses people off. I like to piss off the women [who work at Mi Nueva Casa], Grupo Beta [the special Mexican police force], and the green chilies [the US Border Patrol]. It frustrates them."

The graphic and deep inhaling of paint and other synthetic products was invaluable to the youths as was their visibility in sewers, with all its scatological, shitty associations. Such practices signified how they embraced being irredeemable, opting into an abhorrent space of refusal (see fig. 5).

Certain traditions of scholarship—infiltrated with paternalistic imaginings, as well as certain deracinated approaches to political economy—neglect "bad subjects" such as those living in Barrio Libre. For Louis Althusser, however, "bad subjects" invited the interventions of a repressive state apparatus.[2] At the new frontier, the criminal depths of incomplete sovereignties and accompanying nightmares render such matters more complicated.

Discipline and Punish: The Birth of a Prison by Michel Foucault, Althusser's one-time disciple, remains arguably the most influential work in the contemporary study of prison systems. Nevertheless, despite its subtitle, it privileges not prisons per se but the disciplinary regimes perfected in penal institutions, which have been extended to other institutions such as schools and factories. In Foucault's history, the relegation of sovereign spectacles of punishment to the cruel interiors of the prison led to the perfection of rendering humans compliant with power relations. Unsure of whether they are being watched, "subjects" or humans become their own wardens. They become "the

5. Other pathological (w)rites. Photo by author.

principle of their own subjection."[3] Far more insidious is the fact that pervasive forces discipline inmates and civilian populations alike into submission, such as the control of space and time involved in work schedules, in the army, and in the classroom. The controversial thesis of *Discipline and Punish* is that liberal critiques of torture and other spectacular regimes of punishment ultimately lead to the perfection of such practices rather than ending them. And in their perfection, modern subjects are made.

Yet, empirically, sites such as prisons in the United States and indeed what I call the new frontier birth quite the opposite reaction. State violence against the nightmares of the new frontier proves inextricably linked to the youth's descent into the Free 'Hood, refuting the cool rationality of inwardly turned subjection, as imagined by Foucault and the army of his followers. The inhabitants of Barrio Libre would certainly refuse any characterization that approaches docility.

It is in this respect that the available critical vocabulary struggles to communicate the nature of the Free 'Hood and contemporary vexing criminalities. They cannot be mistaken for a history from below—not even way, way below—or that of anticolonial criminality, which inspired E. P. Thompson, Ranajit Guha, Robin Kelley, and the subaltern scholars of Latin America.[4] The youths of Barrio Libre are not protean revolutionaries. They do not embody nascent forms of anticolonialist consciousness, or politically immature, inarticulate forms of struggle. Nor are they the imagined soldiers of a latent cultural war. They are neither automatons of political and economic forces nor autonomous, self-caring subjects, fantasized by the architects and ideologues of this latest iteration of liberalism. The constellation of discourses and practices that comprise the Free 'Hood refuse conventional analysis of resistance, which would romanticize them.[5]

Rather, the Free 'Hood must be taken as a delinquent refusal because of the manipulation of the body and criminal violence. Such a refusal embraces the inevitably short and cruel nature of criminal lives at the new frontier. Criminal and pathological practices give them a dark, grandiose sense of refusal to the new exercises of sovereignty, the war making of this late moment of the ongoing neoliberal era, that coalesces in and oozes through the necessary, jagged fissures of the neoliberal age, forming a space of inevitable, pathological death. In poisoning themselves by breathing toxic, mind-numbing fumes, the inhabitants of Barrio Libre defy sovereign powers and material forms of subjugation of living normal lives, of submitting to power and its ends.[6]

To embrace an imminent end to their young lives is to simultaneously embrace their delinquent freedoms, the violations of other bodies and boundaries, the abuse of street drugs, and the flowing through a transnational underground terrain and its both real and imagined channels. They, too, are "never meant to survive."[7] Their confounding delinquent practices, their transnational subterranean movements, and their grand claims to territory stretching from these bowels of the new frontier through Tucson, Los Angeles, Chicago, and beyond constitute an embrace of imminent death as a political act, a pathological, delinquent refusal, a refusal to live life as a normal subject of neoliberalism. Barrio Libre captures one avenue where the grossly dispossessed and grossly marginalized retain some power in conditions of neoliberal governmentality and the accompanying new exercises of sovereignty. Their identifications, desires, fantasies, and imaginaries gestate in the moist darkness of the transnational sewer system, whose radically circumscribed agency provides its inhabitants space and avenues for refusal, survival, and at times pleasure in the darkened realms that shadow the militarized managements of bodies up above and down below the new frontier.

Pathological (W)rites

Inevitably, an ethnographic research project on regimes of dispossession and state violence and their birthing of criminal violence, pathology, "death wishes," and similarly loaded concepts about marginalized, predominantly Mexican youth—particularly by a scholar on the border of anthropology and Latina/o studies—calls forth the controversial concept of the culture of poverty. And it is to this concept that I now turn my attention.

Drawing on ethnographic methods, the late anthropologist Oscar Lewis described the culture of poverty as subcultures formed as "both an adaption and a reaction of the poor to their marginal position in a class-stratified, highly individuated, capitalistic society." Once it comes to be, "it tends to perpetuate itself from generation to generation because of its effect on the children. By the time slum children are age six or seven . . . they have absorbed the basic values and attitudes of their subculture and are not psychologically geared to take full advantage of changing conditions or increased opportunities which may occur in their life-time."[8] It entangles those children in its clutches, passing dysfunctional dynamics from generation to generation and suffocating the children in strong feelings of "marginality, of helplessness, of dependence, and of inferiority."[9] According to Lewis, only some impoverished populations exhibit the culture of poverty. He held that a lack of cultural richness and self-organization of the globe's poor prevented their concerted political mobilization for social change. He extolled tightly organized primitive and peasant societies, because they offered lives rich with meaning to their members.[10]

Critics hold Lewis responsible for initiating a resurgence of Social Darwinism in the academy. His ascription of causality to the behavior of the poor effectively "blamed the victim": it was not social, political, or structural forces that overdetermined the reproduction of poverty, but the practices of the poor themselves. Lewis's ideas did prove extremely pernicious, particularly in the policy arena. The idea of the culture of poverty affirmed liberal beliefs about the poor and the underclass, rationalizing the US government's War on Poverty in the 1960s.[11] The culture of poverty and its derivatives—ideologies of the underclass, cultural deficit, and related iterations—remain central to the debate about the status of African Americans, Latinos, and other urban poor in the United States since the 1960s. The premises of the culture of poverty later affirmed the conventions of the dismantling of the welfare state, first under neoliberal orthodoxies, and later under neoconservative governments. The poor were deemed unworthy of public assistance, while it became part of the ideological arsenal to legitimate the policing and vast regimes of incarceration, deportation, and related oppressions exercised against nightmarish figures.

The culture of poverty strangles critical thought in the academy and in public discourse to this day. Images of welfare queens, absentee fathers, and welfare-abusing migrants draw on the culture of poverty's pernicious legacy and reproduce haunting demonizations and discourses that reproduce middle-class sensibilities about the impoverished and the unworthy, pathological poor. Its influence is now remarkably unremarkable; it is where most mainstream discourses about poverty begin, rather than the regimes of dispossession and accompanying power relations that characterize these moments. The widespread influence of the culture of poverty problematically illustrates anthropology's greatest contribution to the public sphere: the instrumentalization of liberal social sciences about Latinos and other racialized communities to their detriment.[12]

That is, the culture of poverty is far more than simply a pernicious and politically potent class discourse. As scholars, such as Kamala Visweswaran, have noted, conceptually, "culture" can do the work of racism, despite its noble origin as a term to contest "race." The term "culture" often holds too much coherence, as is the case in Lewis's formulation. It is all too determining in its deployment in anthropology and other disciplines, generally, and as held in the popular imagination within the United States and in Mexico.[13] That is, culture as a concept generally and culture of poverty specifically constitute a shift away from the biological determinism of modern racisms to the muted, hegemonically mobilized discourses about irreducible and incommensurable cultural difference. And, in the case of the culture of poverty, what is taken as an impoverished population's internally produced pathologies become the subject of study. The culture of poverty and its pernicious and pervasive derivatives are a scholarly reaffirmation of the unstated commonsense, which is backed by the iron fist of state violence, incarceration, and their banal permutations in the punishments of daily life.[14] The culture of poverty effectively criminalizes social problems rather than addressing them.

The culture of poverty shares certain premises with structural functionalism, one of the predominant schools of anthropology in the twentieth century. Problematically, this school understood culture as internally produced, failing to address broader arrangements of power and connection. Culture is taken as shared values, meanings, or images among a community; they are autonomous and self-organizing. Moreover, it is noteworthy that Lewis exemplified conventions of anthropology as he engaged in these practices of knowledge production. He conducted research on the impoverished or the dispossessed — not the poor — among Native Americans, as well as in Mexico, Puerto Rico, Cuba, New York, and India.

Urban anthropologists, anthropologists of crime, and — most forcefully — scholars from outside anthropology have challenged the idea of the culture of poverty. They offer complex analyses of poverty and crime, often pointing to the overdetermination of economies and policies rather than to a pathological inheritance. Pernicious values, they hold, such as individualism, hedonism, materialism, and violence, penetrate — or some similar top-down term — these subcultures of poverty.[15] For example, Philippe Bourgois's *In Search of Respect,* an ethnography of crack dealers in a Latino neighborhood in New York City, holds that crack dealers reproduce many of the dominant values of corporate America.[16] Meanwhile, Jean and John Comaroff suggest that in neoliberal South Africa, those young people who are denied full citizenship grow frustrated: "[They] take to the streets[,] . . . often the only place where, in an era of privatization, a lumpen public can be seen and heard." The profile of these populations reflects also the feminization of post-Fordist labor, which further disrupts gender relations and domestic reproduction among working people, creating a concomitant "'crisis of masculinity': a crisis as audible in U.S. gangsta' rap as in South African gang rape."[17]

Limón seizes on the complex notions of class struggle, consciousness, and state power in Antonio Gramsci's coded and scattered prison writings and on the anticolonialist fury of Franz Fanon to suggest that the historical marginalization of Mexicans in Texas generates a latent social war. It involves acts of questionable political character and ranges from social banditry early in the twentieth century to the more mundane, sometimes internally directed acts such as substance abuse and masculinist joking practices rife with both hetero- and homosexual as well as sexist innuendos, and it is full of relations of dominance.[18]

Several other social theorists, in this respect, have noted the correspondence between morality, ethics, and the economic relations of society. Gramsci long ago noted the ethical and moral leadership of the hegemonic bloc, or the alliance of class fractions, that spearhead a hegemonic social formation. Accordingly, as Stuart Hall noted in his critical grappling with the work of Gramsci, the state adapts "the civilization and the morality of the broadest masses to the necessities of the continuous development of the economic apparatus of production."[19] Arturo Escobar suggests that development discourse, the latest manifestation of which appears in neoliberalism, associates poverty with qualities such as mobility, vagrancy, independence, promiscuity, ignorance, and the refusal of social duties and work. Notably, to him, the management of poverty calls for interventions in health, hygiene, education, morality, and employment.[20] Moreover, although Hall and his coauthors, as well as Paul Gilroy, long ago argued the political salience of mugging as a form of social protest,[21] theirs were subjects who, at least, they suggested, mugged people from the dominant group. But, methodologically speaking, they did not interview the black muggers. Other scholars adopt a functionalist position in their interventions, where "pathological" or criminal practices are seen as a release from order, a release of steam, darkened in this case.

The furiously delinquent lords of the mobile, scatologically flowing Free 'Hood—who traffic in the underground and purvey circulating racisms, participating as they do in an asymmetrical economy of violence—interrupt such well-intentioned, politicizing analyses of criminalities. The young men and women dwelling in Barrio Libre exercise a radically conditioned choice—but not a choice in the liberal sense of the term. Rather, the high-intensity militarized policing of the US Border Patrol and special Mexican police units, in tandem with neoliberal conditions, incite and provoke new defiant subjectivities. These are evident in the youths' affects, fantasies, and imaginaries; sensibilities of unbridled freedoms and grandiose powers; and dehumanizing, dense degradations in the dominant order. Barrio Libre is a refusal. It is a reluctant acceptance of the short lives of the criminal and criminalized at the new frontier, captured in the paint-breathing formation of Barrio Libre.

What I have underscored throughout this text is a perverse proximity or a perverse relationship between the birth of Barrio Libre and the necessarily incomplete exercises of sovereignty by both the US and Mexican nation-states. In this chapter, I follow Judith Butler's call to approach the gendered subject as a site of ambivalence, where power and primary violence both enact and press on it, so as to grapple with the complex question of delinquent, criminal, and in this case, pathological death-embracing agency. "Agency" does not in itself sufficiently grasp the complexity that I am trying to address, but it represents my uncomfortable compromise with the available critical vocabulary in terms of subject effects, or how people are made subjects in relation to power.

The term "agency" refers to "the assumption of a purpose unintended by power"; "a reversal and concealment occurs and power emerges as what belongs exclusively to the subject (making the subject appear as if it belongs to no prior operation of power)."[22] That is, the Barrio Libre — and related sites of pathology, delinquency, and criminality — that can be discerned in the points of view, images, utterances, affects, and fantasies of those living in it constitutes a critical opting into a delinquent, dark, parallel realm and out of the life-demands of neoliberalism. In so doing, such refusals disrupt certain critical orthodox modes of cultural analysis and modes of representation within anthropology and certain postdisciplinary intellectual formations.

"Choosing" Barrio Libre

After one of his many stays in the youth authority in Nogales, Sonora, an exhausted, enraged Román — then eighteen years old — says to me: "I don't wanna go back to Guadalajara. . . . I don't wanna go back home. . . . I want to be here . . . in Barrio Libre. I want to maintain contact with my dad. I want to find a job, raise my daughters, marry Margarita. But I'm going to need my papers . . . like high school papers [diploma] . . . but I only did primary [elementary school]. . . . I want to be in my barrio, Barrio Libre."

Román and the other youths knew that they needed certain credentials to enter into a better life. As I discussed in chapter 2, in the wake of NAFTA, the gutting of Mexico's welfare state, and the production of vast new migrant flows, those who inhabited Barrio Libre and who worked on the streets panhandling or performing menial labor suddenly found themselves subject to policing for not having *credenciales*. They spent much of their time when they were not in the streets or in the tunnels trying to figure out ways to acquire them. Moreover, Román had been held at a prison run by the Correction Corporation of America. There he had befriended a Chicano prison guard and had perfected his English.

Nevertheless, it bears repeating: Román does not want to return to his parents' home. At least as he describes it, his home in Guadalajara is not characterized by the squalor of conventional bourgeois narratives about street youth. His home life did not force him onto the streets to avoid the painful realities of deprivation. That is, he was not forced onto the streets nor forged into a delinquent, nor did foreign hedonistic or individualistic values penetrate his subjectivity. The cultural field of neoliberalism—despite its dismemberment of the welfare state and, indeed, of the very notion of the social, and its coupling with new forms of violent, warlike, governance—generates a radically circumscribed agency and new forms of delinquent subjectivity. In this case, Román and many other youths in Barrio Libre consciously decided to inhabit the dark, underground, criminal, parallel terrain and economy, and its vertiginous transnational incarnations, both real and imagined.

Another young man, it seems, made a similar "choice." As Tortas tells me while I take mental notes over a game of foosball in downtown Nogales, Sonora, he found the young people's claims of freedom exciting: "I wanted to be free. I wanted to be in Tucson, in Barrio Libre." He appeared to come from a reasonably stable family. Indeed, when he first started spending time with the young people of Barrio Libre, his mother came by Mi Nueva Casa. She expressed her frustration at his hanging out with *estos tipos cholos* (those gangster types).

Rubio and Beto Gonzalez likewise seemed to have "chosen" to inhabit Barrio Libre. Despite being part of Barrio Libre and having regularly literally undermined the border through its subterranean passages, where he sometimes mugged people—Rubio had had a green card at one point in his life. This document would allow him to cross the border through official channels. It had been confiscated by the Tucson Police Department during his time in Barrio Libre of Tucson, when—as he explains—he was up to no good: "I was in Barrio Libre [in Tucson]. Being libre. I was caught shoplifting at Wal-Mart. The police officers caught me. They tore up my papers and deported me." I asked him why he didn't get another green card, but he just shrugged. During the time I worked with the young people of Barrio Libre, he never sought to acquire another one.

Defiance, tempered by a certain inevitability, charged the subjective state of being libre. Indeed, Gabriel, Rubio's younger brother, told me: "I like to anger the authorities, those from Beta [Grupo] and the *migra* [the Border Patrol]. I like to be in the tunnel and frustrate them." Similarly, Loco (the crazy one) stated: "For me, to be Barrio Libre . . . I like to piss off the *doñas* [the women who managed Mi Nueva Casa], los de Beta [the members of Grupo Beta], los chiles verdes [the US Border Patrol]." Rubio's explanation references the multiple forms of subjugation, often too quickly reduced to sovereignty, that subjugate this population.

Loco adds, emphatically: "Somos Barrio Libre" (we are the Free 'Hood). José told me: "We are free because we have no rules. No one tells us what to do." In Nogales, Sonora, during an interview at a time when he was struggling to earn a living washing the windshields of passing vehicles, Toni, who had left his family in Sinaloa and lived on the streets and occasionally in the tunnel, told me they had named it Barrio Libre because "we are free." They lived "anywhere . . . and we would do anything we want." Or, as Román and others would often say, "Barrio Libre es donde nadie te maneje" (Barrio Libre is where no one controls you). Such sentiments garner greater potency when contextualized in the young people's sense of collectivity. The youths frequently said: "Somos Barrio Libre," "Somos libre," or "Libre total." To say "libre" in the singular, as the young people often did, refers to a collective subject in Spanish, a subject that neoliberal power would individuate.

Indeed, the inhabitants of the Free 'Hood relied upon the nightmarish abhorrence that they and their practices produced. They realized that officials in both Mexico and the United States avoided the tunnels, that the daily practices of policing them invited disgust, repulsion, and fear. Indeed, a senior officer of the Border Patrol told me that he would never go into the tunnel without wearing a "haz suit," a reference to his time in the military and to the special clothes that people wear when dealing with toxic waste. He further explained to me that by late 2000, a US government policy prohibited Border Patrol officers from entering the sewer. Before this policy was implemented, agents who entered the tunnel often became ill. One officer reported that when he entered the dark labyrinth he was wearing new boots. When he came out, the boots' soles had melted.

The lived experiences of another youth provide an interesting counterpoint. In contrast to the young people of Barrio Libre who, in some respect, "chose" it or consciously positioned themselves as its subjects, I turn to the youngest Gonzalez brother Lazaro, brother of Güero and Beto. The thirteen-year-old with long hair "chose" *not* to inhabit Barrio Libre. He relied on Mi Nueva Casa for regular meals, and he often spent time with members of Barrio Libre in the community organization, yet he did not accompany them to the rest of the terrain of Barrio Libre. I once asked him why.

> *Lazaro*: Well, I don't know. Because it's a mess. My brothers' lives are messes. They're sick. And the drugs.
>
> *Gilberto*: You have never crossed under the border? Or have you mugged chúntaros?
>
> *Lazaro*: No, never. I just work. I cross the border and go help people clean their houses or pull weeds in the garden. I work for Ms. Montoya. She tells me that she is going to pay for my school. [Lazaro held a green card—the requisite credential to cross the border as a day laborer—the document his brother Güero had lost and refused to pursue.]
>
> *Gilberto*: But what do you think about being part of Barrio Libre?
>
> *Lazaro*: It never really got my attention. I did not want to *be bad* [my emphasis]. To get sick.
>
> *Gilberto*: Have you had any trouble with the police or the Border Patrol?
>
> *Lazaro*: Well, I've been lucky there. I'm not out on the streets that much, and one time Grupo Beta chased me but I was able to hide. Other than that, no. The guys at the border are fucked up. But, no. Not like my brothers. I don't want to die.

It would be both naive and complicit with the individuating logics of self-care of neoliberalism to suggest that Lazaro had greater will or some other quality that allowed him to resist becoming part of the Free 'Hood. Such a position would also echo the conventions of the culture of poverty, which would hold that Barrio Libre and similarly positioned parties practiced internally produced pathology. But the conversation reinforces the fact that the young people exercised a radically circumscribed agency—they did not have a choice in the literal sense of the term. But, seeping under the new frontier and its myriad forms of subjugation, mugging migrants, inhaling spray paint, and consuming drugs constituted a refusal. It was their delinquent refusal of the new frontier. That is, Barrio Libre must be recognized as a political discourse. Granted, it is one with tremendously vexing practices, but it is inextricably linked to a repudiation of policing and the multiple oppressions that the youths associated with it and to a pathological embrace of death.

Gendered Differentials

But ethnographic grounding trumps theoretical closure. Recalling my learned insistence that race must be taken intersectionally, here the cholas of Barrio Libre intervene in my analysis. They ooze out from the sewer tunnel and vastly complicate Barrio Libre as a pathological embracing of death. Two young women, likely high, seep under the new frontier, which they imagine as Barrio Libre. I am at the same restaurant I described in the beginning of this chapter. A few minutes into our conversation, I ask them: "What does Barrio Libre mean for you?"

> *Margarita*: It's that we are all free.
> *Juana*: All free.
> *Gilberto*: Free from what?
> *Margarita*: Well, from . . . well, here we can do what we want. We are totally free.
> *Gilberto*: Free from what?
> *Margarita*: Everything.

As she said this, she looked around, searching for the authorities.

The specificity of the young women's bodies becomes a potent terrain in political and symbolic struggles at the new frontier.[23] It would be all too easy to construct a narrative about the young people of Barrio Libre—particularly the young women—as "victims," echoing critics of the culture of poverty, whether of academic discourse or material circumstance. But my ethnographic observations and conversations with the young women of Barrio Libre interrupt such conventions.

As Margarita exits Mi Nueva Casa following lunch, a young man on the street who was a regular in the Free 'Hood brushes up against her. He starts to grind against her thigh suggestively. Margarita then mobilizes the gendered differential that informs her alignment to the Free 'Hood. She pushes the young man away and exclaims, "Soy libre, cabron!" (I'm free, asshole!). The Free 'Hood surpasses a space of pathology and imminent death. It becomes a site of "dark," subterranean feminism, where women can control their asymmetrically positioned bodies.

Young women's participation in the Free 'Hood by seeping under the new exercises of sovereignty, incomplete though they are at the new frontier, as well as in its collective pathological rites, undermines stereotypical depictions of helpless Third World women.

Criminal violence has largely been represented in the social sciences as a male domain. The young women draw on the pathological anxieties about this delinquent refusal of the new to refuse to be bound to home, tradition, or country. They literally undermined dominant conventions about women of the Global South being bound to oppressive homes and cultural spaces, dominant narratives that "developed in relation to the vision of Western women as secular, liberated, and in total control of their lives."[24]

Margarita described how Barrio Libre had altered her perspective. Following her return to Nogales, Sonora, she told me: "I [decided to] cross again . . . through the tunnel." When I asked why, she replied: "I don't know. . . . I didn't want to go home. . . . I don't know. . . . I preferred the streets . . . but I don't know. . . . I would get bored in my house. . . . I wanted to go to Barrio Libre."

She sought freedom from some of her "womanly responsibilities." She told of being exhausted and of being required to do housework, go to school, and have a job. As La Negra put it, "I would rather be free, go to Tucson, be in Barrio Libre, hang out with my friends." Consequently, they negate the dominant liberal representation of women of the Global South as the passive victims of an oppressive Third World society, as well as its transnational connections to the First World. Margarita and her mother shared household responsibilities, taking turns to provide child care in their small, humble abode, as I described in chapter 2. Margarita's father had left the family years ago in his travels to the United States. When she was not libre, she worked at the same maquiladora as her mother.

Often, when I discuss Margarita's and other young women's ambivalence toward home life, it elicits strong reactions from my audience and raises questions about violent or abusive households. It is noteworthy that many of the young women and some of the young men of Barrio Libre espoused a critical discourse about *padrastros* (stepfathers). The term implicitly refers to and condemns absent, abusive, or bad fathers. This critical perspective could refer to something more akin to a conventional patriarchal heteronormative nuclear family arrangement—although not necessarily in all instances. In either case, what seems clear is that these were in some sense marked and perhaps "problematic" father figures, juxtaposed directly with the figure of a similarly problematic "real" father, terms that certainly echo their treatment by the authorities. Nevertheless, whether taken as referring to matters of sexual violence, heteropatriarchic subordination in the household, or the absent father figure of the Mexican state in the neoliberal epoch, such discourses rendered the Free 'Hood a space not just of pathology and delinquency, but also of critical refusal with certain gendered differentials.

Conclusion

Breathing metallic spray paint, inhaling glue and marker fumes, and mugging chúntaros or neoliberal migrants constitute the pathological space of Barrio Libre. It is a radically circumscribed agency, a delinquent refusal of young men and women who face imminent death as nightmarish human waste at the new frontier. The Free 'Hood mediates agonistic and intimate ways of life and struggles for this particular population. It defies the legacy of pathologizing formulations such as the culture of poverty and its derivatives, which, as their critics rightly maintained, ultimately blame the victim in emphasizing a pathological inheritance that is internal to impoverished grossly marginalized populations. Barrio Libre also defies the subsequent well-meaning academic formulations that have emphasized the macro-political forging of pathological or criminal formations.

Such new liberal conventions erase, rather than confront or explicate, the vexing relations among the nightmares of insecurity of the neoliberal age, the new stratagems of racialization, and the refusals of lives to submit to new orders. They risk erasing the vexed circumscribed agency of those who dwelled in Barrio Libre — their opting into the pathological space of Barrio Libre and its perverse relations to the incomplete sovereign warfare that is the new stratagem of governance of the neoliberal age. To engage in repulsive practices, Barrio Libre inhabited a sewer system, a site of actual pathology, and drew on its scatological associations to participate in criminal violence and to breathe in industrial toxins. Such practices constituted the youths' embrace of an imminent death; it was their delinquent refusal of the new frontier. These lords of a dark, delinquent pathological space, of fleeting powers and dense marginalities, reveal how in a context of neoliberal state violence even those positioned as human waste can exercise agency, make space, and assume terrain — painful, vexing and complicated though the process sometimes is. Their pathological practices help reveal how normativity encodes structural inequalities and how criminal, delinquent, and pathologically vexing practices at the level of the body become refusal.[25] This pathological space of premature death shows the complexity of power and resistance for marginal subjects—the vexing entanglements of subjects with power and the birth of bad subjects with little to lose and much to gain from exercising their own violence and engaging in reviled practices.

Such subjects cannot be accessed without empirical grounding. Their choices speak to the limitations of abstract theoretical discourses and to competing discourses of subjectification, structures, and agencies. Choosing to accelerate their deaths interrupts notions of victimhood and the genre of border studies, predicated on a necessarily struggling subject. That is to say that although not overtly political, Barrio Libre carries with it political resonances. Thus, when Juana, Margarita, Román, Bolillo, Loco, Beto, Güero, and the others who incarnate Barrio Libre invoke freedom, they mean a freedom from the displacement of the neoliberal economy, the manifest violence of homelessness, and particularly the warlike exercises of sovereignty that anchor the new frontier.

It is through such a contaminated grappling with criminal powers and knowledges that the normative power behind structural inequities becomes clear. Kathleen Stewart has called for "contaminated cultural critique."[26] Yet her suggestion, as with most experimental writings in anthropology, is to imbed the anthropologist deeper into the ethnography. My suggestion is that we refuse to erase the production of subjectivities of those mired in complex relations of power, and how they in turn exercise their own power. These youths exercised racialized, entrepreneurial violence and pathology that placed them outside of discourses of victimhood. In doing so, they exhibited a complex, circumscribed, delinquent agency and a vexing political discourse, one that many will refuse to hear.

Nervous Cocks
at the New Frontier

MAY 2008

To my right are about five small pens, constructed of chicken wire and two-by-fours. In them, roosters and chickens flap their wings and cackle. Another rooster, uncaged, has his leg tied to a box. Román is sitting on a chair that he has pulled from inside one of his two shacks, where his youngest child — a three-month-old girl — is sleeping. With a few of his friends, he watches me watch the birds.

Over this past week, Román has recounted to me what he knew about those who once inhabited Barrio Libre. For the young women, it seems, marriage was one way out of this space of impending death. Román explained: "Margarita married another man and left. La Morena, too. La Negra dances [actually strips] at that club." She had explained to me and apparently to Román too that she did not want her children to become delinquentes. Another young woman sells tacos and another works in a maquiladora. Román explains that "some of the guys are living in prison, others are running drugs." Many are dead, part of the fatal logics of neoliberal rule. And some "got out," explains Román. "Simon, he's working as a carpenter in Tucson." Other youths reported having nightmares about the tunnel, dreams of being attacked by spirits from below. Others told of hearing women's screams coming from the tunnels — criminal iterations of la llorona, Mexico's folkloric phantasm of lost children, and of gendered psyches rocked by guilt.

During our conversations this past week, Román has been educating me about the art of cockfighting, an icon of manhood in both Mexico and among certain populations in the United States. To be muy gallo *(very rooster) is to act manly.[1] Suddenly, Román grabs the uncaged bird and begins to stroke it. He explains to me again that the gallos must be raised to be strong. This one will not be ready to fight for over a month, during which time Román will feed him, give him vitamins, and care for him.*

Román goes to one of the pens, opens it, and unleashes another cock. Román explains: "He's my newest one. He's my best one. Look at his claws—they're big." I see that they are several inches long. Holding the bird by its talons, he strokes its back and coos at it.

"I got him yesterday," he says. "I made trade." He rubs his finger and his thumb together, signaling what I take to be a criminal transaction of the drug trade. Every now and then Román's English fails him. He learned the language when he went to school in Washington state, before his father's naturalization status was revoked because he was alleged to have sold cocaine. Román adamantly denies this charge, saying that it was his older brother who dealt.

As the global economy contracted in yet another crisis and the dark, parallel, criminal realm that had once been banished underground seeped upward and into civil society, Román and many of the other young people were repositioned. Román himself and many of his friends were increasingly involved in the deepening drug economy of the new frontier. Even in the post–September 11 intensification of policing, it remains possible to cross the new frontier. Román explains that he heads east and then crosses the new frontier into the deserts, where he then hides drugs at a predetermined drop-off point. As we talk, Román's hand softly cups the bird.

"Look," Román says, "hold him. How much do you think he weighs?"

He hands the cock to me. Having never held a rooster before, I fumble with it, causing Chamuco to laugh. The bird is surprisingly heavy, probably weighing a few pounds.

Román orders Chamuco to hold the bird. Román goes to another pen and pulls out another cock, which appears larger. Román grabs its talons. He strokes the bird slowly, cooing at it. Breathing heavily, I watch the cock throb. Its breast contracts, expands, contracts, expands . . .

Román hands me this cock. Trying to be cool, I reach for it. But I am clumsy. The bird claws me. Blood drips from my wrist. Román laughs and says: "You must learn to handle the gallos better."

The larger cock weighs a couple more pounds than the small one. Román, Chamuco, and Tortas laugh. Román grabs the bird.

Román's little boy has grown agitated and tries to play with a third gallo tied to the door. Román yells at the toddler, while caressing the *cock in his hand. The child starts bawling and runs into one of the small shacks.*

Glancing behind Román, I see two Border Patrol vehicles on a hill in the distance, behind the border wall. I can make out a figure who emerges from one of the vehicles. Below them and just to the west is the Nogales, Sonora, cemetery. I wonder if the agent is watching us.

"Have you seen a pelea de gallos [a cockfight]?" Román asks me. I shake my head no. Having been taught by Román that a good bird can cost up to fifty dollars, I tell him there is no need to hurt his birds on my account. Román dismisses my concern with a wave of his hand.

Cockfights have a weighty role in the discipline of anthropology. Indeed, in the groundbreaking "Deep Play: Notes on the Balinese Cockfight," Clifford Geertz argues for a semiotics of culture in anthropology. It is premised on an understanding of cultural analysis as an exercise in interpretation: practices are to be read like literature, listened to like music, appreciated like art, and represent the Other's daily informal knowledges. Accordingly, passions and conflicts animate social facts and imbue everyday discourses and gestures with cultural meanings garnered from the conceptual structures of the world that others live in.[2] But aside from erasing the materiality of cultural creation,[3] cockfights in this instance revive pathologized masculinities, bringing them some normalcy, at the new frontier.

Román and Chamuco each grab a bird by the tail. They begin to joust, using the birds as living, plumed swords. The birds squawk. Román thrusts; Chamuco parries. Chamuco thrusts; Román parries. Seemingly mimicking the young men's movements, as the birds are put closer together, their heads expand, and they, too, begin to lunge in a sporadic, frenzied, brutal dance. Other roosters in the pens crow, contributing to the clamor.

Román and Chamuco tire of the fight after a few minutes. They put the birds on the ground.

Chamuco commands his bird: "¡Chingalo!" (Fuck him!).

The birds lunge at each other. Each bird tries to jump on the other. Talons ready, they swipe at one another, squawking. Though the smaller bird jumps higher, the larger bird pummels it. Transfixed, we watch the carnal violence of beast against beast. Feathers and cock flesh fly in the air.

Ofelia passes us as she continues to care for the children, ignoring us. Román stops the fight.

"*El grande pega bien*" (*The large cock hits well*), he says. Size, it seems, does matter. The cock begins to crow, and Román gently rubs it.

Border Patrol surveillance towers loom in the distance. With the fight now over, Román lets his cock chase a chicken around behind the shack he calls his penthouse. "*Si, pega bien*," comments Flaco. We erupt in laughter. Warlike relations, to return to my larger framework, infiltrate everyday life.

The New Frontier Thickens

Increasingly, crises of state sovereignty and low-intensity wars enmesh impoverished figures in concomitant regimes of racialization and criminalization, rendering them nightmares. These same phenomena characterize what I call the new frontier, where Mexico and the United States and their respective new projects of sovereignty involve warfare and policing in this late neoliberal moment. In Mexico, haunted, pressured public officials, police, journalists, and scholars call for something to be done about the renewed nightmares of insecurity, "la delincuencia organizada." Under the nightmares of the drug war, cholos are being targeted. The Mexican authorities and drug traffickers dispose of these abject youths, if they are not conscripted by the latter. Indeed, following a massacre at a drug rehabilitation clinic in Ciudad Juárez that has been linked to the ongoing drug war, letter writers in Mexico's progressive newspaper *La Jornada* celebrated the murder of cholos. And that was why I wrote against Mexico.

Yet, as I have argued in this book, since well before September 11, incipient forms of necessarily incomplete security warfare have occurred at this international border, by both the United States and Mexico. They birthed the cholos of the Free 'Hood and the youths' embrace of the pathological ends of their lives in nightmarish dark, fetid, sewers. There, in seething criminal darkness, they inhaled inexpensive urban poisons, painting their lungs gold, and painting gold the freedoms they found in Barrio Libre. There, the youths exercised violence and terror as a means of production, mugging uncouth, mestizaje-derived chúntaros.

Now, following September 11 and the latest aggravations of security concerns, the perverse proximity of criminality and necessarily incomplete wars of sovereignty has intensified. Fittingly, the youths who once lived on the border of the legitimate and the "darkness" of the illegitimate economy now find the latter has seeped upward from the sewers.

Many of the youths have matured into young adults and have found new ways to make a living in Mexico's current drug war. Indeed, Román explained to me in 2008 that his life as a lower-level drug dealer during the narco wars was in some ways "safer than life below [*alla abajo*]" in the subterranean world of Barrio Libre.

> [Now] I sell tacos [by day] . . . tacos *de birria*. Then at night we come back here and pack up the stuff. I put it in my backpack and then I try to cross. We don't go through the tunnels any more. We don't go down there like we used to. We're lost up here. In ten minutes, I can make more money selling coke, marijuana, or crack than working at a maquiladora. The tunnels are too hot. The *polleros* and the *narcos* [the drug traffickers] have taken them over. And [with] the Federal Preventive Police and Border Patrol, we just can't go down there much any more. We run them [drugs] across the border, climbing over the fence or going through the holes, and leave them hidden on the other side. They [the tunnels] are not safe. Many of the exits have been closed off, and the Border Patrol has put up sensors and video cameras and the narcos run them.

Moreover, as Román reminds me, Barrio Libre was never really in the tunnels: "It was everywhere. In Tucson, Phoenix, Los Angeles, Chicago. Barrio Libre was wherever we were, where we weren't controlled."

The latest economic crisis has impoverished sixty million people. Of that number, one in six lives in Latin America. Meanwhile, Mexico's mutation to a neoconservative, authoritarian government, which began in the 1990s but is still ensconced within neoliberal globalization, has intensified its necessarily incomplete exercises of sovereignty in the dramatic drug war. According to Mexico's government, some eighty-two thousand traffickers have been detained. But — once more signaling law enforcement as a suffused form of warfare, involving questions of race and criminality in the late neoliberal age — overwhelmingly those being detained are peasants and indigenous people involved in the cultivation of drugs. They plant marijuana, hallucinogenic mushrooms, and peyote. Lacking resources for defense attorneys, they are sentenced to more than five years in prison, many for being close to (*estar cerca*) the emerging drug economy, while the bleached narco entrepreneurs sneer at law enforcement — sovereignty — on both sides of the border.

Moreover, post–September 11 security concerns have thickened the new frontier with the United States. Jennifer Allen, the executive director of Border Action Network, maintains that the border and its walls have become the

> center point or a sort of symbol of insecurity[,] ... so if you're feeling insecure, what better thing to do than build a fifteen-foot-high solid metal wall? Walls were already in place here prior to 9/11, but with the Secure Fence Act the congressional push is trying to make this country and the people in it feel secure. While border walls were already in place in Arizona, the Secure Fence Act augmented the "walling" of the border. They are now being doubled in southern Arizona and tripled in southern California.[1]

Moreover, the United States has recently agreed to fund Mexican armed forces and police forces under the Plan Merida for the purposes of the war on drugs and fighting organized crime.[2] This plan effectively emerges from talks that began in the context of NAFTA: an effective realization that neoliberal globalization challenged nation-states' rule. Current nightmares of insecurity began in the smoldering ruins of NAFTA.

Meanwhile, the virtual wall—the so-called Secure Border Initiative—amasses new sensors and representatives of military and intelligence agencies at the border.[3] The US Department of Homeland Security (DHS) implemented the Secure Border Initiative as a comprehensive attempt to gain operational control of the country's land border by integrating staffing, interior enforcement, detection technology, and infrastructure, and coordinating activities at the federal, state, local, and international levels. According to Allen, the virtual wall has been "a dismal failure":

> The technology towers [were built] in ravines, but they were too low and failed to [monitor] over the top of hills. So what Boeing said is that they now need to use more advanced technology. Now, they are using unmanned aerial vehicles, $10 million contraptions hovering [in] the sky. ... [There are] still smatterings of National Guard troops on the border.
>
> [The] Border Patrol is continuing to grow, trying to bring more agents on all the time. They've not been able to live up to the congressional mandates for hiring rates ... they try to pull from people with law enforcement or military backgrounds [as] their first priority, and today those with a military background are more likely to be in Iraq or Afghanistan.

And if they're not there, they are probably working for Halliburton or Blackwater, making a lot more than they are going to make at Border Patrol.

They can't pull anyone from [an] existing law enforcement position. It's a pretty miserable job. . . . You're not beloved in the community. It's not like [being] a firefighter. In border communities, with families of green card holders, undocumented [migrants], you don't want them [Border Patrol agents] to get close. They're kind of marginalized and ostracized. Kids don't like them. They've grown up being harassed by them. So, [there are] high turnover rates. An increasing number of agents are being busted as part of smuggling operations, taking bribes. [But the Border Patrol is] still the nation's largest law enforcement agency.

[Border enforcement practices] are designed for failure. We have these young guys—mostly young guys, we do have [some] women—who have tremendous power over whether someone stays in this country or doesn't, and they are out in the middle of nowhere as part of this institution with little accountability. . . . It's fraying massively at the edges, and that fraying is getting closer and closer to the center.[4]

Allen's comments likewise underscore how a taken for granted masculinity is embedded in the managements of undocumented transnational migration that signify sovereignty at the new frontier and involved in the concomitant production of the new nightmares of insecurity. And her observations capture the fact that whether or not state violence occurs in the context of the new frontier, as Giorgio Agamben wrote, depends "not on the law but rather on the civility and ethical sense of the police that act temporarily as sovereign."[5] Moreover, Allen holds that in Arizona, what had been limited to border enforcement now permeates "all the other facets of our community and society." The nightmares of insecurity, of necessarily incomplete exercises of sovereignty, generate a situation in which "even landlords ask about people's status. They have to ask people per state law about their immigration status."[6]

The necessarily incomplete wars of the new frontier hail vigilante groups, white supremacist violence, and regimes of surveillance in the border states and in sites of new migrations across the United States. For example, the Texas state government invited citizens to survey the border through remote camera technology that circulated images on the Internet. If citizens saw something or someone suspicious, they were urged to report it. Immigrant-hunting ranchers in Arizona, the

Border Patrol, and the Mexican authorities situate Other lives in great proximity to death, inaugurating undocumented border crossers as vulnerable life, as life cast as politically organized racial subjects.

The mobilization of the National Guard to the border in 2006 and the construction of a border wall, alongside the collapsing of the categories of immigrant and terrorist, speak to this intensification—this thickening—of the new frontier. The thickening of the new frontier includes the shifting of the Border Patrol to the Department of Homeland Security, specifically to Immigration and Customs Enforcement (ICE). Allen continues: "Their mandate has changed; they still have to follow the Constitution, but now they are draped in this cape of national security that they hang around themselves and . . . they think they have more power. It's used to justify more abuses, but in reality they have no additional power as it relates to them, migrants, and border residents. The Constitution didn't change, but the political rhetoric around what they do has changed, which enables them to go, 'Well, this could be a national security threat.'"[7]

Raquel Rubio-Goldsmith of the Coalición de Derechos Humanos/ Alianza Indígena sin fronteras (the Human Rights Coalition/Indigenous Alliance without Borders) likewise alludes to the "thickening" of the new frontier:

> Even those working immigration and immigrant rights for a long time and being focused on the impact that immigration policy enforcement has on our communities—even those of us doing that kind of work for years and who are aware [of] what militarization has done to the border, when we hear the announcement that immigration passes from the Department of Justice to Homeland Security, it doesn't really register. You say, "Oh yeah, that's terrible." But we don't really realize what that means in terms of the tremendous shift that has taken place. It's really a seismic shift because it's one thing for the movement of people to be controlled through a civil process [and another for it to move] over to a process that is set up for terrorism and militarization. You see, these are two different things.
>
> In the enforcement that is now taking place . . . the domain of civil, bureaucratic [avenues] have closed. If you want to believe that the justice system can do something for someone . . . if you want to believe there are judicial recourses, that people have rights, you can believe it as long as a just administrative civil system is in place. And although the criminalization of migrants has a long history in this country, the actual status of

being unauthorized to cross and live in this country is a civil offense. As advocates for migrant rights, we complain that the immigrant is criminalized. Now DHS indicts selected detained immigrants with crossing at an unauthorized border point, puts them through a sham preliminary hearing where all the accused are advised to waive rights to a trial and declare themselves guilty of the criminal misdemeanor of crossing unlawfully or being unauthorized to be in this country.

But DHS has moved even further. Immigration policy enforcement is now part of a system protecting the country against terrorism as well as part of the military world. Therefore now it's the control of people through a militarized terrorist war. Terrorism is not confronted as a crime. Rather, we declare war on terrorism. We are at war. The people in charge of enforcing immigration policy at the very top, like [Secretary Michael] Chertoff, don't have to care about anybody's rights. They don't have to care about anybody's rights, because their way of looking at the migrant population is only within the context of terrorism and war. For those of us who believe in governance based on human rights to absorb this into our consciousness when we have always seen it in terms of advocating for rights is very difficult. [Given that new ideological background for population control,] I think it's more than one part of the population, but rather the whole population; what is imposed on the immigration population ends controlling the entire population, not just immigrants. *This is a step in the control of the population of this country like we have never conceived.*

There are wars and there are wars. There are wars that reflect violence that is going on. That is why we call the situation on the border a war. We call *this* a war because there is impunity on the part of authorities and impunity on the part of the vigilantes. Violence against immigrants and the community is allowed. So we call it a war. And per one definition of war, that's okay.

But there is also a legal definition of war. And that is when the power of the state can *legally commit violence. On the border, before immigration and security legislation, violations of human rights were considered to be illegal.* Now violations have been legitimized. That's an enormous difference. And when you add to that those names they can put on lists of terrorists, what organizations they can list as terrorist organizations—it's all at their discretion, what does that do to the right of free speech and free association? How much can you really go out and say and do and feel that there won't be any repercussions? We aren't accustomed to feeling that we can no longer appeal to basic rights.

We have moved from the point [where] it is illegal to be deprived of rights to the point where it is legal. And not only that, but the fact is that there is a large constituency that supports it.[8]

This analysis dramatically illustrates the stakes in this global age of incomplete sovereignties, their wars, and the accompanying nightmares of insecurity that they produce. But these illiberal technologies are hardly new. They follow a series of dramatic raids across the country, in states such as in Iowa and Ohio, and there are rumors of more raids to come. Indeed, the apprehension of the undocumented through the criminal justice system is now the primary focus of enforcement. In the last three years, ICE has rounded up more than half a million people through such "criminal alien" programs. Yet there is no legal consensus on what a criminal alien is.

Agamben reminds us in his much-neglected *Means without End* that what enabled the Nazi death camps and related technologies of terror was their designation as a policing operation. The state of exception at the border has been normalized. But it has not become "the rule." As I explained in chapter 4, the new frontier cannot be situated in a European genealogy of death camps and related totalitarian or genocidal practices.

Sovereign, and sometimes criminal, policing and occasional acts of official violence occur along axes of race, class, and gender and are situated within global relations of inequity, which produce further extralegal practices ranging from the corruption of certain officials to the delinquency of Barrio Libre. In the era since NAFTA and September 11, the intensification of militarized policing and the related stratagems of state violence have become mundane, assumed, naturalized, taken for granted. Moreover, policing affects those subjugated citizens who are culturally and phenotypically similar to immigrants. This marks an informal racial governance of particular relevance to liberal democracies, such as the United States, where a close relationship exists among race, normative imaginings of citizenship, and culture.[9]

But the new frontier parochializes Agamben's formulation. The new frontier lacks the closure of a camp. That is, the new frontier can gestate struggles; delinquent refusals, where impending death becomes sites of pathological resistance; and alternative political imaginaries. As we have seen among the youths of Barrio Libre, certain dramatic events spark new political attitudes and desires for alternative imagined communities.

In this respect, diverse organizations at the border—such as the Border Action Network, No More Deaths, the American Friends Service Committee's Immigration Law Enforcement Monitoring Project, and the aforementioned Coalición de Derechos Humanos/Alianza Indígena sin fronteras—contest the militarization of border policing and consequently the multiple discursive, dehumanizing constructions of undocumented migrants, or the ideological fodder for the reproduction of the new frontier. Many of these organizations build on the sanctuary movement of the 1980s, a legacy of the original War on Terror, when President Reagan's declaration against the Soviet Union's alleged support of terrorist networks authorized the so-called dirty wars in Latin America. Migrants to the United States, then primarily from Central America, relied on southern Arizona as a site where they could enter the country without documentation. These organizations challenge the official mistreatment of migrants and other marginalized borderlanders, organize actions, and share resources with the public.[10]

The organizations provide an alternative approach to the new frontier, not viewing it as a site of criminality and sovereign policings. Instead, they cast it as a site of convergence of people engaged in social struggles and everyday practices of resistance to the state of exception in the borderlands. They share knowledge with other nongovernmental organizations and allied organizations that strategize against the militarization of the border. For example, the American Friends Service Committee sponsored the recording of a *corrido* by Esequiel Hernandez. The classical Mexican corrido—a form of poetic song explored in chapter 1—typically documents the struggles of male heroes against injustices.[11] In this case, it documented the Marine shooting of the Mexican American shepherd at the border in the 1990s and the subsequent struggles around this event.

The interventions of these border organizations gesture to an alternative political imaginary. It is not the proverbial withering away of the state, but rather an alternative form of globalization. That is, they embody what could be described as a new, historically specific form of what Gloria Anzaldúa once termed "mestiza consciousness," or, as Agamben put it, certain "coming political communities," already evident elsewhere in the world.[12]

Indeed, the exposure to death and criminal violence as one becomes subject to the economic and racial order of the United States, which I explored throughout this book, seems inextricably tied to recent immigrant rights mobilization. For example, close to five million immigrants and their supporters marched in nearly a hundred US cities between March 10 and May 1, 2006. A variety of constituencies — including those desiring amnesty or citizenship, and others representative of transnational solidarity movements — participated in these marches. Moreover, the specific lineages and linkages of social struggle require investigation, given the peasant and indigenous struggles of the 1970s and 1980s in Latin America as well as the Zapatista struggle of the 1990s; the particular knowledges such struggles produced; and the likelihood that they have migrated northward and merged with, for example, Chicago's distinctive history of working-class activism.[13]

In other words, the new frontier proves to be heterotopic. Its exceptions are of a different order, daily subjugations and dominations generate subject effects, violently inaugurating undocumented border crossers to the US economic and racial order and exposing them to criminal agents both inside and outside of the law. But this space and power relations inaugurate transnational social movements and the emergence of new political imaginaries. Such possibilities disrupt the closures of concentration camps or the transformation of the border — now a new frontier — into a site of warfare.[14] Indeed, however problematically, the space of delinquent violence — the sewer system — also becomes for the youths of the Free 'Hood a site of freedom as they undermine the border and enter the Barrio Libre of Tucson. Thus, deviance, delinquency, and pathology, even one that embraces imminent death and encourages criminal violence, may lay the groundwork for oppositional politics while providing a valuable corrective to certain normative intellectual imaginings of politics. That is, the manipulations of bodies and affects at the new frontiers situate bodies in a new relation of power — be it the youth performing or claiming Mexican American cultural citizenship or more normative political practices — and potentially alternative social and power relations underscore the productivity of an asymmetrical economy of violence and the gestation of political alternatives. Such mutations upon border or actually new frontier crossing gesture to the new horizons of possibilities that a decolonial approach to the Mexico-US borderlands suggests.

Ultimately, the daily lives and discourses of the youths who inhabited Barrio Libre, engaged in criminal violence while living their pathological ends of life, while oozing under the new frontier, tell us much about the new frontiers of nation-states in the age of globalization. Having opted into dark, pathological modes of production and embraced imminent death, the youths' movements through the scatological connections between the United States and Mexico capture the new conditions of the socially exorcised, as well as the criminal depths of contemporary state power. These practices likewise reveal how death and its proximity prove instrumental to the production of alternative imaginaries, be they delinquent, criminal, or radically new and utopian.

Introduction

1. Stallybrass and White, *The Politics and Poetics of Transgression,* 50–66.

2. I choose the term "'hood" instead of "neighborhood" and other alternatives for "barrio" because of the term's significance in regard to social struggle. Barrios in the United States—and in Latin America—have a long history as a site of racial formation and social struggle for Mexican and other Latin American immigrants (Dávila, *Barrio Dreams;* Koptiuch, "Third-Worlding at Home").

3. See Feldman, "Securocratic Wars of Public Safety."

4. A. Gómez, "Resisting Living Death at Marion Federal Penitentiary, 1972"; Achille Mbembe, "Necropolitics."

5. Quoted in Joseph Nevins, "Border Death-Trap—Time to Tear Down America's Berlin Wall," *San Diego La Prensa,* July 30, 2002.

6. See Luis Plascencia's genealogy of the term "undocumented." Despite the troubling history of this term, I have relied on it and related terminology to underline its widespread usage in common parlance (Plascencia, "The 'Undocumented' Mexican Migrant Question").

7. Davidson, *Lives on the Line;* Taylor and Hickey, *Tunnel Kids.*

8. The rate of anencephaly (in which babies lack brains and are stillborn) in Mexican border cities is four to ten times the national average. Nogales, Arizona, has the highest level of lupus recorded in the United States, and the city's incidence of multiple myeloma, a rare bone cancer, is among the highest. On average, forty cases of cancer are diagnosed in Nogales, Arizona, each month, which is five times the national rate (Levesque and Ingram, "Lessons in Transboundary Management from Ambos Nogales").

9. See Feldman, "Securocratic Wars of Public Safety." Nightmares of insecurity and of the excludable others should be juxtaposed with Benedict Anderson's prominent notion of *Imagined Communities.*

10. Vélez-Ibañez, *Border Visions,* 67.

11. Ralph Cintron's inspired ethnography, *Angels' Town,* captures similar discourses about *cheros* there.

12. Dunn, *The Militarization of the U.S.-Mexico Border,* 20.

13. Ibid., 29.

14. Ibid., 31.

15. Feldman, "Securocratic Wars of Public Safety."

16. As Ralph Cintron and others argue, Minutemen and other actors violently guard their all too frequently hailed prerogatives of citizenship.

17. Lugo, "Theorizing Border Inspections."

18. Balibar, "Is There a 'Neo-Racism'?"; Williams, "A Class Act."

19. Aretxaga, "Maddening States"; Trouillot, "The Anthropology of the State in the Age of Globalization."

20. Vila, *Crossing Borders, Reinforcing Borders*.

21. Eithne Luibhéid (*Entry Denied*) captures the historical processes of gendered and sexual policing at the US-Mexico border, and Cynthia Enloe (*Manuevers*) grapples with the effects of the militarization of women's lives in sites around the globe.

22. Das and Poole, *Anthropology in the Margins of the State*.

23. On the rise of the drug economy following NAFTA, see Hill, "The War for Drugs."

24. See Bourgois, *In Search of Respect*; Marez, *Drug Wars*; Nordstrom, *Global Outlaws*; Zilberg, "Fools Banished from the Kingdom"; Vargas, *Catching Hell in the City of Angels*. For recent work on the effects of criminal violence in Central America, see Moodie, "Seventeen Years, Seventeen Murders" and *El Salvador in the Aftermath of Peace*; Binford, "A Failure of Normalization."

25. Agamben, *Means without End*, 42; Foucault, *"Society Must Be Defended,"* 28.

26. Haraway, "Situated Knowledges"; compare Marez, *Drug Wars*.

27. For a discussion of youth in South Africa enmeshed in "violence as a means production," see Comaroff and Comaroff, "Millennial Capitalism" and "Reflections on Youth."

28. Rosas, "The Managed Violences of the Borderlands."

29. Cornelius, "Controlling 'Unwanted' Immigration"; De Genova, "Migrant 'Illegality' and Deportability in Everyday Life"; Dunn, *The Militarization of the U.S.-Mexico Border*; Heyman, "United States Surveillance over Mexican Lives at the Border."

30. Lugo, *Fragmented Lives, Assembled Parts*.

31. See Brown, "Neoliberalism and the End of Liberal Democracy," and Lemke, "Foucault, Governmentality, and Critique," both of which draw extensively on Foucault's *The Birth of Biopolitics*.

32. Alonso, "Borders, Sovereignty, and Racialization."

33. Hardt and Negri, *Empire*.

34. Butler, *Frames of War*.

35. Foucault, *"Society Must Be Defended"*; see also Rabinow and Rose, "Biopower Today," 196. In his lectures at the Collège de France in 1975–76, Foucault maintained that previous thinking on warfare elides the bloody origins of modern states: their instantiation in relations of violence. Both liberal and Marxist theories of the state minimize the state's origins in rela-

tions of war. They both attribute warfare to ideological failure (*"Society Must Be Defended,"* 15–50). This position marks a profound reversal of conventional thinking about warfare, epitomized by Clausewitz's dictum that war is politics by another means (Paret, *Clausewitz and the State*, 373), as Callahan points out ("Mexican Border Troubles"). For Foucault, politics and power relations instead constitute "a sort of generalized war that, at particular moments, assumes the forms of peace and the state." Political power represents the diffusion of warlike relations, the social inscription of relations of war carried forth in institutions, economic hierarchies, language, and bodies (*"Society Must Be Defended,"* 15). Racism, in this formulation, represents an artifact of the state's originary violence. The phenomenon introduces into the social a caesura or demarcation between those worthy of life and those worthy of death: "a way of introducing a break into the domain of life that is under power's control: the break between what must live and what must die" (ibid., 255). Ann Laura Stoler has critiqued Foucault for failing to attend to the nation-making and imperial processes through which the histories of sexuality that he traces emerged (Stoler, *Race and the Education of Desire*). This criticism is directly relevant here: state formation and imperialism relate directly to US immigration control and border policing (Luibhéid, *Entry Denied*, xii). Moreover, this formulation erases the spectacular productivities of punishment by the preeminent institution of terror today, that used by modern states on living racialized bodies, as Joy James has argued (*Resisting State Violence*). Indeed, state and racial formations work in tandem (Goldberg, *The Racial State*), as can be seen at the border. To see how activists and others can reverse these technologies, see Chari, "State Racism and Biopolitical Struggle."

36. Mbembe, "Necropolitics," 17.

37. Winant, *The World Is a Ghetto*.

38. For elaborations on intersectionality, see, for example, Combahee River Collective, "A Black Feminist Statement"; Collins, *Black Feminist Thought*; Moraga, *Loving in the War Years*. Roderick Ferguson, among others, extends this critique from the "queer of color" standpoint (*Aberrations in Black*).

39. Such inspirational works include Angela Davis, *Abolition Democracy*; and Chandra Mohanty, *Feminism without Borders*.

40. I refer to that body of academic discourse inaugurated by *Borderlands/La Frontera: The New Mestiza*, a text that inaugurated border theory, and in which the creative writer Gloria Anzaldúa privileges her experience as a queer-identified, Tejana, Chicana person of color, to deconstruct Chicano cultural heteronationalism. She writes about a transnationalist, Chicana-inspired feminism emerging from her experience in the interstices of these multiple intersecting or oppositional political discourses. Thus, against the mythical or poetic figures like the Aztec warrior prince or

the twentieth-century border warriors of Chicano cultural nationalism, Anzaldúa invokes Coatlalopeuh, an indigenous goddess, as the foundational figure for a new mestiza culture. In so doing, she maps a new, feminist-inspired, anti-essentialist, cultural homeland. New mestiza culture works "below" other powerful discourses—mestizaje and *indigenismo*—potent ideologies of Indo-Hispano fusion that understated that fusion's participation in the domination of the country's indigenous peoples. Several scholars have suggested that Anzaldúa writes ethnography of the border (R. Alvarez, "The Mexican-US Border"; Visweswaran, *Fictions of Feminist Ethnography*). Indeed, her autobiographical montages and textualized renditions of intersectionality do reflect an ethnographic impulse characteristic of members of other sociopolitically marginalized groups who had been dissuaded from pursuing careers in the social sciences and related disciplines. On the other hand, José Limón (*American Encounters*) laments that *Borderlands/La Frontera* empties the border of its political significance, and other scholars from the humanities and social sciences have expressed similar concerns (Heyman, "The Mexico–United States Border in Anthropology"; L. Martinez, "Telling the Difference between the Border and the Borderlands").

41. See Limón, *Dancing with the Devil*.

42. Appadurai, *Modernity at Large*; Basch, Glick-Schiller and Szanton, *Nations Unbound*; Kearney, "The Local and the Global"; Rouse, "Mexican Migration and the Social Space of Postmodernism" and "Thinking through Transnationalism."

43. See Appadurai, "Dead Certainty" and *Fear of Small Numbers*.

44. Comaroff and Comaroff, "Reflections on Youth," 267.

45. Griffin, *Representations of Youth*.

46. Foley, *Learning Capitalist Culture*; Friedman, "The Political Economy of Elegance"; Hebdige, *Subculture*.

47. Cole, "Fresh Contact in Tamatave, Madagascar"; Devine, *Maximum Security*.

48. Cynthia Bejarano's recent work (*Que Onda?*) draws on border theory to grapple with the everyday complexities of identity formation among border youth.

49. Behdad, "INS and Outs."

50. See, for example, Behar, *Translated Woman*; Fregoso, "Toward a Planetary Civil Society"; Saldaña-Portillo, *The Revolutionary Imagination in the Americas and the Age of Development*; Vélez-Ibañez, *Rituals of Marginality*.

51. See Coronil, "Beyond Occidentalism"; Deloria, *Red Earth, White Lies*; Kondo, "Bad Girls"; Mignolo, *Local Histories/Global Designs*; Stephen, *Transborder Lives*.

52. Limón, *Dancing with the Devil* and *American Encounters*; Paredes, *With His Pistol in His Hand*; Tabuenca Córdoba, "Viewing the Border."

53. Limón (*Dancing with the Devil*) and Américo Paredes (*With His Pis-*

tol in His Hand) have largely privileged the marginalized, pathologized, and criminalized populations of south Texas, and primarily Anglo-Mexican ethno-racial conflict (see also Nájera, "Practices of Faith and Racial Integration in South Texas"). In contrast, the recent scholarship of Alejandro Lugo (*Fragmented Lives, Assembled Parts*), Melissa Wright ("Public Women, Profit, and Femicide in Northern Mexico"), Devon Peña (*Terror of the Machine*), and Leslie Salzinger (*Genders in Production*) has investigated the El Paso–Juárez metropolis, as has other scholarship (Hill, "Metaphoric Enrichment and Material Poverty"). Carlos Vélez-Ibañez (*Border Visions*) and Josiah Heyman (*Life and Labor on the Border*), among others (Thomas, "Living Late Capital"), have explored the Arizona-Sonora borderlands.

54. Alonso, *Thread of Blood*; Nugent, *Spent Cartridges of Revolution*.

55. Compare Kelley, *Race Rebels*.

56. Žižek, *The Sublime Object of Ideology* and *The Plague of Fantasies*.

57. Clifford, "Partial Truths." See also Davalos, "Chicana/o Studies and Anthropology"; Marcus and Fischer, *Anthropology as Cultural Critique: An Experimental Moment in the Human Sciences*.

58. The debates on ethnographic representation are complex and numerous. For a limited sampling, see Clifford, "Partial Truths"; D. Gordon, "The Politics of Ethnographic Authority"; G. Hernandez, "Multiple Subjectivities and Strategic Positionalities"; Hurston, *Their Eyes Were Watching God*; Visweswaran, *Fictions of Feminist Ethnography*; Walters, "'He Can Read My Writing but He Sho' Can't Read My Mind'"; Romano, "The Anthropology and Sociology of the Mexican-Americans."

59. Geertz, *The Interpretation of Cultures*.

60. See Behar, *The Vulnerable Observer*.

61. Randal C. Archibold, "In Border Violence, Perception Is Greater Than Crime Statistics," *New York Times*, June 20, 2010.

1. Other Nightmares

1. In *The Comanche Empire*, his revisionist history, Pekka Hamalainen argues that, from 1750 and to 1850, the Comanche were the dominant empire in what is today the US Southwest and the lower Great Plains. According to Hamalainen, the Comanche relegated the representatives of US imperial power to the margins of the expansive Comanche empire, subjugating them militarily, exacting economic tribute, and regulating all commerce among them and neighboring Indian tribes. Also see Saldaña-Portillo, "No Country for Old Mexicans."

2. R. Gutiérrez, "The Erotic Zone."

3. Monsiváis, "'Just over That Hill.'"

4. Alonso, *Thread of Blood*.

5. Ibid.; Nugent, *Spent Cartridges of Revolution.*

6. Flores, *Remembering the Alamo*; Montejano, *Anglos and Mexicans in the Making of Texas.*

7. Carrigan and Webb, "The Lynching of Persons of Mexican Origin or Descent in the United States, 1848–1928."

8. Paredes, *With His Pistol in His Hand*, 15–16.

9. De Leon, *They Called Them Greasers*; L. Gómez, *Manifest Destinies*; Haney-López, *White by Law*; Menchaca, *Recovering History, Constructing Race.*

10. See Paredes, *With His Pistol in His Hand.*

11. Irwin, "Toward a Border Gnosis of the Borderlands."

12. Tinker Salas, "Los Dos Nogales"; Heyman, *Life and Labor on the Border.*

13. Rénique, "Race, Region, and Nation."

14. Sheridan, *Los Tucsonenses.*

15. Nightmares about incomplete sovereignty similarly inform earlier measures. In 1875, for example, the Page Law had banned the entry of contract laborers, felons, and Asians into the United States. The latter quality, meant to exclude Chinese prostitutes, was so vigorously enforced that all Chinese women became subject to it.

16. K. Hernández, *Migra!*

17. I am sincerely grateful to Carlos Vélez-Ibañez for sharing with me his deep knowledge of Tucson's Barrio Libre.

18. Heyman, *Life and Labor on the Border*, 9.

19. K. Hernández, *Migra!*

20. See González and Fernandez, "Empire and the Origins of Twentieth Century Migration from Mexico to the United States."

21. D. Gutiérrez, *Walls and Mirrors*, 44. See also Chavez, *Shadowed Lives.*

22. Coatsworth, "Measuring Influence."

23. Hart, *Revolutionary Mexico.* Hart further argues that Carranza's actions in protection of US property in 1913 tilted the scales in favor of a US policy that supported Carranza and opposed Villa. Important in Hart's analysis of the background to the revolution is the task of documenting the increasing favoring of US interests in Mexico by Liberals, and even more so by the Diaz regime.

24. Hart, *Empire and Revolution*, 148.

25. O. Martinez, *Troublesome Border*; Nadelmann, *Cops across Borders*, 70–72.

26. Paredes, *With His Pistol in His Hand*, 24.

27. Cockcroft, *Outlaws in the Promised Land*, 49.

28. Limón, *Dancing with the Devil*, 29.

29. Cockcroft, *Outlaws in the Promised Land*, 52–54.

30. Nadelmann, *Cops across Borders*, 73.

31. Shortly after these events, Mexico embarked on the original bracero program, which contrasts with the widely recognized one I described (Mireya Loza, personal communication, April 5, 2011).

32. Menchaca, "On the Racial Implications of Another Broken Treaty"; Montejano, *Anglos and Mexicans in the Making of Texas.*

33. Acuña, *Occupied America*; Almaguer, *Racial Fault Lines*; Callahan, "Mexican Border Troubles."

34. See Ngai, *Impossible Subjects.*

35. See De Genova, "The Legal Production of Mexican/Migrant 'Illegality.'"

36. Balderrama and Rodriguez, *Decade of Betrayal.*

37. See Lytle Hernández, "The Crimes and Consequences of Illegal Immigration."

38. D. Gutiérrez, *Walls and Mirrors*, 142.

39. Dunn, *The Militarization of the U.S.-Mexico Border*, 13.

40. Ibid., 16–17.

41. Kitty Calavita (*Inside the State*) argues that the bracero program was central to the configuration and the rising power of the INS.

42. See Fernández-Kelly, *For We Are Sold, I and My People*; Garcia y Griego, "The Importation of Mexican Contract Laborers to the United States."

43. Devon Peña's *The Terror of the Machine* offers a gripping analysis of the politics of labor and gender subordination at a maquiladora in Ciudad Juárez.

44. Nevertheless, during the bracero program, many women moved to the region surrounding the international boundary to be closer to their relatives working in the United States. The women found it hard to find employment in this area and often depended economically on their bracero family member (Loza, "Braceros on the Boundaries").

45. Bartra, *Los Herederos de Zapata*, 97–98.

46. Cockcroft, *Outlaws in the Promised Land* and *Mexico*; Saldaña-Portillo, *The Revolutionary Imagination in the Americas and the Age of Development.*

47. Bartra, *Los Herederos de Zapata*, 103–5.

48. Gutmann, *The Romance of Democracy*, 63–64.

49. Cockcroft, *Outlaws in the Promised Land*, 107–10.

50. Hondagneu-Sotelo, "The History of Mexican Undocumented Settlement in the United States," 118.

51. D. Gutiérrez, *Walls and Mirrors.*

52. J. Gutiérrez, "Chicanos and Mexicanos under Surveillance."

53. See Cockcroft, *Outlaws in the Promised Land*, 121. Also see Escobar, *Encountering Development*, 90.

54. Coleman, "US Statecraft," 190.

55. Dunn, *The Militarization of the U.S.-Mexico Border*, 13.

56. The sector grew from 2,200 plants with 550,000 workers at the end of 1994 to more than 3,000 plants employing more than 800,000 workers as of 1996 (Cooney, "The Mexican Crisis and the Maquiladora Boom"; Dussel Peters, "Recent Structural Changes in Mexico's Economy"). US companies own the vast majority of maquiladoras in Nogales, Sonora (Kopinak, *Desert Capitalism*).

57. Ochoa and Wilson, "Introduction," 6.

58. California's Proposition 187 effectively criminalized Latino and Asian American identity, creating a previously unheard-of legal category—the "suspected" illegal immigrant (Lipsitz, *The Possessive Investment in Whiteness*, 48).

59. Human Rights Watch, "Frontier Injustice," 6–7.

60. Ibid., 4–7.

61. US Cabinet-Level Task Force on Terrorism, *Combatting Terrorism*, 5.

62. Dunn, *The Militarization of the U.S.-Mexico Border*, 106–11. In this recent work, Dunn looks at the human rights implications of the Border Patrol's Operation Blockade in El Paso, Texas.

63. Balibar, "Is There a 'Neo-Racism'?"; Stolcke, "Talking Culture."

64. Here, I am extending Das and Poole's position about the centrality of margins in the production of the state (Das and Poole, *Anthropology in the Margins of the State*). What I call the new frontier has transformed from a margin to a new center.

65. Wacquant, *Punishing the Poor*.

66. Speed and Reyes, "'Asumiendo Nuestra Propia Defensa.'"

67. Janet Reno, "Consider NAFTA a Border Control Tool," *Los Angeles Times*, October 22, 1993.

68. Cited in Andreas, *Border Games*, 75.

69. Agent Silvestre Reyes had implemented similar polices in McAllen, Texas, prior to becoming chief of the Border Patrol in El Paso and implementing Operation Hold-the-Line in El Paso. Peter Brownwell writes: "These operations did not draw Washington's attention until October and November 1993; just before implementation of NAFTA, Operation Blockade caught presidential attention and became the basis for a border-wide strategy" ("Border Militarization and the Reproduction of Mexican Migrant Labor," 278).

2. Against Mexico

1. Abrams, "Notes on the Difficulty of Studying the State," 63.

2. Ruth Gilmore in *Golden Gulag* identifies modern racism as "the

state-sanctioned and/or extralegal production and exploitation of group-differentiated vulnerability to premature death" (*Golden Gulag*, 261).

3. See Armando Bartra, *Dislocados: Los derechos del que migra y el derecho de no migrar, La Jornada*, November 3, 2002, http://www.jornada.unam.mx/2002/11/03/mas-bartra.html.

4. Anzaldúa, *Borderlands*, 3.

5. See Lowe, *Immigrant Acts*; Marx, "Economic and Philosophic Manuscripts of 1844."

6. González Navarro, *Población y sociedad en México.*

7. See Walsh, "Eugenic Acculturation," particularly 124–28.

8. For competing assessments of mestizaje and Gamio's role in its dissemination, see, for example, Limón, *American Encounters.*

9. Gledhill, "Liberalism, Socio-economic Rights and the Politics of Identity."

10. For elaborations on the transformation of the state under neoliberalism, see Rose, *Powers of Freedom*; Harvey, *A Brief History of Neoliberalism*; Trouillot, "The Anthropology of the State in the Age of Globalization." I greatly appreciate Korinta Maldonado's assistance with this passage.

11. Foucault, *Security, Territory, Population.*

12. For example, in 2000 Vicente Fox, then president of Mexico and previously a titan of global industry, visited Nogales, Sonora, and called migrants "heroes."

13. Alonso, *Thread of Blood.*

14. Fregoso, "Toward a Planetary Civil Society."

15. Weismantel, *Cholas and Pishtacos.*

16. See L. Alvarez, *The Power of the Zoot.*

17. Salzinger, *Genders in Production.*

18. Bourgois, *In Search of Respect*; Vigil, *Barrio Gangs.*

19. See Agamben, *Means without End*; and Benjamin, "Critique of Violence."

20. Lugo, *Fragmented Lives, Assembled Parts*, 235.

3. Low-Intensity Reinforcements

1. For a genealogy of Latinos and incarceration in the United States, see D. Hernández, "Pursuant to Deportation."

2. The cholos of Central and North America should not be confused with those of South America (see Weismantel, *Cholas and Pishtacos*).

3. A certain negligence of the Hispanic middle class characterizes Latina/o studies; recent works such as Arlene Dávila's *Latino Spin* have challenged this.

4. Quoted in De Genova, *Working the Boundaries*, 101.

5. Quoted in Stephen, *Transborder Lives*, 164.

6. Quoted in Lugo, *Fragmented Lives, Assembled Parts*, 234–35 (my emphasis).

7. Hale, *Mas que un Indio*, 2.

8. Paz, *The Labyrinth of Solitude*, 14.

9. Scholarship from a range of theoretical traditions have argued that the specificity of women's bodies becomes a potent region in political and symbolic battles over terrain. See, for example, Alarcon, "Chicana Feminism"; and Aretxaga, *Shattering Silence*. In this respect, scholars such as Falcón, "Rape as a Weapon of War," and González-López, "Nunca he dejado de tener terror," and activists have documented how immigrant women have experienced sexual abuse at the hands of the authorities or become vulnerable to such depredations as a result of their undocumented status. In a related vein, for a case study of the pathologizing notions of culture mapped on victims of rape in indigenous Mexico, see Newdick, "The Indigenous Woman as Victim of Her Culture in Neoliberal Mexico."

10. For example, see Andreas, *Border Games*; Dunn, *The Militarization of the U.S.-Mexico Border*; Heyman, "United States Surveillance over Mexican Lives at the Border."

11. Alonso, "Sovereignty, the Spatial Politics of Security, and Gender"; Hansen and Stepputat, *Sovereign Bodies*.

12. Agamben, *Homo Sacer*.

13. Aretxaga, "Maddening States."

14. Rosas, "The Fragile Ends of War."

15. Goldberg, *Racist Culture* and *The Racial State*.

16. Goldberg, *The Threat of Race*.

17. Torres and Whitten, "General Introduction," 15.

18. Alonso, "Conforming Disconformity"; Urías Horcasitas, *Historias secretas del racismo en México*.

19. Boas's position was steeped in German counter-Enlightenment thought and drew on a rigorous historicity that refigures the question of Otherness in terms of temporal rather than cultural alterity. His emphasis on environmental factors questioned the principles of racial hierarchy and white supremacy rooted in the Lamarckian intellectual climate at the turn of the century (Bunzl, "Boas, Foucault, and the 'Native Anthropologist'"; Gamio, *Forjando Patria*; Stocking, *Race, Culture, and Evolution*). Kamala Visweswaran famously holds that Boas's position has been appropriated: the anthropological notion of culture has become the new way of staging race ("Race and the Culture of Anthropology" and *Un/Common Cultures*).

20. Foucault, *The History of Sexuality*; Stoler, "Racial Histories and Their Regimes of Truth."

21. Alonso, "Conforming Disconformity," 251–52.

22. Gamio, "El Segundo Congreso Internacional De Eugenesia" and *Mexican Immigration to the United States*. Such close collaborations of an-

thropology with projects of state rule in Mexico eventually provoked a strong response among later generations of anthropologists; see for example Warman, *De eso que Llaman Antropología Mexicana.*

23. Vila, *Crossing Borders, Reinforcing Borders.*

24. Rodriguez, "Queering the Homeboy Aesthetic," 130.

25. Peña, *The Terror of the Machine;* Salzinger, *Genders in Production.*

26. Flores, "Aesthetic Processes and Cultural Citizenship."

27. Lomnitz-Adler, *Deep Mexico, Silent Mexico.*

28. Aldama, "Surveillance, Abjection and Musical Mestizaje in the Global Age," is one of few scholarly works that addresses the term "chúntaro" and all its permutations.

29. I am grateful to Rolando Romero for his help with the etymology of "chúntaro."

30. Similarly constructed semantic frontiers can be found across greater Mexico. Chúntaros can be found in Northern California, according to Norma Mendoza-Denton (*Homegirls*). And these and similar distinctions speak to those semantic borders that José Limón found among pocho, peon, pachuco, and fuereño, and as far back as Américo Paredes's accentuation of a *Tejano-fuereño* tension (Limón, *Dancing with the Devil*).

Interlude. Post–September 11

1. Andreas, *A Tale of Two Borders.*

2. De Genova, "Introduction" and "The Production of Culprits."

3. A clear example of such racial science in the making occurred during the nineteenth century in south Texas—in the evolutionary anthropology of Captain John Gregory Bourke, a major ethnologist, folklorist, and colleague and friend of Franz Boas (Limón, *Dancing with the Devil,* 21–42). There are strong resonances here with notions of cultural racism, cultural fundamentalism, and similarly problematic essentialist conceptions of cultures as bounded, timeless, and fixed (Baker, *Anthropology and the Racial Politics of Culture;* Koptiuch, "Third-Worlding at Home"; Mamdani, "Good Muslim, Bad Muslim"; Silverstein, "Immigrant Racialization and the New Savage Slot"; Stolcke, "Talking Culture").

4. See Huntington, "The Hispanic Challenge." Such slippery logic similarly fueled his *Clash of the Civilizations.*

5. Anderson, *Imagined Communities.*

4. Against the United States

1. The INS, before it became Immigration and Customs Enforcement (ICE), estimated that seven million unauthorized immigrants were living in the United States in January 2000, and that on average this population had grown by about 350,000 per year from 1990 through 1999. Indeed, there are now twice as many unauthorized immigrants as there were in the early 1990s (Inda, *Targeting Immigrants*, 113).

2. The scholarship on indigenous transnationality and immigrant "illegality" lends itself to my analysis. See for example, De Genova and Ramos-Zayas, *Latino Crossings*; Kearney, "The Local and the Global"; Mountz and Wright, "Daily Life in the Transnational Migrant Community of San Agustín, Oaxaca, and Poughkeepsie, New York."

3. Eschbach et al., "Death at the Border."

4. Joseph Nevins, "Border Death-Trap — Time to Tear Down America's Berlin Wall," *San Diego La Prensa*, July 30, 2002.

5. See Heyman, "Putting Power in the Anthropology of Bureaucracy."

6. See Dunn, *Border War* and "Border Militarization via Drug and Immigration Enforcement"; Dunn and Palafox, "Border Militarization and Beyond"; Heyman, "United States Surveillance over Mexican Lives at the Border"; Nagengast, "Militarizing the Border Patrol."

7. Agamben, *Homo Sacer*, 6.

8. Ibid., 10.

9. Ibid., 122.

10. Agamben, *Means without End*, 41.

11. Butler, *Precarious Life*; Stoler and Bond, "Refractions off Empire"; Žižek, *Iraq*.

12. Michaelsen, "Between Japanese American Internment and the USA PATRIOT Act," 89.

13. Schmidt Camacho, "Ciudadana x."

14. Alonso, "Sovereignty, the Spatial Politics of Security, and Gender."

15. Foucault, *"Society Must Be Defended."*

16. It must be noted that necropolitics does revert; death — be it in African neocolonies or along the new frontier — proves to lie outside the power relationship, as is recognized in rituals and holidays such as the Day of the Dead (Mbembe, "Necropolitics").

17. Stoler, *Race and the Education of Desire*.

18. Foucault, *Discipline and Punish*, 7.

19. US Border Patrol, *Border Patrol Strategic Plan*, footnote 1.

20. Ibid., 4.

21. Ibid., 4–5.

22. Gustavo de la Vina, statement regarding Border Patrol operations and staffing made at Border Academy Conference, University of Arizona, Tucson, June 15, 1997.

23. See Almaguer, "At the Crossroads of Race."

24. See Fox, "Reframing Mexican Migration as a Multi-Ethnic Process."

25. Rosas, "The Managed Violences of the Borderlands."

26. See Arendt, *The Origins of Totalitarianism*; Césaire, *Discourse on Colonialism*; Mbembe, "Necropolitics."

27. See, for example, De Genova and Ramos-Zayas, *Latino Crossings*; De Genova, *Working the Boundaries*.

28. See Mary Weismantel and Stephen Eisenman's theorization of race and racism in the Andes ("Race in the Andes").

29. Guadalupe Castillo, community activist and founding member of the Coalición de Derechos Humanos/Alianza Indígena sin fronteras (the Human Rights Coalition/Indigenous Alliance without Borders), interview with author, Tucson, July 2001.

30. See Flores, "Aesthetic Processes and Cultural Citizenship"; Rosaldo, "Cultural Citizenship, Inequality, and Multiculturalism."

31. Quoted in Meeks, *Border Citizens*, 25.

32. Vélez-Ibañez, *Border Visions*.

33. See Bhabha, *Locations of Culture*.

5. Oozing Barrio Libre

1. Foucault, *Society Must Be Defended*, 248.

2. "As subjects, of subjection to the Subject, of universal recognition and of absolute guarantee, the subjects 'work,' they 'work by themselves' in the vast majority of cases, with the exception of the 'bad subjects' who on occasion provoke the intervention of one of the detachments of the (repressive) State apparatus. But the vast majority of (good) subjects work all right 'all by themselves,' i.e. by ideology" (Althusser, "Ideology and Ideological State Apparatuses," 155).

3. Foucault, *Discipline and Punish*, 202–3.

4. Guha, *Elementary Aspects of Peasant Insurgency in Colonial India*; Kelley, *Race Rebels* and *Yo' Mama's Disfunktional!*; Thompson, *The Making of the English Working Class*.

5. Abu-Lughod, "The Romance of Resistance."

6. This is not an iteration of Freud's death drive. In contrast to a preternatural and universal unconscious, I am emphasizing how these particular subjectivities are produced. See Freud, *Beyond the Pleasure Principle*.

7. See João Vargas, *Never Meant to Survive*.

8. Lewis, *Anthropological Essays*, 188.

9. Lewis, *La Vida*, 53.

10. See Di Leonardo, *Exotics at Home*, 116.

11. See Gutmann, *The Romance of Democracy*; Moynihan, *The Negro Family*.

12. Briggs, *Reproducing Empire*, 162–92. Other scholars in anthropology and public health have grappled with such questions. See, for example, Santiago-Irizarry, "Culture as Cure"; and Viruell-Fuentes, "Beyond Acculturation."

13. See Visweswaran, "Race and the Culture of Anthropology." Paredes had anticipated this critique. In his "On Ethnographic Work among Minority Groups," Paredes documented how certain well-intentioned anthropologists had taken the words of the people of south Texas too literally. Similarly, Rosaldo (*Culture and Truth*), Diaz Barriga ("The Culture of Poverty as Relajo"), and other Latino anthropologists have maintained that the tradition of *relajo* or Mexicano word play exhibits a complexity that a literalist, positivist, anthropology may not be able to decipher.

14. See Di Leonardo, *Exotics at Home*; Goldberg, *The Racial State* and *The Threat of Race*; Winant, *The World Is a Ghetto*.

15. Edmund T. Gordon's critique of what he calls the hegemonic ideology and black masculinity thesis resonates here ("Cultural Politics of Black Masculinity").

16. Bourgois, *In Search of Respect*.

17. Comaroff and Comaroff, "Millennial Capitalism."

18. Limón, *Dancing*. See also Fanon, *The Wretched of the Earth*; Gramsci, *Selections from the Prison Notebooks of Antonio Gramsci*.

19. See Hall, "Gramsci's Relevance for the Study of Race and Ethnicity."

20. Escobar, *Encountering Development*, 23.

21. Hall et al., *Policing the Crisis*; Gilroy, *"There Ain't No Black in the Union Jack."*

22. Butler, *The Psychic Life of Power*, 15–16. There have also been certain calls in Latino and ethnic studies to incorporate psychoanalytic approaches (Cheng, *The Melancholy of Race*; Limón, *American Encounters*; Viego, *Dead Subjects*).

23. Such was also the case when the menses of women prisoners became a symbolic weapon in a prison revolt in Northern Ireland. Aretxaga, "Playing Terrorist."

24. Volpp, "Feminism versus Multiculturalism," 1190. See also Kapur, "The Tragedy of Victimization Rhetoric."

25. Cohen, "Deviance as Resistance."

26. Stewart, "On the Politics of Cultural Theory."

Interlude. Nervous Cocks

1. Rosaldo, *Culture and Truth*, 158.
2. Semiotic analysis of culture becomes a second-, third-, or fourth-hand reading of the others' readings of their world. Largely local meanings suffuse conspiratorial winks, gentle touches, furrowed brows, and nods. In Geertz's influential essay, a cockfight becomes "a Balinese reading of Balinese experience, a story they tell themselves about themselves. . . . What the cockfight says it says in a vocabulary of sentiment—the thrill of risk, the despair of loss, the pleasure of triumph . . . and the disquieting part [is] that the text in which this revelation is accomplished consists of a chicken hacking another mindlessly to bits" ("Deep Play," 448–49).
3. Roseberry, *Anthropologies and Histories*.

Conclusion

1. Jennifer Allen, executive director of Border Action Network, interview with author, Tucson, Arizona, July 8, 2006.
2. In 2008, the United States allocated $48 million for international narcotics control and law enforcement to Mexico under the Merida Initiative. Direct aid to the Mexican police and armed forces constituted over 40 percent of this amount. Most of the money ends up lining the pockets of defense companies for purchases of surveillance, inspection, and security equipment and for training. The Mexican Federal Police Force receives most of the US funding, with customs, immigration, and communications agencies receiving the remainder. See Carlsen, *The Season of Death*.
3. Heyman, "Constructing a Virtual Wall."
4. Allen, interview.
5. Agamben, *Means without End*, 42.
6. Allen, interview.
7. Agamben, *Means without End*, 42.
8. Raquel Rubio-Goldsmith, interview with author, Tucson, Arizona, July 1, 2006.
9. Ong, "Cultural Citizenship as Subject-Making"; Rosaldo, *Culture and Truth*.
10. See Human Rights Watch, "Brutality Unchecked," "Frontier Injustice," "Crossing the Line," and "Human Rights Violations by INS Inspectors and Border Patrol Agents Continue"; Jimenez et al., "Human Rights on the Line"; Paget-Clarke, "The Militarization of the U.S.-Mexico Border"; Koulish et al., "US Immigration Authorities and Victims of Human and Civil Rights Abuses"; Rubio-Goldsmith et al., "The 'Funnel Effect' and Re-

covered Bodies of Unauthorized Migrants Processed by the Pima County Office of the Medical Examiner."

11. Limón, *Dancing with the Devil*; Paredes, *With His Pistol in His Hand*.

12. Anzaldúa, *Borderlands*; Agamben, *Means without End*. For examples, see Mora, "The Imagination to Listen"; Perry, "Global Black Self-Fashionings"; Valencia Ramírez, "Active Marooning." Saldaña-Portillo's compelling critique of Chicana/o mestizaje fails to sufficiently appreciate its specific articulation in the borderlands, particularly its challenge to the hegemonic racial politics of hypodescent ("Who's the Indian in Aztlán?" and *The Revolutionary Imagination in the Americas and the Age of Development*). See also Spivak, "Can the Subaltern Speak?"

13. The emerging literature on these movements includes Aquino-Moreschi, "De la indignación moral a las protestas colectivas"; Rosas, "The Thickening Borderlands"; Zavella, *I'm Neither Here nor There*. Also, see the Pallares and Flores-González collection *Marcha*.

14. Gregory, "The Black Flag."

Abrams, Philip. "Notes on the Difficulty of Studying the State." *Journal of Historical Sociology* 1, no. 1 (1988): 58–89.

Abu-Lughod, Lila. "The Romance of Resistance: Tracing Transformations of Power through Bedouin Women." *American Ethnologist* 17, no. 1 (1990): 41–55.

Acuña, Rudolfo. *Occupied America: A History of Chicanos*. New York: Harper and Row, 1972.

Agamben, Giorgio. *Homo Sacer: Sovereign Power and Bare Life*. Translated by Daniel Heller-Roazen. Stanford: Stanford University Press, 1998.

————. *Means without End: Notes on Politics*. Translated by Vincenzo Binetti and Cesare Casarino. Minneapolis: University of Minnesota Press, 2000.

Alarcón, Norma. "Chicana Feminism: In the Tracks of 'the' Native Woman." In *Between Woman and Nation: Nationalisms, Transnational Feminisms, and the State*, edited by Norma Alarcón and Minoo Moallem Caren Kaplan, 63–71. Durham: Duke University Press, 1999.

Aldama, Arturo J. "Surveillance, Abjection and Musical Mestizaje in the Global Age." In *Rebellious Reading: The Dynamics of Chicana/o Cultural Literacy*, edited by Carl Gutiérrez-Jones, 145–515. Santa Barbara: University of California, Santa Barbara, Center for Chicano Studies, 2004.

Almaguer, Tomás. "At the Crossroads of Race: Latino/a Studies and Race Making in the United States." In *Critical Latin American and Latino Studies*, edited by Juan Poblete, 206–22. Minneapolis: University of Minnesota Press, 2003.

————. *Racial Fault Lines: The Historical Origins of White Supremacy in California*. Berkeley: University of California Press, 1994.

Alonso, Ana. "Borders, Sovereignty, and Racialization." In *A Companion to Latin American Anthropology*, edited by Deborah Poole, 230–53. Malden, MA: Blackwell, 2008.

————. "Conforming Disconformity: 'Mestizaje,' Hybridity, and the Aesthetics of Mexican Nationalism." *Cultural Anthropology* 19, no. 4 (2004): 459–90.

————. "Sovereignty, the Spatial Politics of Security, and Gender: Looking North and South from the US-Mexico Border." In *State Formation: Anthropological Perspectives*, edited by Christian Krohn-Hansen and Knut G. Nustad, 27–54. Ann Arbor, MI: Pluto, 2005.

————. *Thread of Blood: Colonialism, Revolution, and Gender on Mexico's Northern Frontier.* Tucson: University of Arizona Press, 1995.

Althusser, Louis. "Ideology and Ideological State Apparatuses (Notes towards an Investigation)." Translated by Ben Brewster. In Louis Althusser, *Lenin and Philosophy, and Other Essays,* 127–86. New York: Monthly Review, 1971.

Alvarez, Luis. *The Power of the Zoot: Youth Culture and Resistance during World War II.* Berkeley: University of California Press, 2008.

Alvarez, Robert R. "The Mexican-US Border: The Making of an Anthropology of the Borderlands." *Annual Review of Anthropology* 24 (1995): 447–71.

Anderson, Benedict. *Imagined Communities: Reflections on the Origins and Spread of Nationalism.* London: Verso, 1991.

Andreas, Peter. *Border Games: Policing the U.S.-Mexico Divide.* Ithaca: Cornell University Press, 2000.

————. *A Tale of Two Borders: The U.S.-Mexico and U.S.-Canada Lines after 9/11.* La Jolla: University of California, San Diego, Center for Comparative Immigration Studies, 2003.

Anzaldúa, Gloria. *Borderlands/La Frontera: The New Mestiza.* San Francisco: Aunt Lute, 1999.

Appadurai, Arjun. "Dead Certainty: Ethnic Violence in the Era of Globalization." *Development and Change* 29, no. 4 (1998): 905–25.

————. *Fear of Small Numbers: An Essay on the Geography of Anger.* Durham: Duke University Press, 2006.

————. *Modernity at Large: Cultural Dimensions of Globalization.* Minneapolis: University of Minnesota Press, 1996.

Aquino-Moreschi, Alejandra. "De la indignación moral a las protestas colectivas: La participación de los migrantes zapotecos en las marchas de migrantes de 2006." *Norteamérica* 5, no. 1 (2010): 63–90.

Arendt, Hannah. *The Origins of Totalitarianism.* New ed. with added prefaces. New York: Harcourt Brace Jovanovich, 1973.

Aretxaga, Begoña. "Maddening States." *Annual Review of Anthropology* 32 (2003): 393–410.

————. "Playing Terrorist: Ghastly Plots and the Ghostly State." *Journal of Spanish Cultural Studies* 1, no. 1 (2000): 43–57.

————. *Shattering Silence: Women, Nationalism, and Political Subjectivity in Northern Ireland.* Princeton: Princeton University Press, 1997.

Baker, Lee D. *Anthropology and the Racial Politics of Culture.* Durham: Duke University Press, 2010.

Balderrama, Francisco E., and Raymond Rodriguez. *Decade of Betrayal: Mexican Repatriation in the 1930s.* Albuquerque: University of New Mexico Press, 2006.

Balibar, Etienne. "Is There a 'Neo-Racism'?" Translated by Chris Turner. In

Etienne Balibar and Immanuel Wallerstein, *Race, Nation, Class: Ambiguous Identities*, 17–28. London: Verso, 1991.

Bartra, Armando. *Cosechas de Ira: Economía Política de la Contrarreforma Agraria*. Mexico City: ITACA, Instituto Maya, AC, 2003.

Basch, Linda, Nina Glick-Schiller, and Cristina B. Szanton. *Nations Unbound: Transnational Projects, Postcolonial Predicaments, and Deterritorialized Nation-States*. Basel, Switzerland: Gordon and Breach, 1994.

Behar, Ruth. *Translated Woman: Crossing the Border with Esperanza's Story*. Boston: Beacon, 1993.

——. *The Vulnerable Observer: Anthropology That Breaks Your Heart*. Boston: Beacon, 1996.

Behdad, Ali. "INS and Outs: Producing Delinquency at the Border." *Aztlan* 23, no. 1 (1998): 103–13.

Bejarano, Cynthia. *Que onda? Urban Youth Culture and Border Identity*. Tucson: University of Arizona Press, 2005.

Benjamin, Walter. "Critique of Violence." Translated by Edmund Jephcott. In Walter Benjamin, *Reflections: Essays, Aphorisms, Autobiographical Writings*, edited by Peter Demetz, 277–301. New York: Harcourt Brace Jovanovich, 1978.

Bhabha, Homi K. *Locations of Culture*. London: Routledge, 1994.

Bigo, Didier. "Security and Immigration: Toward a Critique of the Governmentality of Unease." *Alternatives* 27, no. 1 (2002): 63–92.

Binford, Leigh. "A Failure of Normalization: Transnational Migration, Crime, and Popular Justice in the Contemporary Neoliberal Mexican Social Formation." *Social Justice* 26, no. 3 (1999): 123–44.

Bleeden, David, Caroline Gottschalk-Druschke, and Ralph Cintron. "Minutemen and the Subject of Democracy." In *Marcha: Latino Chicago and the Immigrant Rights Movement*, edited by Amalia Pallares and Nilda Flores-González, 179–97. Urbana: University of Illinois Press, 2010.

Bourgois, Philippe. *In Search of Respect: Selling Crack in el Barrio*. Cambridge: Cambridge University Press, 1995.

Briggs, Laura. *Reproducing Empire: Race, Sex, Science, and U.S. Imperialism in Puerto Rico*. Berkeley: University of California Press, 2002.

Brown, Wendy. "Neoliberalism and the End of Liberal Democracy." In *Edgework: Critical Essays on Knowledge and Politics*, edited by Wendy Brown, 37–59. Princeton: Princeton University Press, 2005.

Brownell, Peter B. "Border Militarization and the Reproduction of Mexican Migrant Labor." *Social Justice* 28, no. 2 (2001): 269–92.

Bunzl, Matti. "Boas, Foucault, and the 'Native Anthropologist': Notes toward a Neo-Boasian Anthropology." *American Anthropologist* 106, no. 3 (2004): 435–42.

Butler, Judith. *Frames of War: When Is Life Grievable?* London: Verso, 2009.

————. *Precarious Life: The Powers of Mourning and Violence*. London: Verso, 2004.

————. *The Psychic Life of Power: Theories in Subjection*. Stanford: Stanford University Press, 1997.

Calavita, Kitty. *Inside the State: The Bracero Program, Immigration, and the INS*. New York: Routledge, 1992.

Callahan, Manolo. "Mexican Border Troubles: Social War, Settler Colonialism, and the Production of Frontier Discourses, 1848–1880." PhD dissertation, University of Texas, Austin, 2003.

Carlsen, Laura. *The Season of Death*. Americas Program, Interhemispheric Resource Center, 2003.

Carrigan, William D., and Olive Webb. "The Lynching of Persons of Mexican Origin or Descent in the United States, 1848–1928." *Journal of Social History* 37, no. 2 (2003): 411–38.

Césaire, Aimé. *Discourse on Colonialism*. Translated by Joan Pinkham. New York: Monthly Review, 1972.

Chari, Sharad. "State Racism and Biopolitical Struggle: The Evasive Commons in Twentieth-Century Durban, South Africa." *Radical History Review* 2010, no. 108 (2010): 73–90.

Chavez, Leo R. *Covering Immigration: Popular Images and the Politics of the Nation*. Berkeley: University of California Press, 2001.

————. "Immigration Reform and Nativism: The Nationalist Response to the Transnationalist Challenge." In *Immigrants Out! The New Nativism and the Anti-immigrant Impulse in the United States*, edited by Juan F. Perea, 61–77. New York: New York University Press, 1997.

————. *Shadowed Lives: Undocumented Immigrants in American Society*. Fort Worth, TX: Harcourt Brace College Publishers, 1998.

Cheng, Anne Anlin. *The Melancholy of Race*. Oxford: Oxford University Press, 2001.

Cintron, Ralph. *Angels' Town: Chero Ways, Gang Life, and Rhetorics of the Everyday*. Boston: Beacon, 1997.

Clifford, James. "Partial Truths." In *Writing Culture: The Poetics and Politics of Ethnography*, edited by James Clifford and George E. Marcus, 1–26. Berkeley: University of California Press, 1986.

Coatsworth, John H. "Measuring Influence: The United States and the Mexican Peasantry." In *Rural Revolt in Mexico: U.S. Intervention and the Domain of Subaltern Politics*, edited by Daniel Nugent, 64–71. Durham: Duke University Press, 1998.

Cockcroft, James D. *Mexico: Class Formation, Capital Accumulation, and the State*. New York: Monthly Review, 1990.

————. *Outlaws in the Promised Land: Mexican Immigrant Workers and America's Future*. New York: Grove, 1986.

Cohen, Cathy. "Deviance as Resistance: A New Research Agenda for the Study of Black Politics." *Du Bois Review* 1, no. 1 (2004): 27–45.

Cole, Jennifer. "Fresh Contact in Tamatave, Madagascar: Sex, Money, and Intergenerational Transformation." *American Ethnologist* 31, no. 4 (2004): 573–88.

Collins, Patricia Hill. *Black Feminist Thought: Knowledge, Consciousness, and the Politics of Empowerment.* Boston: Unwin Hyman, 2000.

Comaroff, Jean, and John Comaroff. "Millennial Capitalism: First Thoughts on a Second Coming." *Public Culture* 12, no. 2 (2000): 291–343.

———. "Reflections on Youth, from the Past to the Postcolony." In *Frontiers of Capital: Ethnographic Reflections on the New Economy,* edited by Melissa S. Fisher and Greg Downey, 267–81. Durham: Duke University Press, 2006.

Combahee River Collective. "A Black Feminist Statement." In *All the Women Are White, All the Blacks Are Men, but Some of Us Are Brave,* edited by Gloria Hull, Patricia Bell Scott, and Barbara Smith, 13–22. Old Westbury, NY: Feminist Press, 1982.

Cooney, Paul. "The Mexican Crisis and the Maquiladora Boom." *Latin American Perspectives* 28, no. 3 (2001): 55–83.

Cornelius, Wayne. "Controlling 'Unwanted' Immigration: Lessons from the United States, 1993–2004." *Journal of Ethnic and Migration Studies* 31, no. 4 (2005): 775–94.

Coronil, Fernando. "Beyond Occidentalism: Toward Nonimperial Geohistorical Categories." *Cultural Anthropology* 11, no. 1 (1996): 51–87.

Coutin, Susan Bibler. *Nations of Emigrants: Shifting Boundaries of Citizenship in El Salvador and the United States.* Ithaca: Cornell University Press, 2007.

Das, Veena, and Deborah Poole. *Anthropology in the Margins of the State.* Santa Fe, NM: School of American Research Press, 2004.

Davalos, Karen Mary. "Chicana/o Studies and Anthropology: The Dialogue That Never Was." *Aztlan* 23, no. 2 (1998): 13–45.

Davidson, Miriam. *Lives on the Line: Dispatches from the U.S.-Mexico Border.* Tucson: University of Arizona Press, 2000.

Dávila, Arlene. *Barrio Dreams: Puerto Ricans, Latinos, and the Neoliberal City.* Berkeley: University of California Press, 2004.

———. *Latino Spin: Public Image and the Whitewashing of Race.* New York: New York University Press, 2008.

Davis, Angela Y. *Abolition Democracy: Beyond Empire, Prisons, and Torture; Interviews with Angela Y. Davis.* New York: Seven Stories, 2005.

De Genova, Nicholas. "Introduction: Latino and Asian Formations at the Frontiers of U.S. Nationalism." In *Racial Transformations: Latinos and Asians Remaking the United States,* edited by Nicholas De Genova, 1–22. Durham: Duke University Press, 2006.

168   *Bibliography*

———. "The Legal Production of Mexican/Migrant 'Illegality.'" *Latino Studies* 2, no. 2 (2004): 160–85.

———. "Migrant 'Illegality' and Deportability in Everyday Life." *Annual Review of Anthropology* 31 (2002): 419–47.

———. "The Production of Culprits: From Deportability to Detainability in the Aftermath of 'Homeland Security.'" *Citizenship Studies* 11, no. 5 (2007): 421–48.

———. *Working the Boundaries: Race, Space, and "Illegality" in Mexican Chicago*. Durham: Duke University Press, 2005.

De Genova, Nicholas, and Ana Y. Ramos-Zayas. *Latino Crossings: Mexicans, Puerto Ricans, and the Politics of Race and Citizenship*. London: Routledge, 2003.

De Leon, Arnoldo. *They Called Them Greasers: Anglo Attitudes toward Mexicans in Texas, 1821–1900*. Austin: University of Texas Press, 1983.

Deloria, Vine. *Red Earth, White Lies*. Golden, CO: Fulcrum, 1997.

Devine, John. *Maximum Security: The Culture of Violence in Inner-City Schools*. Chicago: University of Chicago Press, 1996.

Díaz Barriga, Miguel. "The Culture of Poverty as *Relajo*." *Aztlan* 22, no. 2 (1997): 43–65.

Di Leonardo, Micaela. *Exotics at Home: Anthropologies, Others, American Modernity*. Chicago: University of Chicago Press, 1998.

Dunn, Timothy J. "Border Militarization via Drug and Immigration Enforcement: Human Rights Implications." *Social Justice* 28, no. 2 (2001): 7–30.

———. "Border War: As the U.S. Military Melds with Civilian Police Agencies, the First Casualties Are Immigrants." Global Exchange, 2000.

———. *The Militarization of the U.S.-Mexico Border, 1978–1992: Low-Intensity Conflict Doctrine Comes Home*. Austin, TX: CMAS Books, 1996.

Dunn, Timothy J., and Jose Palafox. "Border Militarization and Beyond: The Widening War on Drugs." *Borderlines* 8, no. 4 (2000): 14–16.

Dussel Peters, Enrique. "Recent Structural Changes in Mexico's Economy: A Preliminary Analysis of Some Sources of Mexican Migration to the United States." In *Crossings: Mexican Immigration in Interdisciplinary Perspectives*, edited by Marcelo Suarez Orozco, 53–78. Cambridge: Harvard University Press, 1998.

Enloe, Cynthia. *Maneuvers: The International Politics of Militarizing Women's Lives*. Berkeley: University of California Press, 2000.

Eschbach, Karl, et al. "Death at the Border." *International Migration Review* 33, no. 2 (1999): 430–54.

Escobar, Arturo. *Encountering Development: The Making and Unmaking of the Third World*. Princeton: Princeton University Press, 1995.

Falcón, Sylvanna M. "Rape as a Weapon of War: Advancing Human Rights for Women at the U.S.-Mexico Border." *Social Justice* 28, no. 2 (2001): 31–50.

Fanon, Franz. *The Wretched of the Earth*. New York: Grove, 1963.

Feldman, Allen. "Securocratic Wars of Public Safety." *Interventions* 6, no. 3 (2004): 330–50.

Ferguson, Roderick A. *Aberrations in Black: Toward a Queer of Color Critique*. Minneapolis: University of Minnesota Press, 2004.

Fernández-Kelly, María Patricia. *For We Are Sold, I and My People: Women and Industry in Mexico's Frontier*. Albany: State University of New York Press, 1983.

Flores, Richard R. "Aesthetic Processes and Cultural Citizenship: The Membering of a Social Body in San Antonio." In *Latino Cultural Citizenship: Claiming Identity, Space, and Rights*, edited by William V. Flores and Rina Benmayor, 124–51. Boston: Beacon, 1997.

———. *Remembering the Alamo: Memory, Modernity, and the Master Symbol*. Austin: University of Texas Press, 2002.

Foley, Douglas. *Learning Capitalist Culture: Deep in the Heart of Tejas*. Philadelphia: University of Pennsylvania Press, 1990.

Foucault, Michel. *The Birth of Biopolitics: Lectures at the Collège de France, 1978–79*, edited by Michel Senellart. Translated by Graham Burchell. Basingstoke, England: Palgrave Macmillan, 2008.

———. *Discipline and Punish: The Birth of the Prison*. Translated by Alan Sheridan. New York: Vintage, 1979.

———. *The History of Sexuality*. Translated by Robert Hurley. New York: Vintage, 1990.

———. *Security, Territory, Population: Lectures at the Collège de France, 1977–78*, edited by Michel Senellart, François Ewald, and Alessandro Fontana. Translated by Graham Burchell. New York: Palgrave Macmillan, 2007.

———. *"Society Must Be Defended": Lectures at the Collège de France, 1975–76*, edited by Mauro Bertani and Alessandro Fontana. Translated by David Macey. New York: Picador, 2003.

Fox, Jonathan. "Reframing Mexican Migration as a Multi-Ethnic Process." *Latino Studies* 4, no. 1 (2006): 39–61.

Fregoso, Rosa Linda. "Toward a Planetary Civil Society." In Rosa Linda Fregosa, *MeXicana Encounters: The Making of Social Identities on the Borderlands*, 1–29. Berkeley: University of California Press, 2003.

Freud, Sigmund. *Beyond the Pleasure Principle*, edited by James Strachey. New York: W. W. Norton and Company, 1961.

Friedman, Jonathan. "The Political Economy of Elegance: An African Cult of Beauty." *Culture and History* 7 (1990): 101–25.

Gamio, Manuel. *Forjando patria (pro nacionalismo)*. Mexico City: Porrúa Hermanos, 1916.

————. *Mexican Immigration to the United States*. New York: Arno, 1969.

————. "El Segundo Congreso Internacional de Eugenesia." *Ethnos* (1920): 251–52.

Garcia y Griego, Manuel. "The Importation of Mexican Contract Laborers to the United States." In *Between Two Worlds: Mexican Immigrants in the United States, 1942–1964*, edited by David G. Gutiérrez, 45–85. Wilmington, DE: Scholarly Resources, 1996.

Gaspar de Alba, Alicia. "The Maquiladora Murders." *Aztlan* 28, no. 2 (2003): 1–17.

Geertz, Clifford. "Deep Play: Notes on the Balinese Cockfight." In Clifford Geertz, *The Interpretation of Cultures: Selected Essays*, 412–54. New York: Basic, 1973.

————. *The Interpretation of Cultures: Selected Essays*. New York: Basic, 1973.

Gilmore, Ruth W. "Globalization and U.S. Prison Growth: From Military Keynesianism to Post-Keynesian Militarism." *Race and Class* 40, no. 2–3 (1998–99): 171–88.

————. *Golden Gulag: Prisons, Surplus, Crisis, and Opposition in Globalizing California*. Berkeley: University of California Press, 2007.

Gilroy, Paul. *"There Ain't No Black in the Union Jack": The Cultural Politics of Race and Nation*. Chicago: University of Chicago Press, 1991.

Gledhill, John. "Liberalism, Socio-economic Rights and the Politics of Identity: From Moral Economy to Indigenous Rights." In *Human Rights, Culture and Context: Anthropological Perspectives*, edited by Robert Wilson, 70–110. London: Pluto Press, 1997.

Goldberg, David Theo. *The Racial State*. Malden, MA: Blackwell, 2002.

————. *Racist Culture: Philosophy and the Politics of Meaning*. Oxford: Blackwell, 1993.

————. *The Threat of Race: Reflections on Racial Neoliberalism*. Oxford: Blackwell, 2009.

Gómez, Alan Eladio. "Resisting Living Death at Marion Federal Penitentiary, 1972." *Radical History Review* no. 96 (2006): 58–86.

Gómez, Laura E. *Manifest Destinies: The Making of the Mexican American Race*. New York: New York University Press, 2007.

González, Gilbert G., and Raúl Fernandez. "Empire and the Origins of Twentieth Century Migration from Mexico to the United States." *Pacific Historical Review* 71, no. 1 (2002): 19–57.

González-López, Gloria. "'Nunca he dejado de tener terror': Sexual Violence in the Lives of Mexican Immigrant Women." In *Women and Migration in the U.S.-Mexico Borderlands: A Reader*, edited by Denise A. Segura and Patricia Zavella, 224–48. Durham: Duke University Press, 2007.

González Navarro, Moisés. *Población y sociedad en México (1900–1970)*. Mexico City: UNAM, 1974.

Gordon, Deborah. "The Politics of Ethnographic Authority: Race and Writing in the Ethnography of Margaret Mead and Zora Neale Hurston." In *Modernist Anthropology: From Fieldwork to Text*, edited by Marc Manganaro, 146–62. Princeton: Princeton University Press, 1990.

Gordon, Edmund T. "Cultural Politics of Black Masculinity." *Transforming Anthropology* 6, nos. 1–2 (1997): 36–53.

Gramsci, Antonio. *Selections from the Prison Notebooks of Antonio Gramsci*, edited and translated by Quintin Hoare and Geoffrey Nowell Smith. New York: International Publishers, 1972.

Gregory, Derek. "The Black Flag: Guatanámo Bay and the Space of Exception." *Geografiska Annaler: Series B Human Geography* 88, no. 4 (2006): 405–27.

Griffin, Christine. *Representations of Youth: The Study of Youth and Adolescence in Britain and America*. Cambridge, England: Polity, 1993.

Guha, Ranajit. *Elementary Aspects of Peasant Insurgency in Colonial India*. Durham: Duke University Press, 1999.

Gutiérrez, David G. *Walls and Mirrors: Mexican Americans, Mexican Immigrants, and the Politics of Ethnicity*. Berkeley: University of California Press, 1995.

Gutiérrez, José Angel. "Chicanos and Mexicanos under Surveillance: 1940–1980." In *Renato Rosaldo Lectures Series Monograph 2: 1984–1985*. Tucson: Department of Mexican American Studies, University of Arizona, 1992.

Gutiérrez, Ramón A. "The Erotic Zone: Sexual Transgression on the US-Mexico Border." In *Mapping Multiculturalism*, edited by Avery F. Gordon and Christopher Newfield, 253–62. Minneapolis: University of Minnesota Press, 1996.

Gutmann, Matthew C. *The Romance of Democracy: Compliant Defiance in Contemporary Mexico*. Berkeley: University of California Press, 2002.

Hale, Charles R. *Más que un Indio: Racial Ambivalence and the Paradox of Neoliberal Multiculturalism in Guatemala*. Santa Fe, NM: School of American Research Press, 2006.

Hall, Stuart. "Gramsci's Relevance for the Study of Race and Ethnicity." *Journal of Communication Inquiry* 10, no. 2 (1986): 5–27.

Hall, Stuart, et al. *Policing the Crisis: Mugging, the State, and Law and Order*. London: Macmillan, 1978.

Hamalainen, Pekka. *The Comanche Empire*. New Haven: Yale University Press, 2008.

Haney-López, Ian. *White by Law: The Legal Construction of Race*. New York: New York University Press, 1996.

Hansen, Thomas Blom, and Finn Stepputat. *Sovereign Bodies: Citizens, Migrants, and State in the Postcolonial World*. Princeton: Princeton University Press, 2005.

Haraway, Donna J. *Simians, Cyborgs, and Women: The Reinvention of Nature.* New York: Routledge, 1991.

Hart, John Mason. *Empire and Revolution: The Americans in Mexico since the Civil War.* Berkeley: University of California Press, 2002.

———. *Revolutionary Mexico: The Coming and Process of the Mexican Revolution.* Berkeley: University of California Press, 1987.

Harvey, David. *A Brief History of Neoliberalism.* Oxford: Oxford University Press, 2005.

Hebdige, Dick. *Subculture: The Meaning of Style.* London: Routledge, 1991.

Hernández, David Manuel. "Pursuant to Deportation: Latinos and Immigrant Detention." *Latino Studies* 6, no. 1 (2008): 35–63.

Hernández, Graciela. "Multiple Subjectivities and Strategic Positionalities: Zora Neale Hurston's Experimental Ethnographies." In *Women Writing Culture*, edited by Ruth Behar and Deborah A. Gordon, 148–65. Berkeley: University of California Press, 1995.

Hernández, Kelly Lytle. "The Crimes and Consequences of Illegal Immigration: A Cross-Border Examination of Operation Wetback, 1943 to 1954." *Western Historical Quarterly* 37, no. 4 (2006): 421–44.

———. *Migra! A History of the U.S. Border Patrol.* Berkeley: University of California Press, 2010.

Heyman, Josiah McC. "Constructing a Virtual Wall: Race and Citizenship in US-Mexico Border Policing." *Journal of the Southwest* 50, no. 3 (2008): 305–33.

———. *Life and Labor on the Border: Working People of Northeastern Sonora, Mexico, 1886–1986.* Tucson: University of Arizona Press, 1991.

———. "The Mexico–United States Border in Anthropology: A Critique and Reformulation." *Journal of Political Ecology* 1, no. 1 (1994): 43–66.

———. "Putting Power in the Anthropology of Bureaucracy: The Immigration and Naturalization Service at the Mexico–United States Border." *Current Anthropology* 36, no. 2 (1995): 261–87.

———. "United States Surveillance over Mexican Lives at the Border: Snapshots of an Emerging Regime." *Human Organization* 58, no. 4 (1999): 430–38.

Hill, Sarah. "Metaphoric Enrichment and Material Poverty: The Making of 'Colonias.'" In *Ethnography at the Border*, edited by Pablo Vila, 141–65. Minneapolis: University of Minnesota Press, 2003.

———. "The War for Drugs: How Juárez Became the World's Deadliest City." *Boston Review*, July–August 2010, 19–23.

Hondagneu-Sotelo, Pierrette. "The History of Mexican Undocumented Settlement in the United States." In *Challenging Fronteras: Structuring Latina and Latino Lives in the U.S.*, edited by Mary Romero, 115–34. New York: Routledge, 1997.

Human Rights Watch. "Brutality Unchecked: Human Rights Abuses along the US Border with Mexico." New York: Human Rights Watch, 1992.

———. "Crossing the Line: Human Rights Abuses along the U.S. Border with Mexico Persist amid Climate of Impunity." New York: Human Rights Watch, 1995.

———. "Frontier Injustice: Human Rights Abuses along the US Border with Mexico Persist amid Climate of Impunity." New York: Human Rights Watch, 1993.

———. "Human Rights Violations by INS Inspectors and Border Patrol Agents Continue: Attorney General Reno Urged to Address Abuse Problem." New York: Human Rights Watch, 1997.

Huntington, Samuel P. *The Clash of Civilizations and the Remaking of World Order*. Pocket Books, 1997.

———. "The Hispanic Challenge." *Foreign Policy*, March–April 2004, 30–45.

Hurston, Zora Neale. *Their Eyes Were Watching God*. Reprint ed. New York: Harper Collins, 2006.

Inda, Jonathan Xavier. *Targeting Immigrants: Government, Technology, and Ethics*. Malden, MA: Blackwell, 2006.

Inda, Jonathan Xavier, and Renato Rosaldo. "Introduction: A World in Motion." In *The Anthropology of Globalization: A Reader*, edited by Jonathan Xavier Inda and Renato Rosaldo, 1–34. Malden, MA: Blackwell, 2002.

Irwin, Robert McKee. "Toward a Border Gnosis of the Borderlands: Joaquín Murrieta and Nineteenth Century US-Mexico Border Culture." *Nepantla* 2, no. 3 (2001): 509–37.

Jackson, John L. *Harlem World: Doing Race and Class in Contemporary Black America*. Chicago: University of Chicago Press, 2001.

James, Joy. *Resisting State Violence: Radicalism, Gender, and Race in U.S. Culture*. Minneapolis: University of Minnesota Press, 1996.

Jimenez, Maria, et al. "Human Rights on the Line: A Border Report." Oakland, CA: National Network for Immigrant and Refugee Rights, 2001.

Kapur, Ratna. "The Tragedy of Victimization Rhetoric: Resurrecting the 'Native' Subject in International/Post-Colonial Feminist Legal Politics." *Harvard Journal of Human Rights* 15 (2002): 1–38.

Kearney, Michael. "The Local and the Global: The Anthropology of Globalization and Transnationalism." *Annual Review of Anthropology* 24 (1995): 547–65.

Kelley, Robin D. G. *Race Rebels: Culture, Politics, and the Black Working Class*. New York: Free Press, 1996.

———. *Yo' Mama's Disfunktional! Fighting the Culture Wars in Urban America*. Boston: Beacon, 1997.

Kondo, Dorinne. "Bad Girls: Theater, Women of Color, and the Politics of Representation." In *Women Writing Culture*, edited by Ruth Behar and

Deborah A. Gordon, 49–64. Berkeley: University of California Press, 1995.

Kopinak, Kathryn. *Desert Capitalism: Maquiladoras in North America's Western Industrial Corridor.* Tucson: University of Arizona Press, 1996.

Koptiuch, Kristin. "Third-Worlding at Home." In *Culture, Power, Place: Explorations in Critical Anthropology,* edited by Akhil Gupta and James Ferguson, 234–48. Durham: Duke University Press, 1997.

Koulish, Robert E., et al. "US Immigration Authorities and Victims of Human and Civil Rights Abuses: The Border Interaction Project Study of South Tucson, Arizona, and South Texas." Tucson: University of Arizona, Mexican American Studies and Research Center, 1994.

Lemke, Thomas. "Foucault, Governmentality, and Critique." *Rethinking Marxism* 14, no. 3 (2002): 49–64.

Levesque, Suzanne, and Helen Ingram. "Lessons in Transboundary Management from Ambos Nogales." In *Both Sides of the Border: Transboundary Environmental Management Issues Facing Mexico and the United States,* edited by Jan J. Batema, Linda Fernandez, and Richard T. Carson, 161–82. Dordrecht, Netherlands: Kluwer Academic, 2002.

Lewis, Oscar. *Anthropological Essays.* New York: Random House, 1970.

———. *La Vida: A Puerto Rican Family in the Culture of Poverty—San Juan and New York.* New York: Random House, 1966.

Limón, José E. *American Encounters: Greater Mexico, the United States, and the Erotics of Culture.* Boston: Beacon, 1998.

———. *Dancing with the Devil: Society and Cultural Poetics in Mexican-American South Texas.* Madison: University of Wisconsin Press, 1994.

Lipsitz, George. *The Possessive Investment in Whiteness: How White People Profit from Identity Politics.* Philadelphia: Temple University Press, 1998.

Lomnitz-Adler, Claudio. *Deep Mexico, Silent Mexico: An Anthropology of Nationalism.* Minneapolis: University of Minnesota Press, 2001.

Lowe, Lisa. *Immigrant Acts: On Asian American Cultural Politics.* Durham: Duke University Press, 1996.

Loza, Mireya. "Braceros on the Boundaries: Activism, Race, Masculinity, and the Legacies of the Bracero Program." PhD dissertation, Brown University, 2011.

Lugo, Alejandro. *Fragmented Lives, Assembled Parts: Culture, Capitalism, and Conquest at the US-Mexico Border.* Austin: University of Texas Press, 2008.

———. "Theorizing Border Inspections." *Cultural Dynamics* 12, no. 3 (2000): 353–73.

Luibhéid, Eithne. *Entry Denied: Controlling Sexuality at the Border.* Minneapolis: University of Minnesota Press, 2002.

Maldonado, Salvador. *Los Márgenes del estado Mexicano: Territoriaos ilegales, desarrollo y violencia en Michoacán.* Zamora, Michoacán, Mexico: El Colegio de Michoacán, 2010.

Mamdani, Mahmood. "Good Muslim, Bad Muslim: Post-Apartheid Perspectives on America and Israel." *PoLAR* 27, no. 1 (2004): 1–15.

Marcus, George E., and Michael M. J. Fischer. *Anthropology as Cultural Critique.* Chicago: University of Chicago Press, 1986.

Marez, Curtis. *Drug Wars: The Political Economy of Narcotics.* Minneapolis: University of Minnesota Press, 2004.

Martinez, Luis Manuel. "Telling the Difference between the Border and the Borderlands." In *Globalization on the Line,* edited by Claudia Sadowski-Smith, 53–68. New York: Palgrave, 2002.

Martinez, Oscar. *Troublesome Border.* Tucson: University of Arizona Press, 1991.

Marx, Karl. "Economic and Philosophic Manuscripts of 1844." In *The Marx-Engels Reader,* edited by Robert C. Tucker, 66–125. 2nd ed. New York: Norton, 1978.

Massey, Douglas, Jorge Durand, and Nolan J. Malone. *Beyond Smoke and Mirrors: Mexican Immigration in an Era of Economic Integration.* New York: Russell Sage Foundation, 2002.

Mbembe, Achille. "Necropolitics." *Public Culture* 15, no. 1 (2003): 11–40.

Meeks, Eric V. *Border Citizens: The Making of Indians, Mexicans, and Anglos in Arizona.* Austin: University of Texas Press, 2007.

Menchaca, Martha. "On the Racial Implications of Another Broken Treaty." In *Reflexiones 1998: New Directions in Mexican American Studies,* edited by Yolana Padilla, 52–61. Austin: University of Texas Press, 1999.

———. *Recovering History, Constructing Race: The Indian, Black, and White Roots of Mexican Americans.* Austin: University of Texas Press, 2001.

Mendoza-Denton, Norma. *Homegirls: Language and Cultural Practice among Latina Youth Gangs.* Malden, MA: Blackwell, 2008.

Michaelsen, Scott. "Between Japanese American Internment and the USA PATRIOT Act: The Borderlands and the Permanent State of Racial Exception." *Aztlan* 30, no. 2 (2005): 87–111.

Mignolo, Walter D. *Local Histories/Global Designs.* Princeton: Princeton University Press, 2000.

Mohanty, Chandra Talpade. *Feminism without Borders.* Durham: Duke University Press, 2003.

Monsiváis, Carlos. "'Just over That Hill': Notes on Centralism and Regional Cultures." In *Mexico's Regions: Comparative History and Development,* edited by Eric Van Young, 247–54. San Diego: University of California, Center for U.S.-Mexican Studies, 1992.

Montejano, David. *Anglos and Mexicans in the Making of Texas: 1836–1986.* Austin: University of Texas Press, 1987.

Moodie, Ellen. *El Salvador in the Aftermath of Peace: Crime, Uncertainty, and the Transition to Democracy.* Philadelphia: University of Pennsylvania Press, 2010.

————. "Seventeen Years, Seventeen Murders: Biospectacularity and the Production of Post–Cold War Knowledge in El Salvador." *Social Text* 27, no. 99 (2009): 77–103.

Mora, Mariana. "The Imagination to Listen: Reflections on a Decade of Zapatista Struggle." *Social Justice* 30, no. 3 (2003): 17–31.

Moraga, Cherríe. *Loving in the War Years: Lo Que Nunca Pasó por Sus Labios.* Cambridge, MA: South End, 2000.

Mora-Torres, Juan. *The Making of the Mexican Border: The State, Capitalism, and Society in Nuevo Léon, 1848–1910.* Austin: University of Texas Press, 2001.

Mountz, Allison, and Richard A. Wright. "Daily Life in the Transnational Migrant Community of San Agustín, Oaxaca, and Poughkeepsie, New York." *Diaspora* 5, no. 3 (1996): 403–28.

Moynihan, Daniel P. *The Negro Family: The Case for National Action.* Washington: Department of Labor, Office of Policy Planning and Research, 1965.

Nadelmann, Ethan A. *Cops across Borders: The Internationalization of U.S. Criminal Law Enforcement.* University Park: Pennsylvania State University Press, 1993.

Nagengast, Carol. "Militarizing the Border Patrol." NACLA 32, no. 3 (1998): 37–42.

Nájera, Jennifer Rose. "Practices of Faith and Racial Integration in South Texas." *Cultural Dynamics* 21, no. 1 (2009): 5–28.

Newdick, Vivian. "The Indigenous Woman as Victim of Her Culture in Neoliberal Mexico." *Cultural Dynamics* 17, no. 1 (2005): 73–92.

Ngai, Mae M. *Impossible Subjects: Illegal Aliens and the Making of Modern America.* Princeton: Princeton University Press, 2004.

Nordstrom, Carolyn. *Global Outlaws: Crime, Money, and Power in the Contemporary World.* Berkeley: University of California Press, 2007.

Nugent, Daniel. *Spent Cartridges of Revolution: An Anthropological History of Namiquipa, Chihuahua.* Chicago: University of Chicago Press, 1993.

Ochoa, Enrique C., and Tamara Diana Wilson. 2001. "Introduction." *Latin American Perspectives* 28, no. 3 (2001): 3–10.

Ong, Aihwa. "Cultural Citizenship as Subject-Making: Immigrants Negotiate Racial and Cultural Boundaries in the United States." *Current Anthropology* 37, no. 5 (1996): 737–62.

————. *Neoliberalism as Exception: Mutations in Citizenship and Sovereignty.* Durham: Duke University Press, 2006.

Paget-Clarke, Nic. "The Militarization of the U.S.-Mexico Border: Interview with Maria Jiménez." *In Motion Magazine*, February 2, 1998, http://www.inmotionmagazine.com/mj1.html.

Pallares, Amalia, and Nilda Flores-González. *Marcha: Latino Chicago and the Immigrant Rights Movement.* Urbana: University of Illinois Press, 2010.

Paredes, Américo. "On Ethnographic Work among Minority Groups: A Folklorist Perspective." In *Folklore and Culture on the Texas-Mexican Border*, edited by Richard Bauman, 73–112. Austin, TX: CMAS Books, 1993.

———. *With His Pistol in His Hand: A Border Ballad and Its Hero.* Austin: University of Texas Press, 1971.

Paret, Peter. *Clausewitz and the State.* Oxford: Clarendon Press of Oxford University Press, 1976.

Paz, Octavio. *The Labyrinth of Solitude: Life and Thought in Mexico.* Translated by Lysander Kemp. New York: Viking Penguin, 1985.

Peña, Devon G. *The Terror of the Machine: Technology, Work, Gender, and Ecology on the U.S.-Mexico Border.* Austin, TX: CMAS Books, 1997.

Perry, Marc. "Global Black Self-Fashionings: Hip Hop as Diasporic Space." *Identities* 15, no. 6 (2008): 635–64.

Plascencia, Luis F. B. "The 'Undocumented' Mexican Migrant Question: Re-examining the Framing of Law and Illegalization in the United States." *Urban Anthropology* 38, nos. 2–4 (2009): 375–434.

Rabinow, Paul, and Nikolas Rose. "Biopower Today." *BioSocieties* 1, no. 2 (2006): 195–217.

Rénique, Gerardo. "Race, Region, and Nation: Sonora's Anti-Chinese Racism and Mexico's Postrevolutionary Nationalism, 1920s–1930s." In *Race and Nation in Modern Latin America*, edited by Nancy P. Appelbaum, Anne Macpherson, and Karin Alejandra Rosemblatt, 211–36. Chapel Hill: University of North Carolina Press, 2003.

Rodriguez, Richard T. "Queering the Homeboy Aesthetic." *Aztlán* 31, no. 2 (2006): 127–37.

Romano, Octavio. "The Anthropology and Sociology of the Mexican-Americans: The Distortion of Mexican-American History." *El Grito* 2, no. 1 (1968): 13–26.

Rosaldo, Renato. "Cultural Citizenship, Inequality, and Multiculturalism." In *Latino Cultural Citizenship: Claiming Identity, Space, and Rights*, edited by William V. Flores and Rina Benmayor, 27–38. Boston: Beacon, 1997.

———. *Culture and Truth: The Remaking of Social Analysis.* 2nd ed. Boston: Beacon, 1993.

Rosas, Gilberto. "The Fragile Ends of War: Forging the US-Mexico Border and Borderlands Consciousness." *Social Text* 25, no. 2 (2007): 81–102.

———. "The Managed Violences of the Borderlands: Treacherous Geographies, Policeability, and the Politics of Race." *Latino Studies* 4, no. 4 (2006): 401–18.

———. "The Thickening Borderlands." *Cultural Dynamics* 18, no. 3 (2006): 335–49.

Rose, Nikolas. *Powers of Freedom: Reframing Political Thought.* New York: Cambridge University Press, 1999.

Roseberry, William. *Anthropologies and Histories: Essays in Culture, History, and Political Economy.* New Brunswick, NJ: Rutgers University Press, 1991.

Rouse, Roger. "Mexican Migration and the Social Space of Postmodernism." *Diaspora* 1, no. 1 (1991): 8–23.

————. "Thinking through Transnationalism: Notes on the Cultural Politics of Class Relations in the Contemporary United States." *Public Culture* 7, no. 2 (1995): 353–402.

Rubio-Goldsmith, Raquel, et al. "The 'Funnel Effect' and Recovered Bodies of Unauthorized Migrants Processed by the Pima County Office of the Medical Examiner, 1990–2005." Tucson: University of Arizona, Binational Migration Institute, October 2006.

Saldaña-Portillo, María Josefina. "No Country for Old Mexicans." *Interventions* 13, no. 1 (2011): 67–84.

————. *The Revolutionary Imagination in the Americas and the Age of Development.* Durham: Duke University Press, 2003.

————. "Who's the Indian in Aztlán? Rewriting Mestizaje, Indianism, and Chicanoismo from the Lacandón." In *The Latin American Subaltern Studies Reader,* edited by Ileana Rodríguez, 402–23. Durham: Duke University Press, 2001.

Salzinger, Leslie. *Genders in Production: Making Workers in Mexico's Global Factories.* Berkeley: University of California Press, 2003.

Santiago-Irizarry, Vilma. "Culture as Cure." *Cultural Anthropology* 11, no. 1 (1996): 3–24.

Schmidt Camacho, Alicia. "Ciudadana X: Gender Violence and the Denationalization of Women's Rights in Ciudad Juárez." *New Centennial Review* 5, no. 1 (2005): 255–92.

Sheridan, Thomas. *Los Tucsonenses: The Mexican Community in Tucson, 1854–1941.* Tucson: University of Arizona Press, 1986.

Silverstein, Paul A. "Immigrant Racialization and the New Savage Slot: Race, Migration, and Immigration in the New Europe." *Annual Review of Anthropology* 34 (2005): 363–84.

Speed, Shannon, and Alvaro Reyes. "'Asumiendo nuestra propia defensa': In Our Own Defense; Globalization, Rights and Resistance in Chiapas." *PoLAR* 25, no. 1 (2002): 69–89.

Spivak, Gayatri Chakravorty. "Can the Subaltern Speak?" In *Marxism and the Interpretation of Culture,* edited by Cary Nelson and Lawrence Grossberg, 271–316. Urbana: University of Illinois Press, 1988.

Stallybrass, Peter, and Allon White. *The Politics and Poetics of Transgression.* Ithaca: Cornell University Press, 1986.

Stephen, Lynn. *Transborder Lives: Indigenous Oaxacans in Mexico, California, and Oregon.* Durham: Duke University Press, 2007.

Stewart, Kathleen. "On the Politics of Cultural Theory: A Case for Contaminated Cultural Critique." *Social Research* 58, no. 2 (1991): 395–412.

Stocking, George W., Jr. *Race, Culture, and Evolution: Essays in the History of Anthropology*. Chicago: University of Chicago Press, 1982.

Stolcke, Verena. "Talking Culture: New Boundaries, New Rhetorics of Exclusion in Europe." *Current Anthropology* 36, no. 1 (1995): 1–23.

Stoler, Ann Laura. *Race and the Education of Desire: Foucault's History of Sexuality and the Colonial Order of Things*. Durham: Duke University Press, 1995.

——. "Racial Histories and Their Regimes of Truth." *Political Power and Social Theory* 11 (1997): 183–206.

Stoler, Ann Laura, and David Bond. "Refractions off Empire: Untimely Comparisons in Harsh Times." *Radical History Review* 2006, no. 95 (2006): 93–107.

Tabuenca Córdoba, Maria Socorro. "Viewing the Border: Perspectives from the Open Wound." *Discourse* 18, nos. 1–2 (1995): 146–48.

Taussig, Michael. *The Nervous System*. New York: Routledge, 1992.

Taylor, Lawrence, and Maeve Hickey. *Tunnel Kids*. Tucson: University of Arizona Press, 2001.

Thomas, Tresa. "Living Late Capital: Hierarchy and Desire along the U.S.-Mexico Border." *PoLAR* 23, no. 1 (2000): 148–54.

Thompson, E. P. *The Making of the English Working Class*. New York: Vintage, 1963.

Tinker Salas, Miguel. "Los dos Nogales." In *Encuentro en la frontera: Mexicanos y nortreamericanos en un espacio común*, edited by Manuel Ceballos Ramirez, 259–82. Mexico City: El Colegio de Mexico, 2001.

Torres, Arlene, and Norman Whitten Jr. "General Introduction: To Forge the Future in the Fires of the Past." In *Blackness in Latin America and the Caribbean*, vol. 2, edited by Arlene Torres and Norman Whitten Jr., 3–33. Bloomington: Indiana University Press, 1998.

Trouillot, Michel-Rolph. "The Anthropology of the State in the Age of Globalization: Close Encounters of a Deceptive Kind." *Current Anthropology* 42, no. 1 (2001): 125–38.

Tsing, Anna Lowenhaupt. *Friction: An Ethnography of Global Connection*. Princeton: Princeton University Press, 2005.

Urías Horcasitas, Beatriz. *Historias secretas del racismo en México*. Mexico City: Tusquets Editores México, 2007.

US Border Patrol. *Border Patrol Strategic Plan: 1994 and Beyond, National Strategy*. Washington, DC, 1994.

US Cabinet-Level Task Force on Terrorism. *Combatting Terrorism: The Official Report of the Cabinet-Level Task Force Chaired by Vice President George Bush*. Rancocas, NJ: Defense Information Action Network, 1987.

Valencia Ramírez, Cristóbal. "Active Marooning: Confronting Mi Negra and the Bolivarian Revolution." *Radical History Review* no. 103 (2009): 117–30.

Vargas, João H. Costa. *Catching Hell in the City of Angels: Life and Meanings of Blackness in South Central Los Angeles*. Minneapolis: University of Minnesota Press, 2006.

———. *Never Meant to Survive: Genocide and Utopias in Black Diaspora Communities*. Lanham, MD: Rowman and Littlefield, 2009.

Vasconcelos, José. *The Cosmic Race/La Raza Cósmica*. Baltimore: Johns Hopkins University Press, 1979.

Vélez-Ibañez, Carlos G. *Border Visions: Mexican Cultures of the Southwest United States*. Tucson: University of Arizona Press, 1996.

———. *Rituals of Marginality: Politics, Process, and Culture Change in Urban Central Mexico, 1969–1974*. Berkeley: University of California Press, 1983.

Viego, Antonio. *Dead Subjects: Toward a Politics of Loss in Latino Studies*. Durham: Duke University Press, 2007.

Vigil, James Diego. *Barrio Gangs: Street Life and Identity in Southern California*. Austin: University of Texas Press, 1988.

Vila, Pablo. *Crossing Borders, Reinforcing Borders: Social Categories, Metaphors, and Narrative Identities on the U.S.-Mexico Frontier*. Austin: University of Texas Press, 2000.

Viruell-Fuentes, Edna A. "Beyond Acculturation: Immigration, Discrimination, and Health Research among Mexicans in the United States." *Soc Sci Med* 65, no. 7 (2007): 1524–35.

Visweswaran, Kamala. *Fictions of Feminist Ethnography*. Minneapolis: University of Minnesota Press, 1994.

———. "Race and the Culture of Anthropology." *American Anthropologist* 100, no. 1 (1998): 70–83.

———. *Un/Common Cultures: Racism and the Rearticulation of Cultural Difference*. Durham: Duke University Press, 2010.

Volpp, Leti. "Feminism versus Multiculturalism." *Columbia Law Review* 101, no. 5 (2001): 1181–218.

Wacquant, Loïc J. D. *Punishing the Poor: The Neoliberal Government of Social Insecurity*. Durham: Duke University Press, 2009.

Wade, Peter. "Race in Latin America." In *Blackwell Companion to Latin American Anthropology*, edited by Deborah Poole, 177–92. Oxford: Blackwell, 2008.

Walsh, Casey. "Eugenic Acculturation: Manuel Gamio, Migration Studies, and the Anthropology of Development in Mexico, 1910–1940." *Latin American Perspectives* 31, no. 5 (2004) 118–45.

Walters, Keith. "'He Can Read My Writing but He Sho' Can't Read My Mind': Zora Neale Hurston's Revenge in Mules and Men." *Journal of American Folklore* 112, no. 445 (1999): 343–71.

Warman, Arturo. *De eso que llaman antropología Mexicana*. Mexico City: Nuestro Tiempo, 1970.

Weismantel, Mary J. *Cholas and Pishtacos: Stories of Race and Sex in the Andes*. Chicago: University of Chicago Press, 2001.

Weismantel, Mary J., and Stephen F. Eisenman. "Race in the Andes: Global Movements and Popular Ontologies." *Bulletin of Latin American Research* 17, no. 2 (1998): 121–42.

Williams, Brackett. "A Class Act: Anthropology and the Race to Nation across Ethnic Terrain." *Annual Review of Anthropology* 18 (1989): 401–44.

Wilson, Tamara Diana. "Anti-Immigrant Sentiment and the Problem of Reproduction/Maintenance in Mexican Immigration to the United States." *Critique of Anthropology* 20, no. 2 (2000): 191–213.

Winant, Howard. *The World Is a Ghetto: Race and Democracy since World War II*. New York: Basic, 2001.

Wright, Melissa. "The Dialectics of Still Life: Murder, Women, and Maquiladoras." *Public Culture* 11, no. 3 (1999): 453–74.

———. "Public Women, Profit, and Femicide in Northern Mexico." *South Atlantic Quarterly* 105, no. 4 (2006): 681–98.

Zavella, Patricia. *I'm Neither Here nor There*. Durham: Duke University Press, 2011.

Zilberg, Elana. "Fools Banished from the Kingdom: Remapping Geographies of Gang Violence between the Americas (Los Angeles and San Salvador)." *American Quarterly* 56, no. 3 (2004): 759–79.

Žižek, Slavoj. *Iraq: The Borrowed Kettle*. London: Verso, 2004.

———. *The Plague of Fantasies*. London: Verso, 1997.

———. *The Sublime Object of Ideology*. London: Verso, 1989.

Agamben, Giorgio, 71, 101–102, 143, 144
agriculture, 34–35, 43
Allen, Jennifer, 139–41
Althusser, Louis, 117
Ambos Nogales, 52; race in, 79, 80. *See also* Nogales (Ariz.); Nogales (Son.)
anthropologists/anthropology, 124; and border studies, 18–22, 149n40; and cockfighting, 135; and culture of poverty, 120–23; Latin American, 74
Anzaldúa, Gloria, 18, 144, 149n40
Apache, 31, 33, 52
Arizona: anti-immigration measures in, 27, 51, 139–40, 144; decline of crime in, 27; and old frontier, 33–34. *See also* Nogales (Ariz.); Tucson
Arizona Rangers, 36

Barrio Libre: condition of tunnels in, 3, 126, 138; formation of, 16, 51–52, 58, 71, 110, 114; imagined geography of, 3, 108, 110, 119, 138; notions of freedom in, 52, 111, 124–27, 131, 145; as refusal, 12–13, 109, 117–19, 123–31; as site of feminism, 128; substance abuse in, 115–17; Tucson's, 33, 34, 99, 109. *See also* cholas; cholas/os; cholos; violence; youths
Beto/Chamuco, 89, 90, 125; at cockfight, 133; death of, 97–99
biopolitics/biopower, 100–102, 148n35; bodily mediation of, 76–77, 88; definition of, 17; and racism, 17, 88, 149n35
blanqueamiento, 77–79
Boas, Franz, 78
Bolillo, 68, 111
border, 76; decline in crime at, 27; flow of weapons across, 12; inspections, 10–11; militarization of, 4, 8–9, 27, 41, 49, 77, 141; modern, 38–47; as

new frontier, 47–52, 75; old frontier, 31–38; policing of, 40–52, 55–59, 66–70, 77, 90, 103–4, 113 14, 139–42; surveillance at, 95–96, 99; US fortification of physical, 46, 139–42. *See also* new frontier
Border Coverage Program, 45
border crossings: author's attempt at, 3–5, 10; Beto/Chamuco's attempts at, 97–99; chúntaro vs. cholo, 85; criminalization of, 51, 104, 141–43; deaths during, 56, 97; expectations of violence during, 103–6; as expression of freedom, 51; filming of, 99–100; into Nogales, Ariz., 100–101; subjugation during, 76, 84–85, 114; undocumented, 16–17, 96, 103–6
Border Industrialization Program, 42
Border Patrol. *See* US Border Patrol
border patrol stations, 106–7
border studies, 18–22, 149n40
bracero program, 40, 42

California: anti-immigrant violence, 35; Operation Gatekeeper, 51
Chavo, 112
cheros, 8
Chinese Exclusion Act of 1882, 33, 35
cholas: of Barrio Libre, 128–30; employment, 81; fashion, 61, 81, 87; as mothers, 81
cholas/os: criminalization of, 60–61, 67, 71, 73–74, 76–83, 137; empathy toward chúntaros, 86; fashion, 61, 80–83, 87; identity, 71; passing for US citizens, 83; perceptions of, 6, 67, 73–74, 80; as reflection of sovereignty-making warfare and policing, 74; violence against, 66–71, 137; violence against chúntaros, 77, 84–85, 87. *See also* youths

cholos: fashion, 61, 80–83; passing for US citizens, 83, 109; use of term, 60, 67, 80
chúntaros, 8, 99; empathy for, 86; fashion styles of, 84; perceptions of, 75, 84–85, 87; use of term, 83–84; violence against, 77, 84–85, 87
civil rights movement, 50, 53
clothing. *See* fashion
Coalición de Derechos Humanos/ Alianza Indígena sin fronteras, 48, 141, 144
cockfighting, 133–36
COINTELPRO, 45
colonias, 7
corridos, 33, 144
Cortez, Gregorio, 33, 52
crime: as act of resistance, 33, 119; decline in, at border, 27; as economic opportunity, 3, 7, 62–67, 71, 85, 92, 137. *See also* violence
criminalization: of border crossers, 38, 51, 104, 141–43; of cholos, 60–61, 66, 72–76, 80–83, 87–88, 137; of immigrants, 38, 57, 69; as means of asserting sovereignty, 32, 69, 137; of *serranos*, 32, 60
culture of poverty, 120–23

decolonization movements in US, 44
deportation, 41; and illegalization of undocumented labor, 40; as voluntary departure, 98, 100, 108
detention of minors, 12, 49–50, 98, 108
Diaz, Porfirio, 35
Discipline and Punish (Foucault), 117–18
disease, 7, 147n8
drugs: cultivation of, 138; smuggling of, 51; trafficking of, 16, 104, 137, 138; transporting and selling of, by Barrio Libre youth, 63, 65, 93, 134, 138; use of, 63, 82, 115–17, 119, 127, 130; and US fears of traffickers, 9, 53, 101; war on, 15, 55, 137–39, 142
Dunn, Timothy, 8, 9

ejidos, 50
Elmer, Michael, 47, 48
emigration, to US, 56, 58

employment: clothing expectations for, 82; discrimination in, 61; in Nogales, Son., 7; opportunities for Barrio Libre youth, 8, 62–66, 82, 115. *See also* labor
Escobar, Arturo, 123
ethnography: author's approach to, 21, 22, 24–27; of cholos, 81; practice of, 123, 131

fashion: cholas/os, 61, 80–83, 87; chúntaro, 75, 84, 87
Federal Bureau of Investigation (FBI), 45
femicide, 9, 55, 102
femininity, 81, 82, 128, 149n40
Foucault, Michel, 95, 102–3, 117–18, 149n35
Franco, 67, 68
Free 'Hood. *See* Barrio Libre

Gabriel, 66, 125, 126
Gamio, Manuel, 58, 78, 79
gangs. *See* cholas; cholas/os; cholos
GATT (General Agreement on Tariffs and Trade), 46
gender, 18; in Barrio Libre, 128–29; and chola aesthetic, 61; and chúntaro renderings, 75; relations and employment, 42, 61; relations at border, 68, 92, 112. *See also* femininity; masculinity
General Agreement on Tariffs and Trade (GATT), 46
Gentlemen's Agreement of 1907, 33, 35
Gilroy, Paul, 19
Giuliani, Rudolph, 74
graffiti, 3–5, 74, 84, 100, 115
Gramsci, Antonio, 123
Grupo Beta, 4, 5, 60, 77; criminal acts by, 58, 59, 67–69; harassment of youth by, 67–69, 85, 127. *See also* police
Güero, 65, 66
Guerrero, Práxedis G., 4
Gutiérrez, Ramón, 29

Hall, Stuart, 19
Hart, John Mason, 36

homo sacer, 100–102, 105, 106
huffing, 115–17, 119, 130
Human Rights Coalition/Indigenous
   Alliance without Borders, 48, 141,
   144

IDENT system, 107
immigrants: criminalization of, 38, 57,
   69; deaths of, 97; increase in arrests
   of, 44; minor, 98, 108; rights groups,
   141–44; violence against, 47–48, 57,
   90, 140. *See also* chúntaros
immigration: along Arizona-Sonoran
   border, 34; attempts to control,
   33–35, 40–42, 46, 51, 107, 140–43;
   criminalization of, 103–6, 142–43; increase in undocumented, 40, 41, 44,
   96; as means to *mestizaje*, 79; after
   Mexican Revolution, 37; SB 1070, 27
Immigration and Nationalization Service (INS), 40, 51; criminal prosecut-
   ing of, 45; detention of minors by,
   49, 50
Immigration Reform and Control Act
   (IRCA), 46
incarceration, 12, 96, 117–18; of drug
   cultivators, 138; of Latinos, 73;
   Román, 64, 91, 124
indigenous populations: in *mestizaje*
   discourse, 78; subjugation of, 31, 32;
   in Tucson, 34; unrest among, 43
INS (Immigration and Nationalization
   Service), 40, 51; criminal prosecut-
   ing of, 45; detention of minors by,
   49, 50
intersectionality, 18, 42, 81, 128, 140

Javi, 61, 62, 66, 67
Jesús, 63, 70
Johnson-Reed Act of 1924, 38, 39
Juana, 108, 128
Juárez, Benito, statue of, 61, 62

"killing deserts," 9, 56, 97, 105, 107, 114
Ku Klux Klan, 44

labor: Asian, 35; *bracero* program, 40,
   42; declining need for agricultural,
   43; demand for migrant, 8, 34, 35,
   40; drug cultivation, 138; fear of

mobilized, 58; illicit, 67; increase in
   undocumented, 40, 41; *maquiladora*,
   42, 47; racialized, 105. *See also* employment
labor activism, 36
landownership, 31, 32, 35, 50
La Negra, 129
Lazaro, 126–27
Lewis, Oscar, 120–22
Limón, José, 19, 122
Loco, 125, 126
Louie: clothing, 83; empathy toward
   chúntaros, 86; employment, 82
low-intensity conflict (LIC), 8, 9
low-intensity warfare, 13, 101; border
   policing as, 7–9, 76, 85; as characteristic of new frontier, 137; in creation
   of Barrio Libre, 12, 13, 51. *See also*
   policing
lynching, 32

maquiladoras, 93; appropriate attire in,
   82; employment at, 61–63, 65, 138;
   growth of, 6, 7, 42, 46, 47
Margarita, 51; employment of, 63, 129;
   familiarity with police, 69; on meaning of Barrio Libre, 108, 128; as parent, 64; police harassment of, 68;
   substance abuse by, 63, 116; time
   spent in Tucson, 110
masculinity: cholo, 80; and cockfighting, 133; crisis of, 122; as dominance,
   68, 122, 140; and drug running, 63;
   and fatherhood, 129, 130; serrano, 32;
   undermining of, by police, 68
media disinterest, 48
mestizaje, 77–80
Mexican Revolution of 1910–20, 36,
   37, 44
Mexico: and colonial northern frontier, 31–38; as coproducer of new
   frontier, 15, 16, 40, 55–59; decline in
   government programs, 21, 50, 51, 65;
   economic decline of, 45–47, 97; economic reliance on migrants, 13, 40,
   59, 67; industrialization of, 42, 43;
   modernization of, 35; rural unrest in,
   43; as threat to US national security,
   15; and Tlatelolco massacre, 43, 44;

Mexico (*continued*)
    turn to neoliberalism, 14–15, 46, 47,
    50, 59–61; US investment in, 35, 42;
    violence in, 55
Mexico City, 15, 16
Mexico-US border. *See* border
migrant labor: activism, 44; *bracero*
    program, 40, 42; demand for, 8, 34,
    35, 47; Mexico's reliance on, 13, 40,
    59, 67
migrants: criminalization of, 104, 141;
    deaths of, 45, 106, 113; dehumaniza-
    tion of, 76; female, 42; increase in,
    40, 44; minor, 98, 108; movement of,
    along old frontier, 31–38; protection
    of, 71; racialization of, 60, 84, 105–6;
    rights advocates for, 142; violence
    against, 7, 85, 99, 103, 105–6. *See also*
    chúntaros
migration: freedom from, 56; as na-
    tional security issue, 9; along old
    frontier, 31–38; and relation to neo-
    liberalism, 22, 49–51, 113
militarization: of border, 8–9, 27, 41,
    49, 141; of police, 9, 16, 60, 66, 77
Militarization of the U.S.-Mexico Border
    (Dunn), 8, 9
military personnel as border patrol,
    139, 140
minors. *See* youths
Mi Nueva Casa, 25, 51, 93, 112
Mono Biche statue, 61, 62
Murrieta, Joaquin, 33, 52

NAFTA (North American Free Trade
    Agreement), 4, 46, 50, 51
Negro, 82
neoliberalism: defined, 14; in Mexico,
    14–15, 46–50, 59–61; and migration,
    22, 49–51, 105, 113; in United States,
    50, 53
new frontier, 4; Barrio Libre as, 51, 52;
    definition of, 5, 16, 137; as hetero-
    topia, 145; militarized policing of,
    96–101, 104, 106–7; porousness of,
    143; race at, 49, 60, 84, 88, 105–6;
    rise of, 29, 47–53; and rise of Barrio
    Libre, 71; as site of delinquent re-
    fusal, 12, 118–19, 130, 143; subversion

of sovereignty in, 108–12, 113–14;
    thickening of, 137–43
9/11 attacks. *See* September 11, 2001,
    attacks
Nogales (Ariz.): Border Patrol station
    in, 106–7; crossing into, 100–101; dis-
    ease in, 7, 147n8; relationship with
    Nogales, Son., 5, 34. *See also* Ambos
    Nogales
Nogales (Son.), 53; living conditions
    in, 7; maquiladoras in, 6, 7, 47; re-
    lationship with Nogales, Ariz., 5, 34;
    tourist industry in, 6; vice in, 92;
    youth employment in, 62–66. *See*
    also Ambos Nogales
norteños, 31
North American Free Trade Agree-
    ment (NAFTA), 4, 46, 50, 51

Ofelia, 93
old frontier, 31–38
Operation Gatekeeper, 51, 103
Operation Hold-the-Line, 51, 103
Operation Safeguard, 51, 97
Operation Wetback, 41

pachucos, 74
paramilitary groups, 44, 90
Paredes, Américo, 29, 32, 33
Partido Liberal Mexicano (PLM), 36,
    37
passing: as adult, 98, 108, 112; as US
    citizen, 108, 109, 111, 112, 114
Paz, Octavio, 74
Plan Chihuahua, 57
Plan Merida, 56, 139
police: brutality, 5, 58, 59, 67–68;
    harassment by, 51, 66–69; militari-
    zation of, 9, 16, 38, 41, 49, 58, 60, 66,
    77, 103; US funding of Mexican, 139,
    161n2. *See also* Grupo Beta
policing: border, 40–46, 66–69, 77,
    103–4, 113–14, 139–42; cholas/os as
    reflection of, 74; of informal econ-
    omy, 66; as low-intensity warfare,
    7–9; and proximity to Barrio Libre
    delinquency, 67–69, 74, 81, 85, 87–89,
    108–11, 114, 123; and race, 49, 60, 103;
    after September 11, 2001, attacks,
    90–94, 139–40, 143

political activism, 144, 145; in rural Mexico, 43; in southwestern US, 44
polleros, 70, 138
Posse Comitas Act, 49
prison. *See* incarceration

race: anxieties, 29; and biopower, 17–18; as culture, 121; as difference, 80; immigrant knowledge of, 90; and *mestizaje*, 77–80; at new frontier, 16–18, 60, 88, 105–6, 111, 143; as skin color, 84; in southwestern US, 32–33
racial profiling, 143; author's experience with, 92–94; at border, 69; by Mexican police, 69, 92; after September 11, 2001, attacks, 90
racial violence, 33, 36, 52
racism, 17; as anti-immigrant discourse, 103; and biopower, 17, 102–3, 149n35; and chúntaros, 75, 79, 88; cultural, 49, 121; as exercise of sovereignty, 36; state, 79, 102–3; subjection to, by migrants, 144
railroads, 35
remittances, 56, 59, 71
Román, 5, 20; attempt to pass for US citizen by, 112; and choice to dwell in Barrio Libre, 124–25; on chúntaros, 85; clothing, 83, 109; at cockfight, 133–36; employment, 62, 93; illicit activities of, 70, 115, 117, 138; migrant experience of, 63–64, 95, 109; as parent, 64; on September 11, 2001, attacks, 89–91; time spent in Tucson, 110; on US Border Patrol, 69
Rosaldo, Renato, 18
Rubio, 82, 125
Rubio-Goldsmith, Raquel, 141–42, 143

SB 1070, 27
Secure Border Initiative, 139
Secure Fence Act, 139
September 11, 2001, attacks, 8; and exercising of sovereignty, 76; increase in border security following, 90, 139, 143; viewing of televised reports on, 89–91
Sergio, 3
serranos, 31, 52; criminalization of, 32, 60

Sonora: and old frontier, 33–34, 51, 139–40, 144; US investment in, 47
sovereignty: and criminalization, 32, 69, 137; at modern border, 38–47, 52; at old frontier, 31–38, 52; production of, 7–9, 11, 15–16, 49; relationship with violence, 32, 101, 113–14, 143; reliance on biopower and biopolitics, 16–17; and rise of new frontier, 48–52; subversion of, 108–10, 119, 128
Spenser, Gary, 90
state of exception, 100–101, 103
substance abuse, 115–17, 119, 130
surveillance, 95–96, 99; at Border Patrol station, 106, 107; of Mexican expatriates, 37; by Texas citizens, 140; by US Army at border, 49

Task Force on Terrorism, 48, 53
Teporron, 109
terrorism: and border reinforcement, 90, 141–42; of Texas Rangers, 36
terrorists, 29, 142; migrants as, 9, 10, 141; youths as, 48, 49, 53
Texas, 140; marginalization of Mexicans in, 122; and old frontier, 31, 52; racial conflict in, 32–33
"Texas Legend," 32
Texas Rangers, 36, 37, 41
Tlatelolco massacre, 43, 44
Tortas, 125
Tratado Libre Comercio. *See* NAFTA (North American Free Trade Agreement)
Tres por Uno, 59
Tucson, 8, 33; Barrio Libre in, 34, 109–10

unemployment, 42, 46, 47
United States: and border policing, 40–41, 44, 49, 103–4, 113–14, 139–42; and colonial Mexican frontier, 31–38; criminalization of undocumented migrants in, 40; demand for migrant labor in, 35; history of dependency on migrant labor, 35; immigration to, 44; insurgency in southwest, 37; military collaboration with US Border Patrol, 49; move to neoliberalism, 50,

United States (*continued*)
53; public sentiment in, 50, 53; southwest, 32–34
US Border Patrol, 30, 38, 44, 97; as bus ride back to Mexico, 69; collaboration with US military, 49; criminal acts by, 47–48, 140; hiring of military personnel by, 139, 140; increase in funding to, 46; life-preserving services of, 113; origins, 38, 52; strategies of, 103–4; tactics of, 40–41, 51; in Texas, 90
US-Mexico border. *See* border

Valenzuela, Dario Miranda, 47, 48
Victor, 66, 111
Villa, Pancho, 32, 37
Vina, Gustavo de la, 104
violence: against Barrio Libre youth, 5, 8, 66–70, 71, 137; biopolitics of, 113–14; against chúntaros, 77, 84–85, 87; expectations of, at border, 103–6; as governance, 17, 18; against immigrants, 33–35, 47–48, 57, 90, 140–43; "managed," 13; in Mexico, 55; against migrants, 7, 57, 67, 85, 95, 103, 105–6; by police, 5, 58, 59, 67–68; by *polleros*, 70; racial, 36, 52; relationship with sovereignty, 32, 101, 113–14, 143; by US Border Patrol, 41, 47, 48. *See also* crime
voluntary departure, 98, 100, 107, 112

War on Drugs, 15, 55, 137–39, 142
War on Terror, 76, 142, 144
whiteness, 60; aspiration to, 53; and *blanqueamiento*, 77–79; maintenance of, 40
With His Pistol in His Hand (Paredes), 29, 33
women: in Barrio Libre, 128–29; economic opportunities for, at border, 92; employment of, 82; femicide, 9, 55, 102; gender expectations of, 129; increase in migrant, 44; as *maquiladora* labor, 42. *See also* cholas; femininity

youth culture studies, 19, 20, 81
youths: anxieties concerning, 19–20, 48, 50, 53; criminalization of, 20, 22, 66–72; detention of, 49, 50, 98, 108; economic activities of, 61–66, 82, 137–38; embrace of death by, 108–12; migrant experience of, 61–66; notions of freedom, 52, 111, 124–27, 131, 145; passing as adults, 98, 108, 112; passing as US citizens, 108–12, 114; as potential terrorists, 48, 49, 53; substance abuse by, 115–17; subversion of sovereignty by, 108–12, 119; violence against, 5, 8, 58–59, 66–71, 137. *See also* cholas; cholas/os; cholos; *individual names*